Alfred Egmont Hake, O.E. Wesslau

Free Trade in Capital

Alfred Egmont Hake, O.E. Wesslau

Free Trade in Capital

ISBN/EAN: 9783744725057

Printed in Europe, USA, Canada, Australia, Japan

Cover: Foto ©ninafisch / pixelio.de

More available books at **www.hansebooks.com**

FREE TRADE IN CAPITAL

OR

FREE COMPETITION IN THE SUPPLY OF CAPITAL
TO LABOUR, AND ITS BEARINGS ON THE POLITICAL
AND SOCIAL QUESTIONS OF THE DAY

BY

A. EGMONT HAKE

CHAIRMAN OF THE FREE TRADE IN CAPITAL LEAGUE

AND

O. E. WESSLAU

London
REMINGTON & CO.
HENRIETTA STREET, COVENT GARDEN
1890

The rights of translation and reproduction are reserved

CONTENTS

INTRODUCTION

PAGE

Scientific methods everywhere except in government—The first triumph of Political Economy—The lavish promises of the economists—Great causes of inflation in trade overlooked and attributed to Free Trade—How Political Economy became the 'dismal science'—The new sentimental Economy—Government interference mistaken for freedom—Free Import not Free Trade—The chief feature of our civilisation not explained by Adam Smith—The *laisser faire* policy blamed for consequences of monopolies—Free Trade system incomplete without Free Trade in Capital 1

CHAPTER I

THE IMPORTANCE OF CAPITAL

Different meanings of the word Capital—Distinction between commercial and economic capital not made by economists—The true definition of capital—Political Economy deals with material things only—Modern division of labour renders capital indispensable—The effectiveness of labour depends on capital 14

vi   FREE TRADE IN CAPITAL

CHAPTER II

DIVISION OF LABOUR

PAGE

Origin of division of labour—Division of labour led to trades and professions—Co-operation in the North and in the South—Compulsory division of labour in ancient Empires —The ancient Empires a warning against applying Domestic Economy to the State—How modern co-operation works through exchanges—Difficulties in the way of exchanges— The demand for workers should be immense, but is small —Strong inducements for an inquiry into the workings of the exchanges 24

CHAPTER III

VALUE-MEASURERS AND MEDIUMS OF EXCHANGE

Inconvenience of barter—Exchanges facilitated by a value-measurer—Only goods in great demand suitable for value-measurers—The tendency of value-measurers to become mediums of exchange—Necessity of distinguishing between them—Coin nothing but stamped metal—Mistakes resulting from Adam Smith's use of the word 'money' .   . 33

CHAPTER IV

COIN, THE WORST MEDIUM OF EXCHANGE

Confusion produced by the word 'money'—Such vague terms would be disastrous in other sciences—Credit, not coin, the chief medium of exchange—Bi-metallists misled by the word 'currency'—Coin, as a value-measurer, need not exist in quantities—The Mark Banco of Hamburg an excellent value-measurer because not coin—The use of gold as a medium of exchange expensive and unreasonable— Small government notes could replace coin—The introduction of small government notes not an economic but a fiscal question—Government notes and private free notes can circulate side by side 41

CONTENTS

CHAPTER V

THE IMPOSSIBILITY OF INCREASING THE QUANTITY OF COIN BY IMPORTATION

PAGE

Other mediums of exchange than coin an old institution— Imported coin subject to same economic laws as imported goods — Examples — Imported coin returns quickly to whence it came—Proofs supplied by the variations of the rates of exchange—The trade balance maintained by the rates of exchange—The different ways in which imported coin affects markets—Each market has sufficient coin 59

CHAPTER VI

GOVERNMENT PREJUDICES AND THEIR CONSEQUENCES

Why gold leaves the gold-mining districts—Imported gold prevents productive work in the same way as gold-mining— Historical examples of the baneful influence of gold—What became of the French milliards—The Gründerzeit and the Crash — Effects on Germany and on France — Foreign statesmen import gold instead of improving banking . 75

CHAPTER VII

THE IMPORTANCE OF CREDIT

Credit in olden times—Accounts current of limited application —Indirect credit—Drafts—Money-lending the beginning of banking—Baneful effect of State interference with interest—Removal of State interference a blow to usury— Storage of coin and deposits—The bankers become the mediators between capital and labour—How drafts circulated—Promissory-notes the forerunners of bank-notes— The London goldsmiths the first issuers of bank-notes— What experience taught the goldsmiths—The useful effect of their business on London trade 87

CHAPTER VIII

SIR ROBERT PEEL'S MISTAKE

PAGE

The goldsmiths sacrificed for Bank monopoly—A splendid opportunity missed by the founders of the Bank of England—Note-issuing restricted by the Bank Act of 1844—The amount of the uncovered notes arbitrarily fixed—The note-issuing of the Bank of England in no proportion to the requirements of commerce—Prohibition of note-issuing banks in new-rising centres—No notes of amounts suitable to productive trades—Present defenders of monopoly more to blame than Sir Robert Peel—His object to make production profitable—The cutting of the Gordian knot—What Peel did not see and ought to have done—The teachings of experience in Scotland and England not understood—Security in Scotland through freedom, panics in England through Government interference—Mill's farcical conclusion—Freedom in Scotland effected what Peel desired to accomplish in England 100

CHAPTER IX

HOW OUR BANKING SYSTEM DIVORCES CAPITAL AND LABOUR

The real purpose of banking—The two missions of banking—Other mediators between capital and labour than banking inadequate—English banking is deposit banking—Who are the customers of an English bank ?—English banking unsuitable to the productive trades—Small chance for capital to reach the working man—The consequences to capital of its divorce from labour 119

CONTENTS ix

CHAPTER X

HOW OUR BANKING SYSTEM DESTROYS PROFITS AND PROMOTES POVERTY

PAGE

The inability of our banks to work the exchanges in the country—Absence of banks suitable to productive trades—Productive trades compelled to use coin—High cost of production and low price of sale—High cost of production means low wages—The deadlock produced by the Bank Act of 1844—The result to farming and the leading industries 134

CHAPTER XI

THE SWEATING SYSTEM

Slavery in England—Great demand for wealth and small demand for the labour which produces it—Scramble for few foreign markets and destruction of good markets at home—Low wages the cause, not the effect, of pauper immigration—The East-End Jews the benefactors of the English workers—The two systems of middle-men oppressing the workers — The middle-men replacing the capitalist — Labour as necessary to capital as capital is to labour—The Sweating System points to defective banking . . . 142

CHAPTER XII

THE EXCHANGED ATTITUDE OF PARTIES

The threatened evils worse than the actual ones—Political aims overshadowed by political means—Economic evils the origin of political agitation—The barrenness of political reforms—The Conservative party yielding to the socialistic clamour—The Liberals aim at subjecting the individual to State tyranny—Political Economy abandoned by the Liberals—The Conservatives now the upholders of individual freedom—The effects of the old party warfare after the exchanged attitude of parties 162

CHAPTER XIII

STATE SOCIALISM AND TRADE

The faith of the ignorant in the omnipotence and omniscience of government—How bureaucratic tyranny arises—The solidarity of humanity ignored—How solidarity operates in a great city—The disturbing effect of the introduction of Domestic Economy into the mechanism of Division of Labour—Friends of working men opposing the Factory Acts—Factory Acts useless when times are bad, and superfluous when times are good—The Factory Acts a contributing cause of the Sweating System—State interference between the harsh landlord and poor tenant—The demonstration of the pit-girls—The ruinous effect of the Merchandise Marks Act 178

CHAPTER XIV

THE PERSECUTION OF THE CHILD BY THE STATE

The cry 'Let us educate our future masters'—The experiences of National Education abroad misunderstood—Cramming is not education—The effect of our compulsory school system on poor children—The injustice inflicted on parents—Good State education only possible under complete Socialism—Willing parents prevented from properly educating their children—State Socialism in banking compels State Socialism in education—The theatrical children—Children placed in the position of useless slaves under harsh masters—State Socialism paving the way to complete Socialism 204

CHAPTER XV

THE SOCIALISTIC MIRAGE

Mr. Plimsoll's Bills—What effective supervision over ships means—Only effective under complete Socialism—The British sailor protected out of existence—Complete Socialism held up as the goal—All attempts to systematise

Socialism have failed—Socialism without compulsory labour impossible—Disastrous commercial and economic effects of State-supervised production — Universal Socialism means universal war—The creation of a powerful bureaucratic class—Socialism a calamity to the working man—By aiming at Socialism we shall arrive at despotism—Is the Post Office an example of successful State Socialism ? 223

CHAPTER XVI

THE SOLUTION OF THE CAPITAL AND LABOUR PROBLEM FOUND

Banking the mechanism of exchanges—Freedom alone can supply the required number of banks—Note-issuing a paying business—The losses of producers for want of banking accommodation—Free banks would aim at a large circulation—Distinct on between Government-supervised notes and free notes—Banks alone can circulate notes—The experiment in Jersey and its lessons—Free notes can only circulate in the district of the issuing bank—The banks will give preference to producers—Economic laws compel the issuing banker to avoid wealthy customers—Free banking a capital-distributing system—Free note-issuing system the opposite in every respect to the deposit system—Low cost of production and high wages the result of free issuing banks 249

CHAPTER XVII

FREE TRADE IN CAPITAL IN SCOTLAND BEFORE 1844

All economists praise the Scotch free system—Its effect in Scotland—Unsuccessful attempts of the Scotch banks to over-issue—Reservation clauses on the notes—The causes which led to the use of very small notes in Scotland—The jealousy of the larger banks—The Royal Commission of 1756—The small notes blamed for the bankers' mistakes—Parliament strikes the first blow at the free system in Scotland—How branch offices arose—Peel's Bank Act of 1844 destroyed the free system 275

CHAPTER XVIII

THE FRENCH BANQUIER SYSTEM

Beneficial effect of the *banquier* system—Misgovernment in France—Effect of the *banquier* system in Germany—Advantages to the working classes—The Bank Act of 1844 prevents the *banquier* methods in England—Free Trade in Capital would combine the advantages of the *banquier* system and the Scotch free system 293

CHAPTER XIX

ABUSE OF FREE NOTE-ISSUING AN ECONOMIC IMPOSSIBILITY

Universal prohibition of rational banking—The fear that free note-issuing should be abused—The origin of prejudices against Free Banking—The causes of the great bank panics in England and America—The American public misled by its government—Can a free issuing banker fail or run away with advantage to himself?—How banks buy gold—Free note-issuing does not increase the gold-stock of the banker—The granted cash-credits always in excess of the note-circulation—Free note-issuing a floating book-keeping—The present deposit-system more productive of panics than the free note-issuing system—The dangers of only one gold-reserve in the country—How the Bank of England protects its gold at the expense of commerce and the working classes—The raising of the rate of discount a self-acting check on prosperity—Forgeries highly unlikely under a free system 309

CHAPTER XX

THE IRISH QUESTION

Vitiated Economy must produce discontent—Political agitators seldom economists—Patriotism and Home Rule—Parliament alone responsible for poverty in Ireland—Failure of the Irish leaders to produce an economic programme—The protective spirit engendered the Home Rule agitation— What Mr. Parnell did when he dominated Parliament— Did Mr. Gladstone introduce his Irish Bills in order to destroy Home Rule?—Mr. Gladstone's proposition would have produced a new set of formidable grievances—The Irish Question not a Land Question—Transition from a feudal to a commercial system in Ireland—The ruinous effect of vitiated banking on land-holding peasants—Where the banking is best, there the peasants are least indebted— The fallacies of Land Nationalisation—The effect of compulsory reduction of rents and royalties—The Irish Question a Capital Question—The effects of free competition in the supply of capital on the landlords and farmers—*La petite culture* in France impossible without the *banquier* system—With Free Trade in Capital the farmers would resent any interference with their contracts—The term Home Rule involves a contradiction 335

CHAPTER XXI

HOW THE ANCIENT PROSPERITY OF EGYPT COULD BE REVIVED

The probability of an understanding between the Mahdists and the discontented Egyptians—Is England to be Egypt's enemy?—Prosperity in Egypt would satisfy all parties concerned—History proves Egypt capable of prosperity— The usury system producing the same effect in Egypt as in Ireland—Extensive division of labour the secret of success among ancient administrations—Free Banking supplies a far superior system of division than the ancient compulsory system—No serious obstacles to Free Banks in Egypt . 384

CHAPTER XXII

PRACTICAL IMPERIALISM

How the State-socialistic bias has caused British statesmen to neglect British territories—Many and strong reasons for a closer union—The present bonds are bonds of sentiment—The economic advantages derived from our possessions a mere fraction of what they ought to be—The squandering of the wealth represented by the Colonies—Bonds of sentiment should be strengthened by bonds of interest—Protection duties in the Colonies the greatest obstacles to perfect union—The protective system of our Colonies means ruin to the natural industries—The protected industries mere shams—Protection destroys industry instead of furthering it—The working men under a Protective system suffer from the same injustice as slaves—The advantage of pensioning-off protected manufacturers—The fundamental principle of the Imperial Constitution should be economic and individual liberty—Temporary animosity would wear away as in North and South America—England lost America through vitiated Economy—Protection, if allowed in Canada, will lead to the loss of that Colony—The great advantages of one closely-united free-trading Empire 405

FREE TRADE IN CAPITAL

INTRODUCTION

It is a characteristic phenomenon of the age that civilised nations strive to establish the most accurate scientific theories for all that has to be accomplished, and that no trade or profession is looked upon as thorough and serious if not guided entirely by scientific knowledge. Promotion in Government offices depends on competitive examinations in all sciences which can possibly be applied to administration. Scientific knowledge is expected in men little above the labouring class, such as plumbers, engine-drivers, &c. Dentists, in order to be entrusted with the extraction of a tooth, have to guarantee a scientific education by the display of diplomas. With the view to cookery chemistry is taught in girls' schools. Hospital nurses, Government inspectors, farmers' assistants, game-

B

keepers, soldiers, and many others of similar grades are expected to have their smattering of science. Competition has made it almost impossible to succeed in any branch of production unless the latest scientific discovery is fully exploited.

While science is thus becoming more and more a qualification in so many branches, it is a remarkable fact—and one over which future historians will pause with wonder—that the science which deals with the laws regulating the material happiness of individuals, nations, nay, of humanity itself, is not respected, and only rarely and fitfully obeyed—namely, Political Economy. Whether Political Economy is an exact science or not, is a hackneyed question which shall be left undiscussed here; the reply to it does not depend on what Political Economy is, but on what the definition of an exact science is. It will at least be recognised that Political Economy is a branch of human knowledge, the truths of which, if not all of them, at least a great number, are as trustworthy as the truths of any exact science, and as amenable to tests as these.

In no country have the truths of Political Economy received greater recognition than in

England, and when it is considered that some decades ago hardly any educated Englishman cared to confess that he doubted the laws of Economy as expounded by the leading economists, and that by practical legislation in obedience to these laws, an unprecedented prosperity was begun, it seems a matter of surprise that it should have lost hold over the minds of men to such an extent as is at present the case. This is all the more remarkable, seeing that no theories have been established which even pretend to disprove the fundamental principles of Political Economy, and no fact can be pointed to as warranting the disrepute into which it has fallen.

It will therefore not be without interest to consider the circumstances, the events, and the strange methods of reasoning, which have destroyed men's faith in Political Economy.

It should at first be admitted that many political economists have committed mistakes; but, although such mistakes may have in many individual cases helped to undermine the reputation of the science, they cannot be looked upon as an essential cause of modern scepticism as to its truths. Innumerable and egregious mistakes have been made and are still being made in many a science without in the slightest degree destroying its influence. Nor can incompleteness have been of importance, because Political Economy has this in common with all the natural sciences. The prestige of Political Economy has suffered from more special and more powerful causes. The great crime of which it stands accused is that of having disappointed humanity. Long after its foundations were laid by Adam Smith it continued to be regarded with suspicion by the old school of statesmen, by routine-ridden financiers, and all the champions of vested interests, as a clever system of theories impossible of application. It was not until the middle of this century that it became the guide of practical politicians. It found ardent and genial apostles in Villiers, Cobden, Bright, and their large following. The new vista which it opened up at this time, the fearful evils which it was called upon to remedy, and the brilliant confirmation elicited, were well calculated to rouse enthusiasm —the great reform which was contemplated, could not have been carried without it—and many free-traders were enthusiasts at the time. The teachings of political economists, such as they were then, had never been put to a practical test; but most of them were, when looked at in the abstract, irrefutable, and promised enormous benefits, if obeyed. No wonder, therefore, that its enthusiastic votaries, confirmed in their faith by improvements already become remarkable, should prophesy great things in the name of Political Economy. Labour was to be emancipated, capital was to rapidly increase, production was to be easy, life cheap, competition insignificant, taxes were to be light, profits were to be large and wages high, and poverty was to disappear. The one indispensable condition for the attainment of all this, was that the laws of Political Economy should have free play, and consequently Government interference was strongly deprecated. All that the economists demanded from Government was that it should do as little as possible beyond protecting individual freedom and the sacredness of contract, and let all things take their natural course. For this demand the economists had a good excuse in the nature of all such laws and regulations which had been passed before for the encouragement and protection of trade and industry; for these enactments were, almost without exception, of an incredible imbecility when regarded in the light of the new science. In this way originated the individualist policy which has been nicknamed the 'Laisser Faire' policy. The new freedom succeeded well at first, and for about thirty years the Economist school triumphed. Even when our trade ceased to advance in leaps and bounds, and times became bad, the economists could point to deliberate infringements of the laws of Political Economy as the causes of depression in trade. Some of the greatest nations of the world, such as France, Germany, Spain, Italy, and the United States, deserted the principles of Free Trade which they more or less had adopted, and went back to excessive Protection. This reacted on English trade in two ways, one direct and one indirect: in a direct way by reducing through high protective duties the import of British goods into the protected countries; and in an indirect way by increasing the poverty of their inhabitants and thus lessening their power of consumption in general, and consequently their consumption of British goods.

This explanation did not satisfy the English people, especially as the economists declared that Free Trade would enrich England even if all other nations maintained Protection. Moreover, the general disappointment was intensified by a mistake which the economists had committed. They had rashly attributed the immense expansion of trade and industry during the thirty years which followed the abolition of the corn laws to the Free Trade reform, and consequently reckoned on the continuance of the expansion as the population and the national capital increased.

They had rashly omitted to take into account the many great causes for trade inflation which set in after 1844. Though railways were introduced earlier, it was only after that period that the civilised world became covered by a network of rails, the materials for which were supplied by England. The changing of wooden ships into iron steamers, and the establishment of the Trans-Atlantic lines; the development of our agricultural colonies and of the United States, which took place from an almost exclusively English base; the immense consumption of manufactured goods which resulted from the enormous loans which were contracted by governments, towns, communities, and associations —loans which to a large extent were supplied by England in the shape of goods; the sanction by the

Bank Act of 1844 of the establishment of large Joint-Stock Banks in London, and the immense credit these new banks created : all these impulses to industrial and commercial activity in England have slackened, disappeared, and even produced reactions, and it was inevitable that the consequences should be keenly felt in this country. To admit so many causes for trade inflation besides the Free Trade reform may seem to favour the views of protectionists and fair traders ; but it should not be forgotten that when we find in face of their collapse and a severe reaction, in spite of the hostile tariffs in so many countries, that trade and industry have not materially receded, this can only be attributed to the immense advantages which Free Trade gives us.

Unconscious of their mistakes, the followers of Cobden attempted to defend themselves against the attacks of the disappointed people by persistent denial of the existence of trade depression, and by repeated assurances that it was only temporary, and that the progress by leaps and bounds was on the point of being resumed. They loudly deprecated any inquiry into the causes of the depression, because they feared that the state of trade would be made an excuse for anti-economic legislation, that Protection would be revived, that individual freedom and private contract would be attacked.

As the depression continued, and the hopeful prophecies of the economists were falsified, and the latter still obstinately refused to abandon their negative attitude, declining to advocate any step on the part of the Government for the improvement of the condition of the people, it was natural that the anti-economist party should gain the ear of the British nation. As the people became more impatient and exasperated, they turned from the economists and began to side with their adversaries. Their entire want of logic soon put the protectionists and fair traders out of court, but many strange hobbies which had been kept down by Political Economy gained a new lease of life. The advocates of bi-metallism, of State-aided emigration, of free education, land nationalisation, land allotment, national work organisation, State-constructed artisans' dwellings, &c., all secured a following; and all these political sects which danced on the grave of Political Economy, joined hands under the banner of State Socialism and, reversing the current of public opinion, gave a new direction to the so-called progressive party. Any step towards Socialism was now looked upon as progress, and both the Conservative and Liberal party yielded to the temptation of securing popular support by pandering to the socialistic yearnings of the people. The extension of the franchise increased enormously the number of the uneducated voters, and it became extremely difficult to advocate any views requiring the support of abstract Political Economy, while popularity was easily achieved by advocating socialistic measures. As all such would appear absurd if the fundamental truths of Political Economy were admitted, it became the fashion to sneer and jibe at the 'dismal science.'

Meantime the economists continued to sulk, and the younger and more ambitious among them made desperate efforts to reconcile their science with the public sentiments. In this they were encouraged by warm-hearted and able literary men, and the result was an extraordinary *olla podrida* of economics, finance, politics, philosophy, sentimentality, and religion, which its authors were anxious should be recognised as the New Economy.

And thus it came about that the faith of the

English people in individual liberty, free contract, and the great power for infinite progress in the natural economic laws—a faith under the inspiration of which they had achieved so much—began to give place to an entire dependence on Government.

The economists, in their enthusiasm for Free Trade, represented the passing of that measure as the inauguration of the absolute reign of Political Economy, and thus caused this science to be condemned on results achieved by neglect of its complete application. They did not see that the abstract reasoning from which they drew their conclusion in favour of a great and lasting prosperity, pre-supposed a state of things free enough from Government interference to give the economic laws free play to work out their natural results.

Thus, for instance, they were correct in saying that if trade and industry were left free they would flourish, but they failed to notice that the import duties were not the only, nor even the most important Government obstruction. When Free Trade was passed, they said trade is free, and all the while trade was enslaved. There were obstructions the removal of which could not be advocated without the explanation of a set of economic theories which had not yet been established,—those economic laws which govern under our system of civilisation, that is under a system of individual freedom and private property, the most important economic phenomenon, division of labour, or in other words, universal and infinite co-operation.

Adam Smith did not explain these laws, and though later economists have acknowledged that this explanation was wanting to complete Political Economy, it had not, up to a recent date, been found. To its absence it is easy to trace the errors of our economists and the unpopularity of the science, as well as the maintenance of absurd monopolies, unjust prohibitions, unreasonable regulations. This state of things has produced a mass of misery which has been placed to the credit, not of State interference, as it should be, but to the *laisser faire* policy.

The economic explanation of division of labour is now found, and reveals to us that the most important part of Free Trade—Free Trade in Capital—we have never enjoyed; and this being the case we must draw the conclusion, that if Free Trade, partially adopted, has secured to England the immense advantages we know of, the adoption of a complete Free Trade system promises results brilliant enough to induce all thinking men in this country to use their best efforts to bring it about.

But if such efforts are to be effective, if politicians, philanthropists, commercial men, and the press, are to join in the carrying of Free Trade in Capital, the first thing that is required is a clear and complete treatise on what it is, how it can be carried, and what it will achieve; and such a treatise, it is the object of the present volume to supply.

FREE TRADE IN CAPITAL LEAGUE,
Parliament Mansions,
Victoria Street, Westminster, S.W.
November 1889.

CHAPTER I

THE IMPORTANCE OF CAPITAL

THE term capital is so old, and in such general use, that it may seem superfluous to specially explain what the word means when used in an economic sense. But this term, like many others used in Political Economy, has not originated with that science, nor has it been borrowed from an ancient or foreign language for the special benefit of Political Economy. It was first employed in the Latin languages to indicate something partaking of the head, or being the essential part or element. It has long been used as a commercial term, and probably became general all over Europe with the spread of the art of book-keeping invented by the Italians. Adam Smith used it as an economic term, and since his time it has been indispensable to all economists. In our language the noun capital has retained three distinct significations: the chief town of a country, the total wealth at the disposal of an individual or a firm, and its economic meaning. With the first signification we are not concerned, and we ought not to be concerned with the second, but, as the commercial term and the economic term capital have been used by almost all economists indiscriminately, and in a manner most misleading, it is necessary to draw a sharp distinction between the two terms, for, without it, all that we had to say about the economic term capital would rather confuse than explain our meaning. The want of this distinction has been one great stumbling-block to many economists, for it can be easily conceived how dangerous it is to have to employ a word which is capable of two distinct interpretations; it might so easily happen that what has been found perfectly true in the one sense of the word would be blindly admitted as true of the other. This has constantly been the case with the word capital. Thus Dunning Macleod, one of the ablest writers on banking, comes to the conclusion that banks create capital, evidently using the word in its economic sense. At this conclusion he arrives in the following way. Finding that capital, in a commercial sense, is necessary in commercial undertakings when credit can be had, he concludes that credit is synonymous with capital, and when he finds that bankers can create credit, he contends that they can create capital. The confusing effect of this conclusion will be understood when we consider that the correct definition of capital, in an economic sense, is *those material results of previous labour which are consumed in a production*. The corollary of Macleod's conclusion is that, as banks can create capital, humanity is very foolish to work at all. John Stuart Mill, in trying to determine what is capital and what is not, encounters great difficulties through the confusion of the two terms. Finding that education, talent, and right and similar privileges, are a man's capital in a commercial sense, he concludes that they ought to be included in the economic term capital, which inclusion, were it adhered to throughout economic reasoning, would lead to hopeless confusion.

How necessary it is to distinguish between the commercial and the economic term capital might perhaps best be shown by an illustration. Suppose that one child had only tasted one sort of sauce in its life, and this a sweet one, and another had only tasted anchovy sauce, and that the children discussed the question as to whether sauce improved pudding or not, the term sauce would represent an entirely different thing to each, and no amount of discussion would bring them to agreement. The want of a proper definition of capital has caused endless discussions among economists and prevented a clear insight into a comparatively simple question.

It is not merely for the sake of expediency and clearness that the true definition of the economic term capital should exclude any idea of things that are not material, for such exclusion is inevitable, because exact Political Economy deals only with material things.

The term *exact* is used here because recent writers on Political Economy have been prone to stray into the fields of other sciences and yet communicate their researches under the head of Economy. Talents, rights, and similar advantages may enormously influence the economic condition of individuals and nations, but this is no reason why they should be dragged into economics. There are plenty of other immaterial factors which influence the wealth of nations quite as much as talent, education, &c.: for example, politics, laws, religion, amalgamation of races, which no sane man would dream of including in Political Economy. All these subjects may be dealt with in treatises on history, philosophy, &c., in the most intimate connection with Political Economy, but such an incidental concatenation of many branches of human knowledge is no excuse for allowing the laws of the one to confuse the laws of the other, or to destroy the sharp demarcation which, for clearness' sake and scientific purposes, has been drawn round them.

The object of Political Economy is to show us what economic laws have to be obeyed in order to acquire material wealth for all individuals of the community, with the smallest amount of work, and with complete respect for individual freedom and private property. It has nothing to do with any moral, mental, or legal advantages, however important these may be. To set Economy any other task than to explain the laws of the production of wealth is to destroy its practical utility. Such questions as: whether easy production of wealth is good or bad for human beings, whether it furthers or destroys religion or morality, whether it corrupts or elevates the arts, whether it is apt to produce over-population or tends to destroy humanity, are entirely outside Political Economy, as much so as the question of the colour of the paper on which a geometrical figure is drawn is outside geometry. A nation should therefore not ask an economist whether it ought to facilitate the production of wealth or not, but, when it has decided to do so, it should ask the economist how to do it; and he should not be held responsible for any moral consequence that may result from easy production of wealth.

It is evident that nothing can be regarded as capital which is not the product of labour. If we were to speak of the immense stores of raw materials which exist in many countries as capital, we should at once render all economic reasoning impossible because those very countries where great poverty prevails from want of supply of capital might appear as countries best supplied with capital. Very little labour may suffice to transmute natural wealth, or raw material, into capital; but matter on which no labour has been expended either in shaping it, reaching it, or transporting it, cannot be called capital.

Neither is it difficult to perceive that the word capital can only be used when production is spoken of; under any other circumstances it would have no meaning as an economic term : just as the term multiplicator would have no arithmetic sense if there were no multiplication.

The definition we have given of the economic term capital ought to prevent all confusion with the commercial term capital. When in this work the word capital is used, it will be invariably in the economic sense, except when otherwise described.

Capital is a most important factor in production under any form of government or organisation, but in our modern civilisation, characterised as it is by individual freedom and private property, it is of far greater importance than in any other form of society experienced or proposed, and this importance grows with every step we advance.

When better machines, better methods, and more scientific processes are introduced, when production is carried on on a larger scale, when communications are improved, when new territories are laid under cultivation, and when universal co-operation develops, then capital tells more and its value and effectiveness increase.

In a savage country capital has little value because the small amount of work which is done is independent of it. There, there is no division of labour, little or no utilisation of the work of past generations; the individual fashions, through his own labour, the raw materials he finds around him into the objects he desires. But in a civilised country labour is carried on differently. Here we notice a highly developed system of division of labour, which might be said to have two extensions, one in space and one in time.

The first extension establishes a co-operation between innumerable contemporary individuals; whereby one works for millions, and millions work for one. The miner who raises the ore from the mine contributes to the production of the thousand articles to be manufactured from the metal, as well as of the millions of articles that may be manufactured by tools from that same metal. If one nail, directly or indirectly produced by the same metal is used in a trans-Atlantic steamer, the miner has assisted in the production of the steamer and of all the articles that may be manufactured from the goods carried by that steamer.

The second extension—that in time—establishes a continuous co-operation between past, present, and future generations, in such a way that the labour accomplished by the one generation is used by the succeeding one, which thereby saves labour or accomplishes more perfect work with greater ease. It is thus an absolute certainty that, for instance, the pen with which one writes is the product of a series of efforts which began perhaps somewhere in Asia when a primitive man first shaped a twig with a piece of stone, and that this series of efforts has continued without interruption in one unbroken chain down to the time in which we live.

Thus we see that the effectiveness of modern work depends on to what extent it can utilise, firstly, what we may call contemporary co-operation, and, secondly, the result of labour in the past. Any labour carried on independently of these two advantages would be on a par with the labour of a savage, and would be not only ruinous but impossible in a civilised country.

The results of previous labour are the same thing as capital, and to say that modern labour cannot dispense with them is to say that modern labour cannot dispense with capital.

A slight investigation will at once show that the utilisation of contemporary co-operation is also a question of capital. If all our economic life were presided over by one all-powerful will, we should have a compulsory organisation which would supply every worker with such results of his fellow-workers' labour as would be most suitable to his work. But in our civilisation there exists no such authority, nor any general store from which labourers could be supplied with what they require. The whole co-operation is carried on by means of exchanges, and each individual tries to make as favourable exchanges as possible. Now it is evident that favourable exchanges can only be made by those who can offer in exchange such things as are in great demand and who are owners of enough wealth to effect exchanges on a large scale.

Thus we find that the effectiveness of modern labour almost entirely depends on the supply of capital, and that access to capital is of vital importance to labourers in modern communities where no raw material can be obtained, where the result of previous labour cannot be utilised, and where the general co-operation cannot be entered into without the assistance of capital.

CHAPTER II

DIVISION OF LABOUR

It has already been mentioned that in modern civilisation division of labour has reached a high development. But before we can appreciate the importance of division of labour and the extent of the harm which ensues when the function of division of labour, or co-operation, is obstructed, we must first have a clearer insight into its nature. Division of labour was the beginning of civilisation, and has since characterised it throughout. Our remotest ancestors very early discovered that work became both easier and more effective when it was divided among many. If ten men each wanted a bearskin, they could more easily obtain the object of their wishes if they together hunted one bear after the other till ten were killed, while one hunter stood the chance of being killed by the bear. Ten men could easily erect ten log-huts if they worked together, but if each worked alone their labour would be protracted, exhausting, and bad.

There can be no doubt that the advantages of division of labour were a strong inducement to the formation of communities and states; they caused people to divide into different trades and professions. A man fishing, after having made the best possible arrangement for a successful haul, often caught more fish in his net than he and his family required, and by exchanging his surplus fish against surplus game killed by the hunter, saved himself the trouble of going out hunting.

The benefits of such subdivision and co-operation by exchanges were so striking that each individual selected one occupation, and stuck to it for life. Different tribes living under different climatic and territorial conditions entered into the same relation with each other as individuals and families had done, and thus trade arose between tribes and nations. The result was that each individual could, by a slight exertion in his daily efforts, by a slight improvement in his methods, secure an amount of comfort, luxury, and pleasure which, if he had had to acquire by individual effort and without the co-operation of others, would have cost him more work and trouble and risk by far than he would have been willing to expend on them, or they would have been beyond his reach altogether.

Division of labour, as it extended, proved a strong inducement to accumulation. Men had already found that it was inconvenient and dangerous to live without a reserve stock of the necessaries of life, but when such stock was capable of being exchanged against much-coveted goods which individual efforts could not produce, a powerful incentive to accumulation was added. As men began to apply improved methods and instruments, division of labour developed; the division between trades and professions became more marked; and co-operation by exchange became more active. What had been one trade became divided into two, and these two again became further subdivided. Even in the workshops themselves, division of labour became an indispensable condition to progress. When machines were introduced an extraordinarily strong impulse was given to division of labour, and we see in many modern factories, that to give a new shape to a small piece of metal it is passed through a variety of hands.

The different stages of the development of division of labour, which we have here glanced at, have of course, in reality, been intermingled with and interrupted by the various events of history. But in the northern countries of Europe, where development began late, the progress of division of labour can be clearly traced as here described. The case may appear different with the nations of antiquity, for among them the steady development of co-operation by exchanges cannot be so easily traced to be the skeleton of history as in the north. But if we look at events with an unprejudiced eye, we shall discover that the advancement of civilisation in the ancient states runs parallel with the development of division of labour. Co-operation there, as in the north, presented the same tempting advantages, but, thanks to the mildness of the climate and the richness of nature, there was not the same incentive for individuals to possess and accumulate. Counting on the regularity of the supplies of nature, they lived more on the hand-to-mouth system, and thus there was less occasion for exchanges.

But what in the north was accomplished through hard climate, long winters, scarcity of supplies, was in the south accomplished by the sword of the despot and the whip of the slave-driver. Ambition, love of luxury and pleasure, and no doubt in many cases patriotism and the desire to elevate humanity, induced individuals, dynasties, military and religious castes, to give an extension to division of labour which natural circumstances alone would not have so rapidly achieved. Sovereigns and governments could accomplish nothing single-handed. They had to bring masses of human beings under a system of co-operation as the indispensable condition of the realisation of their aims. The free division of labour which we have seen develop naturally in the north of Europe was in the ancient states represented by a compulsory one. The people were divided into castes, with different tasks imposed upon them. The leaders or sovereigns interested the most advanced and the most daring men of their country in their schemes of ambition, conquest, pleasure, and reduced the rest to slaves. Thus, while the despot ruled over a caste of patricians, these had unlimited power over their slaves. Compulsion was the leading feature of the whole system; the object, organised co-operation. The slave-owners, through their underlings, gave each slave his appointed work—gave him that place in the chain of co-operation which benefited the owner most, supplied him with tools, raw materials, food and shelter—such as they were—and disposed of all that the slaves produced. The despot, in his turn, imposed on the slave-owners contributions, special tasks in the way of cultivation, the construction of roads, canals, fortifications, palaces, and temples; at the same time compelling them to supply arms and men for warlike purposes.

But with the ancient method of organised co-operation we are little concerned. Except to use it, as we shall do later, as a warning to those who advocate State compulsion as a substitute for individual freedom, we need not refer to it, because what we are inquiring into is the necessary condition for easy production of wealth under a free system, that is to say, a system which is governed by the subtle laws of Political Economy, and not by the brutal enactments of despots, governments, and castes, who manage the affairs of a nation on the primitive principle of Domestic Economy.

Finding then that, in our system of civilisation, division of labour, outside the boundaries of properties held by individuals or firms, functions by exchanges, the economic conditions of exchanges are what we have to inquire into. Our own country, like many other countries of the world, presents the strongest inducements for such an inquiry. That exchanges are hampered, are made excessively difficult by mistaken legislation, will be proved later on. Here it will suffice to point out that all civilised countries contain large masses of willing workers who possess no capital of their own, and who consequently have nothing to exchange except their labour. There can be no doubt that in most of these countries this exchange is sometimes impossible, generally difficult, and almost always so unfavourable to the man who has nothing but labour to give, as to keep him in a chronic state of want.

If we lived under an artificial organisation, and wanted to lessen the poverty of the working classes, we should simply ask the government to dismiss and replace the officials who managed things so badly, but under a free system we must inquire into what makes the exchanges of labour and wealth so difficult.

There is a tendency now all over the civilised world to take a despondent view of the position of the labourer, to accept his poverty and his dependence as representing an inevitable and natural order of things, for which nobody except the Creator of the world is responsible. We shall later on expose thoroughly in detail, the fallaciousness of such opinions, but in the meantime only point to certain undeniable facts which, if well understood, clearly demonstrate that the man who has work to offer in exchange for wealth ought to be well off; especially in the time we live in, when work through a widely-extended division of labour, with the whole world for its basis and its market, with wonderful machines to render the most difficult work easy, has acquired an effectiveness which almost surpasses our conception.

For we find, on the one hand, that the world offers practically inexhaustible stores of raw material waiting for work to transmute them into enjoyable wealth, and, on the other hand, we find a demand for wealth which has never been more intense, and which amounts almost to a frenzy. In the presence of this enormous supply and this insatiable demand, which can only be satisfied by work, it is impossible not to conclude that the demand for workers ought to be almost as intense as the demand for wealth. When we therefore find large numbers of working people unable to exchange their work for the necessaries of life, we must infer that something makes this exchange difficult. The aspect of the world at present, therefore, offers every inducement to us to inquire into the conditions under which the exchanges take place.

CHAPTER III

VALUE-MEASURERS AND MEDIUMS OF EXCHANGE

WHEN co-operation between man and man, between community and community began, the exchanges by which they came to an understanding were all barters. One kind of goods was bartered in a certain quantity against a quantity of another kind of goods, or against some service. Services also were exchanged, and when there was a disproportion in their values, the difference was made up in goods. In some countries, placed at the edge of the vortex of modern reform, not long ago remnants of such exchanges existed, and may yet exist.[1] Servants, for instance, in those countries some time ago received hardly any wages, but it was agreed that, against their services, they should receive

---

[1] In Norway, Sweden, Denmark, and Finland, some forty years ago, these methods of exchanges were by no means uncommon, and probably still exist in the remoter districts.

food and lodging and certain articles of clothing. Tithes used to be paid in farm-produce, in stipulated quantities, irrespective of market value.

But exchanges by barter caused great inconveniences which were felt more and more as co-operation by exchanges extended. It was therefore a great improvement when the use of a value-measurer was introduced. It was easier to make a bargain when the two kinds of goods to be exchanged were compared as to value with the third kind of goods. If a man wanted to exchange tools against fish, it might be difficult to form an idea how much fish should be given for so many tools; but, if for example fox-skins were the usual value-measurer, the contracting parties would each know the value of their own goods in fox-skins, and the bargaining thus became more to the point. It was natural that only such goods were chosen as a value-measurer for which there was a general demand, and in most cases goods were applied to that purpose for which there was a demand in distant places or over a considerable area.

It has been advanced that the value-measurer need not always consist of goods of real marketable value, but this is a delusion created by a misconception of modern credit-instruments. The only example which is quoted from among primitive value-measurers is that of the cowries used in Central Africa, but this is a bad example, because the cowries were in great demand as ornaments. No goods without marketable value have ever been used as value-measurers.

It was natural that the value-measurer should be selected as the best form in which surplus wealth should be stored, because it could be exchanged more easily than any other kind of goods. Many primitive nations have used awkward value-measurers, which must have given them a great deal of trouble, especially in the case of small exchanges. Thus, for instance, where the unit of the value-measurer was a cow or a reindeer, small exchanges must have been complicated affairs. The desire to store the value-measurer, the necessity of transporting it to considerable distances, and the occasional demand for very small parts of it, caused our ancestors to look about for a value-measurer that would not perish easily, was small in bulk, and could be subdivided without deterioration in value. The metals alone answered these exigencies, and were early selected as value-measurers by progressing nations.

Any goods that were accepted as value-measurers tended to become a current medium of exchange, and the metals were as suitable for this function of mediums of exchange as of that of value-measurers.

It should here be carefully noted that the value-measurer and the medium of exchange, though often represented by the same metal and the same goods, are two distinct conceptions which unfortunately many writers on economics have hopelessly confounded. In this work a sharp distinction will be made between the term value-measurer and the term medium of exchange. A value-measurer used abstractly in a transaction, but which has not been used bodily and has not actually changed hands, is not considered as a medium of exchange.

A couple of illustrations will make this clear. If a man in Manchester sells yarn to a merchant in London to the amount of one thousand pounds, and the London merchant sells simultaneously indigo to the same amount, and the two invoices are balanced one against the other without any remittances of coin or credit-instruments, the pounds sterling in that transaction have been used as the value-measurer, but credit has been the medium of exchange. If an Englishman travelling in Russia buys there a quantity of fur at so many roubles per piece, and pays for them with English sovereigns calculated at so many roubles per sovereign, the value-measurer in that transaction is the rouble, but the English sovereigns are the mediums of exchange. This distinction is often not made by economists, and when a certain coin—say a sovereign, a shilling, or a penny—is used as the value-measurer, for very large transactions, balancing each other with little or no employment of actual coin, they say that in all those transactions the coin has been the medium of exchange. This confusion of two entirely different conceptions is responsible for a great number of erroneous conclusions which have caused the theories of coin, credit, and banking to be looked upon as abstruse and incomprehensible.

One of the reasons why metals lend themselves so easily to current mediums of exchange, is that they receive impressions and retain them well. This quality in the metals led to their coinage.

Considering the exaggerated importance which has been given to coinage and the prestige the word has long enjoyed, it may be useful to note here that the coining of the metals has, or at least had, originally for sole object the impressing of a stamp on small pieces in order to indicate their weight and their alloy, and thus save constant weighing and testing. It should be well remembered that the metals, though coined, remain nothing but small pieces of goods, carrying on their surface their own weight and alloy; for such names as pound, franc, dollar, indicate both the weight and the alloy of pieces of metal impressed with such names, because certain countries passed laws that whenever the name of pound, franc, or dollar is used in speech, writing, or any other way, it shall mean a piece of metal of so much weight and alloy.

It is absolutely necessary to remember, in speaking about coin, that it is goods like all other goods ; for to call it money or currency, and accord to it a prestige which springs entirely from the imagination and attributes which are quite illusory, is to destroy every hope of arriving at a clear insight into this branch of Political Economy. To consider coin as something subject to different economic laws than goods, is an error extremely frequent with economists. One of the very few mistakes Adam Smith committed was to use the word 'money,' which has no distinct meaning, but which may signify a great variety of things of very different and sometimes entirely opposite meanings, and then to liken it to a kind of wheel which moves the business of a country. No economist who has used the words money and currency has arrived at clearness on the subject of coin.

It might be objected against the foregoing statement as to coin bearing a stamp indicating its intrinsic value as a merchandise, that we have coins in England which are very far from having the intrinsic value which is stamped upon them, namely, silver and copper coins; but this fact in no way detracts from the truth of our statement, for our copper and silver coins are, strictly speaking, not coin at all, in either an economic sense or in a legal sense: they are tokens. Economists will range them under the head of credit-instruments made of metal, and the law warns people against them and disallows them as legal tender for amounts of above two pounds.

The introduction of coin extended co-operation

by exchanges very materially. Small exchanges became very easy, especially after a great number of people began to take up as a profession the facilitating of exchanges—that is to say, when merchants, dealers, and shopkeepers came into existence. The effecting of exchanges with coin, as the medium of exchange or as the value-measurer, is called buying and selling.

CHAPTER IV

COIN, THE WORST MEDIUM OF EXCHANGE

WHEN an author of a book on Economy applies the word *money* not only to coins and tokens, but to government notes, national bank notes, government supervised private notes, free notes, bank balances, cheques, treasury bills, bank bills; and when the reader of his book applies the word *money* to commercial capital, wealth, bonds, consols, &c.—it is no wonder that there should be confusion in the mind of author and readers. It is quite a usual thing that attributes which have been proved to belong to coin are without hesitation supposed to belong to all the other conceptions which are popularly covered by the term money; and *vice versâ*.

The absurdity of using names of indistinct and shifting meanings does not always strike people when it is done in treatises on Political Economy, but it becomes glaring in connection with any other science. If, for instance, a chemist were to use the designation 'white powder' for all substances which appear to the eye as white powder, his treatise would be a burlesque of his subject, and each of his experiments, carried out on the strength of his authority, would be likely to produce results most startling and contradictory, from a freezing liquid to a thundering explosion.

The use of such nondescript words as 'money' and 'currency' is to a very large extent the cause of many of the wild theories and strange prejudices which obscure the simple economic laws which underlie the functions of coin. We have already referred to the frequent mistake of considering all transactions in which coin has been the value-measurer as accomplished through coin as a medium of exchange. In a large commercial centre all transactions are made with coin as the value-measurer, but the bulk of them are actually cleared by other mediums of exchange, and in only a very small percentage is coin the medium of exchange. But this fact is often overlooked, and when the mediums of exchange of a country are found insufficient, attention is not given to those mediums of exchange which are used in the ninety-nine cases, but exclusively to the one which is used in the hundredth, namely coin.

When it is deemed desirable to enhance the industrial and commercial activity of a country, little or nothing is done to improve and extend that medium of exchange which all commercial centres prove to be the most important and the only one deserving attention—credit; but the one which can be used only to a very small extent—coin—is recklessly poured into the place. When a new country is judged short of capital and measures are required to supply the supposed want, the word capital is confounded with money and coin is imported, or rather an attempt is made to import coin, for in most cases the effect of such attempt at once influences the rates of exchange enough to stop the actual remittance of coin, to be replaced by shipments of goods which are of little use to the country receiving them and often of the same kind which the importing country could largely produce if the supply of capital had been arranged in a rational way.

When our friends the bi-metallists find that there is an unnatural depression in trade, that this depression emanates from legislation and not from natural circumstances, and when they discover that legislative mistakes have been committed in connection with mediums of exchange, they are misled by the unfortunate term 'currency'; they declare there is something wrong with the currency; we are short of currency; the currency must be expanded, &c., in all of which they would be perfectly right if they meant by currency the mediums of exchange. But this unfortunate word 'currency' entirely destroys their logic, for, coming to the practical remedies they say, currency is coin, and coin must be mended; and thus they set to work to increase that medium of exchange which plays the smallest part in the great business of the world, and which, as a medium of exchange, could be dispensed with almost altogether, as we shall show further on. But the mediums of exchange which are used in ninety-nine per cent. of business in developed centres, and which tend to become the mediums of exchange of the world, those they do not propose to mend or free from most unreasonable restrictions. They arrive of course at this absurd conclusion by using the chameleon word 'currency.' They make it in the first instance stand for the aggregate of the mediums of exchange; afterwards they make it stand only for coin: and the conclusion they draw correctly from the first meaning of the word becomes absurd when they apply it to the second.

The same confusion of two distinct conceptions, coin and mediums of exchange in general, vitiates the reasoning of the bi-metallists throughout. Thus the advantages which they expect from the monetisation of silver constitute excellent illustrations of the danger of defective definitions against which we wish to warn our readers. The bi-metallists expect that they can by universal government enactment bring about an unnatural or at least a stable relation between gold and silver. They say that when silver is money the demand for that metal for coining purposes will be so large that its price will naturally rise. Here they are again led into a mistake by the supposition that because a certain kind of coin is acknowledged as the value-measurer, its circulation should be measured by all the business done on the basis of it. In their imagination therefore a very large quantity of silver would be required. But what is the real fact of the case? No government enactment will remove people's objection to filling their pockets with silver coin or sending cart-loads of it in the case of heavy remittances. The people will handle exactly the amount of silver they do now, and the only extra use that would be found for silver coin in this country would be for increasing the metallic reserve of the Bank of England. It is certain that a number of new devices would be found to transfer claims for silver coin by paper, and that in any case a very strong extra inducement to use cheques would be established. The consequence in other countries would be similar, and the value of silver would remain unchanged.

But, in order to give another illustration, let us suppose that the bi-metallists succeed in doing what cannot be done, namely, to cause silver to circulate at par with gold, without that daily changing gold-rate, which all experienced financiers know would set in, and see whether the expected beneficial result would be possible. The bi-metallists say, at least some of them, that by increasing the quantity of coin in the world, they would increase the mediums of exchange and thereby facilitate business. If we say that by increasing the mediums of exchange we should facilitate business, we should be right, but to increase the coin in the world is not to increase the mediums of exchange, because coin is the value-measurer, and it determines the prices of all other goods by the quantity in which it is present in the market as compared to the quantity present of other goods. The price of goods, quoted in gold, is high because gold is present in small quantity. If gold suddenly became as abundant as granite the price of all other goods, quoted in gold, would be very high. If therefore we succeed in adding all the world's silver to the quantity of the value-measurer now present in the market, the value of the measurer would go down in exact proportion, and as the value of all other goods is measured by this same value-measurer, the nominal price of all goods would rise in exact proportion. We should then have much more coin, but prices being higher in proportion we should not be able to effect a single pennyworth more exchanges than we do now. Thus we find that an increase in the quantity of circulating coin is not an increase in the aggregate of the mediums of exchange which we so sorely want and which the bi-metallists vainly hope to bring about.

The other fallacies of the bi-metallists do not come within the scope of our subject ; but it may be fair to point out that in one of their conclusions the bi-metallists are right, namely, that if a law were passed to make silver a compulsory legal tender along with gold at a higher gold value than it has now, all those who have contracted debts in gold would be allowed, if they choose to be so dishonest, to pay these debts in silver. The interest on the National Debt, and on loans raised by corporations, companies, and individuals, would thus be materially reduced at the expense of the creditors. It is possible that philosophers—not economists—might favour such a general reduction of debt on the ground that it would tend to diminish the unequal distribution of wealth. But, supposing that this advantage were not so debatable as it really is, but firmly established, we must still come to the conclusion that it would be extremely foolish to bring it about by tampering with the value-measurer, involving as it would such an amount of annoyance and confusion to the commercial world, while the same object could be so easily attained by a simple enactment of the government to the effect that all debts should be reduced by so much per cent.!

The mistakes which we have pointed out, and the infinite number of similar ones, would be avoided if we always bore in mind that coin has two distinct functions, that of value-measurer and that of medium of exchange. The first one is by far the more important—is in busy centres infinitely more important than the second one. To fulfil its mission as value-measurer, coin need not be bodily used, but simply supposed and referred to. No quantity is required for this purpose, and the legal enactment stipulating its weight and alloy is sufficient. If by coin of the realm we understand the unit which has been fixed as legal tender, it is quite right to say that gold and silver can fulfil their functions as value-measurers without being coined. There have been examples of such theoretical coin. At the time when the old Bank of Hamburg was founded, the sovereigns of surrounding nations, including a host of princes of neighbouring nations, reserving for themselves a strict monopoly of coinage, under the pretext of keeping it up to its standard, were much given to base coinage. The Hamburg merchants feared

E

that if their new bank were to coin good full-weighted silver pieces, the princes would all counterfeit them in base alloy and thus cause them much annoyance. They therefore resolved that the new value-measurer, the Mark Banco, which they introduced at the time, should not be coined at all. The name was simply recognised as meaning a certain quantity of fine silver. Deposits were received in silver and gold coins of all nations; all descriptions, all alloys, as well as gold and silver plate and ingots. All was valued in Mark Banco and credited in that imaginary coin to the depositors' accounts. The books of the bank were kept and all transactions were carried on in Mark Banco. Drafts on the bank were credited to the bearer, who in his turn could draw on the bank. When coin happened to be actually required from the bank, it was paid out in silver or in such coin as was demanded, as far as the bank had stock of it. The silver or promiscuous coin paid out was calculated in Mark Banco, the latter according to its weight and alloy. In spite of its theoretical nature the Mark Banco was the value-measurer for centuries in all the countries of the north where the Hanseatic League had its business ramifications, as well as the general international value-measurer; and, thanks to the impossibility of debasing it, it proved of immense use to commerce in general. Had Prince Bismarck, instead of destroying the old Bank at Hamburg, profited by the teachings it afforded, he would never have established such a monopoly bank as that of the Imperial Bank of Germany, and would thus have left one monument the less to bear witness to his incredible want of insight into Political Economy.

As banking and business methods develope, the tendency to dispense with the metallic coin as a medium of exchange, while retaining it as a value-measurer, becomes more marked. In the Clearing House of London alone, some thirty million pounds sterling are daily cleared without the handling of coin. But the sight which a London bank presents, with its weighing and counting of coin, shows that there is plenty of room for improvement in this respect. The immense quantity of gold coin which, in England, is constantly subjected to wear and tear, keeps deteriorating, and the sweating of coin, which has lately been revived, materially assists in the process. The loss is now borne partly by the banks, partly by individuals. Part of the burden the government has agreed to take on itself by the re-coinage of the oldest sovereigns and half-sovereigns. But as long as we keep up the barbarous method of wasting the most expensive metal by using it as a circulating medium of exchange, the difficulty of a debased coinage will always be with us; and the more the government thus sacrifices with the object of keeping it up to the standard, the more encouragement will it give to coin-sweaters and to the picking-out of the full-weighted sovereigns which is now done every day by the banks. Neither the banks, nor anybody else, can be blamed for paying out the light sovereigns whenever they can, and for reserving the good ones for such payments as they are called upon to pay in full weight. If the fact were generally recognised that coin can be retained as a value-measurer, but to a very large extent abolished as a medium of exchange, the government might realise a profit of several millions annually on the circulation, instead of suffering the loss they do now, and at the same time save the banks from a considerable loss. The government has only to issue a sufficient number of one pound, ten-shilling, and even five-shilling notes to replace the circulating gold. If the State took the issue of these notes into its own hands, through the Mint or any other government establishment, not allowing the new circulation to interfere at all with the banking of the country, hardly any economic effect would result, and certainly no bad one, while the profit would be secured to the benefit of the taxpayers. A small stock of gold would suffice to meet the demand for metallic coin, which would be mostly for export, and the state of this metallic cash would indicate exactly whether more notes should be issued or a part of them withdrawn. The objections that would be raised against such a scheme would probably be based on the fear that the government paper circulation might, as the paper circulation of so many States has done before, depreciate, and land us in the plight of a gold premium with all its difficulties and demoralising speculations.

It is, however, hardly necessary to explain that a depreciation of the notes is entirely impossible as long as the government pays them on demand. It is impossible to imagine that nowadays a government department could be mismanaged to such an extent as not to meet the small average demand for gold; and as to a panic or a run, such a thing would not happen until the confidence in England, as a State, is shaken. And in case of a panic arising from some great military defeat, or from a social or political revolution, which is extremely remote, or a serious riot, which is quite possible, the government have only to suspend payment for a few days until the funds can be raised, and the notes would not lose a fraction of their value in the meantime, thanks to the confidence which we have in ourselves as a nation. Should the State fall into such a miserable plight, and the country be visited by such serious calamities as to prevent the raising of a couple of hundred millions to pay the notes, there would be other losses, other causes for ruin, before which the loss of the value of the notes would sink into insignificance. The objections on the ground of danger would only therefore be raised by prejudiced people.

But there is another danger which any Chancellor of the Exchequer might well dread, namely, the deluge of schemes and plans which would set in if the replacement of coin by government notes were mooted. We should then see how little it is understood that we do not suffer from any scarcity of what people are pleased to call 'currency,' and that the reform here proposed is simply a fiscal one intended to add to the income of the State, and not an economic one affecting the supply of capital to labour, cost of production and price of sale, credit, enterprise, values, wages, or indeed any of those factors on which the prosperity of a nation depends.

A little calm reflection will show this at once. If the government, instead of inflating the credit of the country by entrusting the issue to a bank or banks, were to use these notes in all its disbursements, wherever these take place in the country, including the interest on the National Debt, and to hand them over to anyone who wished to buy them for gold, the economic effect on the country would simply be as follows. As the notes began to circulate they would affect the market, that is to say, the whole of the country, as would an imported quantity of gold of the same amount; they would cause a momentary demand for goods which at once would be supplied from abroad, and a quantity of gold equal to the quantity of notes would leave the country permanently in payment of the imported extra quantity of goods. When as many notes had been issued as the market could carry, the result would be that a corresponding quantity of coin would have left the country permanently, or at least until the government recalled the gold and withdrew the notes. The chief difference would be that the people and the banks, including the issuing banks, would use the government notes exactly in the same way as they use coin now. Two direct economic effects there would be, but of such slight importance that they would be hardly noticeable in practical affairs. The first would be a slight rise in prices and a slightly increased activity during the interval in which the gold was replaced by the notes; and the second would be a slight increase of the gold-stock outside England, by which the cost of production would be raised for our competitors and their power to purchase British goods would be almost imperceptibly increased.

There would be an indirect economic effect from the fiscal advantages which the government would secure, allowing of a reduction of the taxes in proportion. Besides the interest on the circulating notes, there would be a very considerable profit through the mass of notes which would be destroyed in fires, shipwrecks, and other accidents, forgotten in hiding-places, and sent out into foreign places never to return. The income to the State from lost notes would probably suffice to pay all expenses connected with the issue.

In dwelling upon the advantages of replacing the gold by government notes we may appear to have strayed from our subject; but the proposed system is a good illustration of how little importance the quantity of the gold coin may be in a country with good credit and an intelligent government. Besides, our task would not be complete, and new confusions would not be forestalled by this work, if we did not succeed in making it clear that government notes and notes of private banks, of which we shall treat very fully, are and should be of a totally distinct nature—Government notes being, with regard to all their economic effect on the country, equal to coin from the simple reason that government prestige causes them to circulate freely and to be received with as little formality and hesitation all over the country as coin, and exempts them from all the economic laws to which other notes are subjected. We have, therefore, spoken of them in connection with coin. Private bank notes are and should be pure credit-instruments, and of them we shall speak when we deal with credit. We shall then be able to show that there is nothing to prevent government notes from circulating in as large a quantity as the country can use, side by side with free-notes of private banks issued in as large a quantity as the issuing banks find to their own advantage, and that yet immutable economic laws will prevent over-issue by a single pound-note.

CHAPTER V

THE IMPOSSIBILITY OF INCREASING THE QUANTITY OF COIN BY IMPORTATION

We have seen how co-operation by exchanges, the leading phenomenon of our civilisation, on which all prosperity depends, was enormously facilitated by the introduction of coin; also how the greatest advantage we derive from coin is the measurement of value; how the use of coin, as a medium of exchange, is of secondary consideration, and can with intelligent organisation be dispensed with altogether.

The introduction of other mediums of exchange than coin is almost as old as coin, and is not optional but absolutely necessary in every community where the economic activity rises above that of a savage country. Why this is so can be easily explained. We have already pointed out, in our remarks on bi-metallism, that if the quantity of the coin in the world were increased, the prices of all other kinds of goods would go up in proportion. Now, if the quantity of coin in one country or in one market is increased, the same thing would happen there, and the effect would be permanent, if that country or that market were entirely isolated and had not commercial relations with other countries or other markets; or, in other words, if it were a world by itself. But our country, like most other countries, is not isolated, but in the closest business relations with all the rest of the world.

The question then presents itself, What would happen if we imported a quantity of precious metal in order to increase our stock of coin? If we bear in mind that coin is goods, we can at once answer, that the same would happen to coin as would happen to any other kind of goods, an extra quantity were suddenly imported without a corresponding increase in consumption. The price of this kind of over-imported goods would go down. A slight fall would, in our times of keen competition, attract buyers from abroad, and the superfluous quantity of the imported goods would soon begin to leave the country, continuing to do so until the level of the supply, and consequently of the price, had been resumed. This is exactly what would happen to coin, with this only difference, that the discrepancy in the value of coin here and abroad would act more quickly, and the return of the gold to the market whence it came would be so much prompter and less influenced by the cost of re-shipment and insurance.

But it seems natural to raise the following objection to these conclusions. 'A large quantity of goods—say coffee—might be suddenly imported into a market, without lowering the price of coffee in that market, if there is a great, or at least a corresponding demand, which need not imply great consumption. In the same way coin may be imported into a country without going down in value, on condition that there is a strongly-felt demand for money.' We use the word 'money' here expressly, because the above objection would only be raised by some one whose ideas about financial and economic matters had been muddled by the word 'money.' It is easy to show the fallaciousness of the objection. What is popularly called 'a want of money' is not the want of coin. Those who require 'money' and will gladly accept coin, do not consume it nor leave it in their strong boxes, but they want it to exchange it against something else or to pay a debt. In the first place, it is self-evident that it was not coin they required, but goods; and in the second case, the creditor who expects to receive the coin does not consume it, but wants it to buy something with or to invest it. In either case, the coin purchases some kind of goods, and it was actually goods the creditor wanted.

The demand for 'money' is therefore actually a demand for capital, and many things may be capital, but coin regarded as coin cannot, because it is not consumed in a production. To the dentist, the goldsmith, the photographer, coin may be capital when it is consumed by them. The people who want capital but say that they want money, and try to get coin, would be just as well served and just as well satisfied, if they obtained the capital directly, instead of first receiving coin and then changing it into capital. But in most countries the supply of capital is so hampered and the trade in credit so restricted, that the idea of obtaining capital without first receiving coin comes into few people's heads, and the result is that the trading classes all over the world are, to use their own expression, in a chronic state of 'want of money.' It is therefore evident that a country may be choked full of coin—that is to say, may contain its full complement, which in fact every market always does—and at the same time the supply of credit and capital may be terribly inadequate, thanks to bad laws and bad institutions. But this would not prevent the people from demanding a further supply of coin. It is then only natural that the imported coin should go down in value, because the want of it was only illusory, and what the people needed was a very different thing, namely, other goods or capital.

If, therefore, coin is imported into a country in an extra quantity, it is bound to go down in value and therefore returns quickly whence it came. The rates of exchange confirm this in so striking and minute a manner, that the sensitive way in which they constantly keep changing is to the experienced business man, who works with foreign countries, a complete proof of the impossibility of disturbing, even to the smallest extent, the level of the world's coin-supply.

The fluctuations of the rates of exchange demonstrate every day, every hour almost, the economic law which says *that every market has the exact supply of coin which it can carry*, and that it is beyond the power of government, beyond human power altogether—except by violence—to suspend the natural consequences of this law. If by any forcible means, or by the varying incidents of commerce, the level of the supply of coin should tend to be disturbed so that one market would have more and another less than is natural to it, there would at once be a rise in the price of coin, or—which is the same—a general fall in the prices of all other goods, in the market where the coin threatens to become too scarce; and the opposite effect would be produced in the market where it tends to be too plentiful.

The price fluctuation affects not only goods as distinct from coin, but even the value of coin compared with coin, so that a foreign coin which contains the same alloy and has the same weight as a native one may, through the varying of the rates of exchange, have to be sold for less or may fetch a higher price than the native coin. In these times, when thousands of keen business men are constantly watching for opportunities to make profits, the fluctuations of the international exchanges, as well as of the prices of goods in general, seldom become excessive, because the reaction from each variation sets in so very rapidly. Wherever goods or coin are sold under their universal market value, they are at once picked up and sent to those markets where they are scarce. Thus the natural level is maintained all over the world.

But to the non-commercial reader it may be interesting to see how the rates of exchange act as inexorable regulators of the universal coin-level. If a forcible transfer from one country to another of a considerable amount of coin, or of those precious metals of which coin is made, were contemplated, the real metallic coin would be shipped only in very exceptional cases. If, for example, an amount corresponding to one hundred thousand pounds were to be sent from Hamburg to London without any countervailing shipments in goods, the sender in Hamburg would buy on the Exchange there drafts on London amounting to one hundred thousand pounds, at the best rate of exchange obtainable. The price he would have to pay for these hundred thousand pounds in drafts would depend on the supply of drafts on

England and on the demand by people who, like himself, had remittances to make to England. If the supply and demand were average before the sender came on the Hamburg Exchange, the hundred thousand pounds he is looking out for would intensify the demand, harden the market, and encourage the sellers to ask for a higher price. The rate of exchange on London would rise. This rise in the Exchange would affect all business with England; would-be importers of English goods to Hamburg would at once consider that, through the rise in the rates of exchange, their goods would cost them more than an hour before, and the least eager ones would reduce or postpone their orders.

The exporters of Hamburg goods to England would, on the contrary, take into consideration that by the risen rate of exchange they could now obtain a higher price for the drafts in pounds sterling, which they could draw if they exported, than they could an hour earlier, and this would decide the more eager ones to ship their goods. Now what is the result of all this? The shipment of goods from England to Hamburg has lessened, the shipment of goods from Hamburg to England has increased, the hundred thousand pounds which our sender wanted to go to London, and which was represented in the draft he remits, have actually gone from Hamburg to London in the shape of goods.

Thus all intended remittances of coin from one country to another generally resolve themselves, through the action of the rates of exchange, into shipments of goods. Should too high a rate of exchange be demanded the coin may be actually sent, but this happens more and more seldom, because in all business centres there are firms which carry on a kind of business often called arbitration. They are always on the look-out to sell drafts on any foreign place when the exchange becomes favourable to them, and the competition between these firms, which are generally satisfied with a very small profit, say $\frac{1}{4}$ per cent., prevents the exchange from rising high even in the face of sudden and large demands.

The trade balance which arises between two countries is not settled by shipment of coin as might be supposed, because the variations of the rates of exchange at once begin to check the import in the one country and the export in the other, until the level is again established. This will be evident from another example.

Let us suppose that France exported more goods to England than England exported to France, and that, for the moment, the other markets were neutral factors. The result would, of course, be that sellers of drafts on France (or francs), would be able to obtain a good price for their drafts, because the great import of French goods would have to be paid for, and exporters with few drafts to offer would have only a small supply to meet a great demand. The sellers of francs would consequently raise their price, that is, the rate of exchange on France would go up. If the value of francs were to rise very much in England, it would pay the importer of French goods to send English coin to France to be melted and sold as metal. The cost of transport and of re-coining the gold may therefore be said to be the limit of the fluctuations of the rates. But long before any such limit is reached, the reaction which the rates produce has re-established the level, because for each fraction that the rate of exchange on France goes up, the import from that country becomes less profitable, and export thither more profitable; the disproportion in the two branches of commerce with which they started would thus be destroyed and the balance restored. We find then that it is not only the forcible shifting of coin from one market to another which causes the rates of exchanges to fluctuate, and thereby produces the reactions described, but that even a slight tendency towards disturbing the level of the international coin-supply suffices to set the rate to work and prevent any actual movement in coin or precious metals.

Large quantities of coin, or coin-metal, can be imported into a country without affecting prices, if they are employed in such way as to be kept out of commerce, the Mint, and the banks. For example, if they were melted for the purpose of constructing a gold or silver statue, and for other ornamental purposes. The effect of the transfer in that case would be limited to the market or markets whence the precious metal or coin was taken, in so far that it would tend to lower the prices of all other goods.

But if coin, or coin-metal, is imported and allowed to flow into the usual channels of commerce, the rise in prices and in the cost of production, as described, is inevitable. Though this is proved by the variations of the rates of exchange, it may be satisfactory to our readers to take a glance at the ways in which this rise of prices and its consequences come about.

We will suppose a market in a normal state—say London. Mr. Smith, from Australia, settles in this normal market and brings with him his whole fortune in gold, which he has accidentally found in Australia. His fortune is not of the slightest use to him so long as it remains gold. He has to get rid of the gold as soon as possible, in order to secure an income from his possession. Moreover he dreads robbers. He takes it to the bank, or he has it coined and pays the sovereigns into the bank.

This increases the metallic cash of the bank, and, as it is the interest of the bank to keep its metallic cash as low as it dare, this abnormal influx of gold induces the manager to grant more liberal credits, and thus, in its turn, the bank at once gets rid of the gold. The people who have obtained the extra credit from the bank may draw the amounts in gold, but they draw as little as they can, and whatever they draw they spend at once. They buy goods or services, and as any amount paid for the latter finally resolves itself into an expenditure for goods, we need only consider the former, that is the purchase of goods. These purchases might have for object either consumption or production: in either case, a certain quantity of goods is taken out of the market—that is to say, from out of the stock, that stock which is held for sale. The extra demand for goods which has thus arisen tends to harden prices, and when the habitual holders find that their stock is smaller, and the demand better, they become anxious to replenish their stock, even by paying a higher price for the goods. All those they buy from are influenced in the same way, and thus the tendency of the rise in prices spreads all over the market like the ripple on a calm sea.

We have only noticed certain and inevitable consequences, but there are a host of incidental ones, all of which tend to send up prices.

Thus the extended facility for credit might cause the enterprising business man to take a sanguine view of the state of trade, and to strain all his resources and all his credit in order to extend his business or his production, whereby greater voids would be caused in the goods market, and a greater number of hands would be employed at higher wages, which again would increase consumption. The habitual holders of goods, finding that there is a rise in the market, may conclude that a yet greater rise is at hand, and secure large quantities of goods in order to take advantage of it; and this would give a strong impulse to the rise.

In the mean time, we see that nobody wants to keep the gold, and that, with the exception of some few hoarders among a million, everybody is anxious to get rid of it as soon as possible. Thus it soon reappears in the bank and encourages the granting of more credits, that is, new causes for a rise in prices. But this is not all. The abundance of gold appears to every individual so much greater than it really is, because it circulates so rapidly from hand to hand, and it is a well-known fact that, wherever large quantities of gold are handled, there arises a tendency to lavishness in personal expenditure; this tendency is powerfully stimulated when trade is good and profits are easy. It is no wonder, then, that the extra gold which Mr. Smith has brought with him from Australia has caused a wave of enhanced prices which will more or less affect the whole country before it goes abroad.

The effect of this general rise in prices is twofold: it makes production dearer, and causes the import of foreign goods to be more profitable. Export thus becomes less and import greater, and so there remains a balance due to foreign countries which is paid in the extra gold which Mr. Smith brought into the market. When we say that the gold goes abroad, this does not imply that in all cases the gold would be actually shipped in return, but, what is more usual and what is more likely to happen, that the normal import of gold from the gold-producing countries becomes less until the quantity which Mr. Smith brought into the market is balanced. We thus find that, whether we look minutely into the actual process by which forcibly imported gold finds its way back, or whether we rely on those immutable witnesses, the rates of exchange, the increase of the normal supply of coin in a market is an economic impossibility, and that the economic truth that each market has sufficient, may be well considered as proved.

It is of course impossible to express in figures the amount of coin that is natural to a market, though with the mass of evidence before us, we cannot doubt that it is very strictly limited. It depends on many circumstances, such as the size of the market, its population, its wealth, its government, and above all, the' supply of other mediums of exchange besides coin. Any change in the condition of a market will naturally affect its capacity for holding coin. A discovery of mineral wealth, the presence of men of great commercial ability, treaties of commerce, the abolition of hampering legislation—all these may tend to increase the normal circulation of coin. But misfortunes and commercial disasters may produce temporarily the same effect. A crisis causing banks to fail, shaking the general credit, and thus destroying a great number of mediums of exchange other than coin, compels a prompt increase in the circulating coin as the only means of re-establishing prosperity. During the great commercial crises which, since 1844, have caused the Bank Act to be suspended, the quantity of coin and coin-notes—that is Bank of England notes—in the London market was probably larger in proportion to the business done than during any other period.

CHAPTER VI

GOVERNMENT PREJUDICES AND THEIR CONSEQUENCES

THE tendency of gold to take its level in all the markets of the world will be seen operating in the distribution of gold from the gold-mining districts. There, where a rich gold mine is situated, the gold is cheaper, and the average price of other goods dearer, than in any other place in the world. Were this not the case the gold would not leave the pit-mouth, because if it were as dear there as in London it could not bear the expenses of freight, insurance, and commissions which its shipment involves. Other goods must be dearer there than anywhere else, because the value-measurer by which their price is determined is cheaper than anywhere else. It is this low price of gold and high price of goods which causes the gold to stream out and the goods to stream in. As to the ways in which this operates, it suffices to remember that where men can earn a large amount by digging for gold, they will do no work which is less paid, and any production attempted near a rich gold mine will be the dearest production in the world.

We find then that the production and export of other goods than gold are prevented or lessened by the gold coming out of the ground in the gold-mining districts, just as production and export of goods are reduced by the presence of imported gold in any other district. It is therefore evident that the efforts of a patriotic government should be directed towards the use of other mediums of exchange than gold, and to reduce it in the market to that minimum which is consistent with safety and expediency.

This can best be done by encouraging other mediums of exchange. From what we have said, it should be clear that the sanguine expectations which have been raised by the discovery of gold in Wales are based on fallacious opinions, and that of all the minerals we may discover in this country gold will benefit us the least. If the whole of Snowdon were found to be one vast nugget of gold, it would probably demoralise and destroy England as a nation, would benefit us much less than the removal of those restrictions on credit from which our country now suffers.

The baneful influence of the importation of gold on Empires of the past may be traced in history, though perhaps not sufficiently noticed by historians. When the centre of the Roman Empire became saturated with the gold drawn by taxes from all the conquered countries, productive labour and healthy industry decayed. The people became divided into two classes, those who spent gold in the gratification of their taste for luxury, enjoyment, and vice; those who ministered meekly to such tastes. The result could only be that fearful corruption which made the Roman Empire an easy prey to barbarians.

Before Spain had acquired its gold and silver producing colonies in America, it was the leading country in industry, art, and commerce; but when these precious metals began to pour in from America, a change for the worse set in. The gold which was landed in Spain had to find its level in all the European markets. The excessive supply in Spain made it cheap there, everything else dear. Spanish products became too expensive to be imported, even to be consumed in the country, and import of foreign goods received an enormous impulse. Other countries, such as France, Germany, Holland, and England, with their small supply of gold and consequent low prices of production, found wealthy and willing customers in Spain, and had thus the strongest inducement to practise those Spanish industries which now began to decay.

Recent historical events supply some striking illustrations of the evil consequence of importing coin. Prince Bismarck, like many of the old school of politicians, is not aware that everything is wealth except coin, which only represents it. He hoped to enrich Germany and to weaken France by the milliards he exacted as war indemnity in 1871. The large quantity of gold expected from France he intended to use for many purposes, among others for the introduction of a new gold coinage. But when the remittances from France began to arrive they were not in gold, but mostly in drafts on German commercial firms and drafts from France or foreign firms and banks. As the remittances continued the proportion of gold they contained became less and that of drafts on Germany larger; finally, when Prince Bismarck wanted the gold for his new coinage he had to buy in the Bank of England, out of which transaction the tendencies of a panic arose which many still remember.

To those who are wedded to the old-fashioned fallacies about gold and wealth, it ought to seem strange that the Germans, after receiving hundreds of millions sterling from France, should have to buy what gold they wanted for coinage out of the small stock kept by the Bank of England.

What happened to France and Germany with regard to the war indemnity was this. When the first remittances arrived the Berlin rate of exchange in Paris was excessively high, as the French government had come upon the market for drafts, and the Paris rate of exchange on Berlin was low in comparison. All exporters of German goods to France, finding that they got a very low price for the francs in which their goods were paid for in Paris, and that this deprived them of their profit, a great number ceased to send goods to France at all. But the importers of French goods into Germany, finding on the contrary, that they could buy francs extremely cheaply, had an extra profit on their importations without paying an extra price to their suppliers in France, and thus increased the imports from France to the utmost.

In the mean time the demand for French and all other foreign goods in Germany became intense. The government did not keep the drafts and gold received from France. The uses for the newly acquired treasure were manifold. Heavy debts contracted during the war had to be met; war-material had to be renewed; the artillery had to be reconstructed; pensions and large national rewards had to be paid to officers and officials, including the lower grades.

All the government departments, all the receivers of national rewards, all the enriched contractors, were spending coin wildly. The demand for all kinds of goods became intense, and everybody in trade realised large profits, and consumed and spent in proportion. The price of all real property rose quickly; the proprietors, finding themselves suddenly rich, increased their consumption. A large amount of capital was in search of investment, an immense crop of companies grew up, all demanding goods for building purposes and for reproduction, counting on the continuance of the inflated state of trade. The working classes received higher wages, not to work for the export traders, but for the enormous demand for goods at home. The whole of Germany was thus a focus of consumption. It could be carried on without disaster for a time, because France was supplying all the imports and making good the gigantic waste—in fact, Germany was feverishly engaged in eating up the milliards which Prince Bismarck had intended as a basis of future German prosperity.

Such was the famous *Gründerzeit* in Germany. It was very pleasant so long as it lasted. But it only lasted until the final remittance of the war indemnity had arrived from France and was spent. The import for a little while went on as briskly as ever, for in Germany, as here, commercial men have a lofty disdain for Political Economy, and sometimes have to pay for it.

When the last of these excessive imports had to be remitted for, the exchange on Paris had again righted itself and the price of francs was no longer cheap. The German importers had to compete for drafts on foreign places in order to pay for the imports, and as the immense source of capital in Paris on which the Germans had drawn ceased to yield, the rates of exchange on all foreign places went up in Germany; the German banks which had assumed lavish habits towards their customers, no longer being replenished by government funds, had to depend entirely on drafts paid in by German exporters in order to balance their accounts abroad; as the export had collapsed such drafts were scarce, and the German banks were chary of supplying drafts on foreign places to the importers except for coin. This naturally produced a great demand for it all over the country: consequently the rise in prices was checked, and the fall began. The ruined state of the German export trade prevented it for a long time from making up for the collapsed remittances from France, and the consumption in Germany fell off rapidly. The mass of foolish undertakings by companies and others had started with such heavy expenses and had wasted so much capital that dividends were out of the question. Many of these enterprises came to grief, the shareholders lost their capital, and they, too, had to restrict their consumption. The working classes were thrown out of employment in very large numbers, and had to live on next to nothing. Prices of all real property fell below the point at which they stood before the *Gründerzeit*, and that great commercial crisis set in which is known as 'the Crash.'

The German export trade, and with it the German industries, had received a tremendous blow, and fully ten years after they had not recovered. What recovery there was sprang from such excessively low wages and such excessively small profits as only a nation driven to desperation could submit to. As to the German Empire and the kingdom of Prussia themselves, they have since the war entered upon a course of huge State loans, and if Germany has not soon recourse to an improved economic system, it is to be feared the new Empire will be shipwrecked on the rock of bankruptcy.

And what was the effect of the war indemnity on France? It was this. The French industries and producers experienced an unprecedented demand for their goods at high prices, and trade in France was never better than during the period of the payment of the war indemnity. New experiences were gained, new works established, improved machinery was introduced, and the foundations of thousands of fortunes were laid.

Thus by ignoring Political Economy Germany

was deprived of the rewards of victory, while defeated France was largely assisted in paying off her debt.

All large transfers, or attempts at transfers of gold from one country to another have proved a curse to the receiving country. Yet it is a common occurrence that the Minister of Finance of a foreign State, finding that the resources of his country are undeveloped and that the inhabitants are poor and short of work—in reality the consequence of legislative restrictions on commerce, industry, and banking—comes to what he deems no doubt the wise conclusion that the country is short of capital, that capital is money, and money is coin; and so he proposes a foreign loan, which is generally accepted with acclamation.

London has been the place where the bulk of such loans has been raised, and we know by experience that very little of the capital thus lent by England leaves this country in the shape of gold. What we send out in return for interest-bearing bonds of foreign States are English goods. The explanation we have given of the rates of exchange shows that this could not be otherwise, because every attempt to send coin would resolve itself into the shipment of goods. In a small treatise on Free Trade by the late Mr. Mongredien, published by the Cobden Club, statistics are given which clearly demonstrate that the extra export from England during the years in which foreign loans had been granted by this country tallied exactly with the amounts of such loans.

Almost every considerable international transaction in coin thus confirms the economic axiom that every market has sufficient coin.

This axiom, however, is far from being recognised by the governments of the world, and hence a mass of mistakes with the most serious consequences to humanity. Instead of facilitating healthy and rational mediums of exchange, the presence of which would considerably reduce the demand for the use of coin, they adhere to the old fallacy of the trade-balance, and maintain a host of obsolete laws all of which have the futile object of retaining more gold than possible in the country.

All protectionist enactments presuppose that coin alone is wealth and foreign goods are not wealth, and that if import can be lessened and export be increased the country will be better off. Governments thus try to enrich their people by compelling them to give to foreign countries very large quantities of the product of their labour for a small quantity of the product of foreign labour. It is this blindness to an evident truth that causes the disgraceful protective system in some of our Colonies —a system established by a ring of unscrupulous politicians and selfish and short-sighted manufacturers which ruins all the natural industries, especially farming, and impoverishes all the working people in some of our Colonies, destined by nature to enjoy extraordinary prosperity. The Sugar Bounty system is an outcome of the same mistake. The enormous amount of foreign loans which, though they momentarily benefit England, are yet a curse to humanity and especially to the nations that obtain them, are a result of the same cause.

If statesmen and parliaments can only be taught that in the first place they cannot, by artificial means, increase the quantity of the circulating coin; and, secondly, that the importation of a large quantity of coin is a source of ruin, they would soon perceive the folly of all their anti-economic enactments, and these formidable causes of poverty and misery would soon disappear.

CHAPTER VII

THE IMPORTANCE OF CREDIT

In the remote past, when other mediums of exchange than coin were introduced, the economic law which we have dealt with in the preceding chapter—that it is impossible to increase the quantity of circulating coin by importation—was as immutable as it is now, though its actions were slow owing to the insignificance of business relations and exchanges, difficulty of communication, and a primitive state of things in general.

In one way the barbarous condition of the people furthered the introduction of a medium of exchange, which has been and is still one of the most important in the world, namely, current accounts. Robbers, pirates, absence of roads, and defective navigation, &c., made the transmission of coin extremely dangerous, and it was found far more convenient to send the goods from one place to another, and not to receive the payment in coin, but to await a return-envoi of goods.

At first no doubt the differences were brought in coin, but the custom of keeping current accounts between merchants living at a distance from each other is a very old one. Such accounts may run for short or long periods, and numbers of them have been running for generations without any remittances of coin. The same method is still kept up all over the civilised world, and our whole import and export trades are cleared in this way, with the exception of rare and small shipments of gold or coin.

But the use of accounts current as mediums of exchange is, for obvious reasons, limited to such cases in which the contracting parties have a certain commercial standing, and are known to each other as honest and trustworthy. In the incomparably more numerous cases in which buyers and sellers were not known to each other, current accounts were impossible, because the contracting parties dared not accord each other credit. All the large number of transactions between people who did not know each other, or between people who had scant credit when they were known, between people who could not afford to spare capital enough to grant credit to their customers—all such transactions always had to be accomplished by the passing of metallic coin if no method had been devised by which to secure to all these classes of people some way of using credit instead of coin.

Such a method was found in indirect credit. A man who had not enough credit where he wanted it, contracted with the man who had. A man desiring to travel on business, and perhaps to buy goods, in places where he was unknown, because of the danger of carrying a large amount of coin with him, or perhaps because he could not raise all the coin he required, would go to a wealthy man well known in the places he intended to visit, and ask him for drafts on his friends in those places. These drafts were only payable to the traveller himself and of no value to robbers. On arrival at his respective destinations he could either get the goods he wanted or the coin from the people on whom the drafts were drawn with which to purchase them. Thus trade in credit, or indirect credit, arose.

Though a considerable amount was cleared by

indirect credit, without the use of coin, there remained a far larger amount of business transactions in which coin could not be dispensed with. A man wanted, for instance, a lot of goods which seemed to him advantageous, but the seller could not afford to part with them except against cash, or he did not know the buyer sufficiently well to trust him. The buyer, though a man of good standing, might not have the cash handy, and in order to accomplish his purpose, he went to some wealthy man and borrowed the coin. As the bargain secured the buyer a good profit he could well afford, and was quite willing, to pay interest, discount, or commission to him who supplied him with the coin. As such transactions became more general, money-lending developed into a business, and the same people who carried on the trade of money-lenders often at the same time dealt in credit. Thus banking arose.

As long as the banker had to limit the loans he granted in coin to the extent of his own fortune, his turn-over and his profits were small while his charges had to be high. The history of every country bristles with examples of the animosity aroused by the exorbitant charges of money-lenders, and a mass of enactments were passed by governments to restrict usury and fix a legal rate of interest.

Such State-socialistic interference in times gone by produced exactly the same results as our modern State-socialistic enactments do: they increased the evil they were intended to remedy, and made matters worse for those they intended to protect. It is natural that when a legal interest was fixed which did not apply to all the risks, the business of money-lending should not pay if carried on according to law. All sorts of subterfuges were consequently adopted, the trade became so disreputable as to cause respectable people to withdraw from it, and when the money-lending business was entirely in the hands of the Shylocks, matters reached such a state that high-minded merchants often refused to charge any interest at all, and to do so was denounced by preachers as a deadly sin.

Such a state of affairs was, of course, a curse to society, as it prevented enterprising men and employers of labour from extending their activity beyond the capacity of their own capital. Those who had to borrow coin were obliged to submit to the expensive subterfuges of the Shylocks from whose net, once caught, there was little chance of escape. It is a well-known fact that the most telling blow ever dealt at usury was the repeal of the Acts which were intended to suppress it.

By-and-by a new development of banking allowed of the bankers charging a moderate interest, and of yet realising a good profit. Wealthy people and others who had considerable stocks of coin to spare, dreading the risk of keeping their treasure at home, found it convenient to entrust it to the bankers, who took good care to have safe places for its storage. The stock of coin at the bankers thus accumulated, and when they found that the daily drawings of their customers were nearly balanced by fresh deposits, they used, without any risk to themselves, and without any inconvenience to their clients, the large stock of coin which remained unclaimed in their safes. They therefore lent this coin and kept the interest as their own profit.

Thus bankers became the mediators between those who had coin to spare and those who wanted it. As the coin was acquired and deposited with the object of storing capital, and was borrowed from the bankers by their customers with the object, in some cases, of increasing the capital of their business or production, the bankers thus early became the mediators between capital and labour as well, though they did not handle the capital itself, but only its representative, coin. The deposit business was so profitable to the bankers that at length they began to pay a small interest on the amounts entrusted to them, and thereby increased materially the in-flow of capital, as well as the services they rendered to labour, by sometimes serving customers who were employers of labour.

While the bankers impelled the circulation of the coin which existed in the country by receiving deposits and granting loans, they also facilitated the business by extending their trade in pure credit, which they created in several ways. We have already mentioned the selling of drafts on other places, and drafts, especially on the Continent, gradually became important credit-instruments of far wider application than current accounts.

Payments were often made in drafts, which frequently circulated through many hands in the same way as coin before they became due for payment. By means of these drafts credit was created in exact proportion to the capital to be transferred.

An example will illustrate this. If a merchant in Venice desiring to sell a cargo of goods to a merchant in Marseilles were unable to spare the capital during the long term a sailing ship took in a voyage to Marseilles, he could arrange with a banker in Marseilles to draw for the whole amount on him, say at three months. Drafts on a well-known banker were easily negotiable in Venice, especially if the credit allowed by the Marseilles banker were confirmed by letter. The merchant, then, would sell his draft to the Venice banker, pay for his cargo, and thus re-enter into the disposal of his capital, ready to renew the transaction at once. The Marseilles banker would accept the draft and charge the Venice merchant with a commission for doing so. While the draft was circulating, or awaiting maturity in the portfolios of some banker, the cargo of goods would arrive in Marseilles, be sold, and the amount paid in to the Marseilles banker, who would thus be in possession of the coin before the draft was due. Thus the credit created by the acceptance of the Marseilles banker would have been the means by which a considerable transfer of capital from hand to hand would have been effected, and the draft would have been the credit-instrument called into existence for the purpose, to die when its work was done.

The promissory note was another credit-instrument which was early adopted and which has remained in use up till now. It probably originated as a bond for a debt, but being endorsed by one bearer in favour of another, or being made out from the beginning to the bearer, it could be used and was used as a medium of exchange in the same way as coin.

It was the promissory note which demonstrated more clearly than any other credit-instrument before the bank-note that coin could be replaced in its capacity of a medium of exchange while it was retained as a value-measurer. It was found that accounts could be settled with the promissory notes of trustworthy people just as well as, if not better, than with coin. In districts where division of labour had opportunities of extending, but where coin was scarce and the education of the inhabitants not advanced enough to work business with accounts alone, small promissory notes circulated very widely and for long periods, and without coming back to be exchanged for coin. In modern times the I O U's of traders in thinly-populated and poor districts have been used to settle the accounts from sheer want of change, and such I O U's have remained for years in circulation in the neighbourhood, and have even been found in the secret places of hoarders.

Such experiences naturally suggested the use of bank-notes.

By the introduction of bank-notes an excellent way was found for extending considerably co-operation by exchanges—that is to say, business—without increasing the circulating coin. The banker created credit by the issuing of notes, and held this credit at the disposal of those who required it and deserved it at a cheap rate and yet with good profit to himself. When we come to treat of note-issuing free from State interference, we shall see that these advantages, though of great importance in themselves, are not the only ones, nor perhaps the most important, which a community might derive from note-issuing.

The receipts of the London goldsmiths were the pioneers of bank-notes in England. Before the establishment of the Bank of England, these goldsmiths acted as the bankers of the city. Their banking business grew naturally out of their jewellery business. Their skill in testing metal made them the keenest buyers of foreign and debased coin of all descriptions, and the valuers of plate, ornaments, and objects made of precious metals. Their business compelled them to keep spacious safes and strong-rooms of which the wealthy classes willingly availed themselves for the storage of their valuables as well as their coin.

With such good security in their hands the jewellers could without risk make advances to the proprietors of the valuables, and thus became money lenders. Those of their customers who had deposited their coin with the goldsmiths, or who had obtained a credit on the strength of their pledges, found it convenient to make their payments either with the receipts of the goldsmiths which they transferred or with drafts on them, that is to say, a letter requesting the goldsmiths to pay the bearer so much.

The experience of the goldsmiths was that the receipts circulated in the same way as coin, and that they were presented for payment in only a small proportion to their number. When therefore they wanted to oblige a customer who was in want of capital, and their stock of coin was low, they lent him a fictitious receipt which served the customer just as well. As the banker charged the same interest for lending his receipts as for lending coin, this new form of business proved very profitable, and the goldsmiths naturally circulated as many receipts as possible. In fact, they created credit and lent it to those who needed it, and these used it exactly as they would have used coin.

Experience taught the goldsmiths, as it tells all issuing bankers, that there was a limit to their issue which could not be exceeded, and their natural instinct of self-preservation caused them to avoid over-issue—that is, to refrain from the issue of more receipts than the trade of London could use: for if they did go beyond their limit their receipts were at once presented for payment in larger quantities than the goldsmiths found it convenient to redeem.

Reckless issue would have meant instantaneous bankruptcy to the goldsmiths, and this perhaps while in possession of wealth which, though considerable, might not be available at a moment's notice. It stands to reason that any man who had sense enough to work up such a business would not commit so senseless an action as to ruin himself by over-issue. There were in fact very few failures among the goldsmiths; those which did happen were not important enough to in any way undermine their popularity, and, when a failure occurred among them, it was not due to over-issue but to over-lending.

The services these issuing goldsmiths rendered to the city of London and to British trade and shipping, at a time when it assumed its supremacy over other large ports in the world, cannot be exaggerated. They enabled a very large business to be carried on without the constant attempt to overfill the market with gold from abroad. London industries were thus enabled to flourish and expand side by side with the larger commerce. The damage done to the London trade and industry was very great when these useful, prudent, and active creators of credit were sacrificed to the Baal of monopoly.

CHAPTER VIII

SIR ROBERT PEEL'S MISTAKE

WHEN the Bank of England was founded the issuing business of the goldsmiths had acquired a considerable extension. Their large profits, and the jealousy these inspired, no doubt had a great deal to do with the establishment of Bank monopoly in this country. The price the government obtained for the monopoly was a large and perpetual loan, which formed, so to say, the commercial capital of the Bank.

The various motives which led to the compact we need not review here. The whole affair was a huge mistake, but there is no occasion to detract from the praise which has been lavished upon the founders of the Bank of England, for they, no doubt, had the best intentions of being useful to the country, and their excuse must be that they did not know what they were about. They had a splendid opportunity of establishing a large model bank in a place offering an enormous scope for it, on a principle that would have allowed it to extend with the circumstances; a pivot round which a free and healthy banking system might have functioned.

But this was, perhaps, not to be expected in those days, when sound economic theories were unknown, and when a government monopoly was regarded as the *sine quâ non* of every important undertaking. How the Bank of England was established, how the charters were renewed, how mistakes after mistakes were committed, all these facts have been related over and over again, and need not be referred to. We are not dealing with the history of events, but rather with the history of progressing ideas and acquired experiences.

The history of a monopoly bank can have little interest for economists, and though discussions, enactments, reforms, the merits of rival methods, in connection with the Bank of England, form a huge literature, it, however, moves and has its being exclusively within the narrow limits of the peculiar and artificial circumstances created by monopoly legislation, and finds no application when matters are regarded from an unprejudiced point of view. To most writers on English finance and banking, the Bank charters are laws of nature, and the Bank of England a part of the scheme of creation. No wonder then that their writings are to sound Political Economy what alchemistry is to chemistry.

Here we shall, therefore, only note that the present system of bank monopoly which prevails in this country originated in the foundation of the Bank of England in 1693, and was last renewed, with a slight concession in favour of Joint-Stock Banks, but unfortunately with considerable additional encroachments on the freedom of note-issuing, as recently as 1844. Thus, during two centuries everything has expanded, improved, developed; but in the all-important matter of banking—the vital mechanism for the supply of capital to labour—we are guided by, and tied down to, the miserable errors and prejudices of our ancestors of two hundred years ago.

What we have to examine is the character of this system, and how it accomplishes those important functions which may be reasonably expected of the banking system of so vast a commercial Empire as ours.

The Act of 1844 puts no restriction on any form of banking except note-issuing. The most beneficial, the most efficient, and the most applicable of all credit-instruments, the pioneers of civilisation and prosperity—bank-notes—are forbidden in Great Britain in any quantity exceeding that which existed forty-five years ago. The Bank of England is allowed to issue notes to the extent of fifteen millions sterling above its reserve stock of precious metals. This arbitrary amount is based on the sum owed by the government to the Bank. Why it is so, and what connection there could possibly be between this debt of the State to the Bank and the want of notes in the English market, are mysteries which no sane man can fathom. No economic or financial reason can be given. The arrangement is one of pure expediency; a bombastic trick intended to convey the impression that the framers of this Bank Act had mastered the most hidden secrets of finance.

That this fixing of these uncovered notes—that is, notes issued above the reserve stock of precious metal—is entirely devoid of sense and innocent of all logic, is evident from the fact that if this amount of notes had to stand in any sensible relation to the business they were intended to facilitate, the quantity should have been determined on the sliding-scale principle, as business expands constantly. Since the promulgation of the Bank Act the export and import of Great Britain have increased more than 600 per cent., and if the uncovered notes of the Bank of England were supposed to be of any use at all to business, their amount must have been enormously too large in 1844, if it was considered sufficient for the probable growth of commerce during the whole term of the charter.

The only reasonable explanation for regulating the uncovered note-issue on the debt of the State to the Bank seems to be that the authors of the Act looked upon such uncovered notes as a great nuisance. But as the State was not prepared to pay its debt there was no escape from allowing the circulation of this nuisance at least up to the amount of the debt. Had the note-issue been fixed before, and the debt contracted afterwards, some excuse for the relation between the two might at least have appeared possible; but as the contrary was the case it is a perfectly hopeless task to look for any reasonable ground for the stipulation.

Besides this uncovered amount of fifteen millions, the Bank of England is magnanimously permitted to issue notes for any quantity of gold and silver stored in the issue department. These notes are consequently equal to warrants, or warehoused gold, and it is not much of a privilege to be allowed to use such warrants when the gold is actually deposited. The Bank also has the right to increase its uncovered issue with the amount of the issue of any private bank which surrenders its right.

From this we must conclude that the amount of notes in the country which was stereotyped by the Act of 1844 must have been considered an extremely nicely calculated amount, exactly responding to the requirements of the country, whatever development might take place in its business—a wonderful calculation indeed! This clause in the Act tempts one to arrive at the contradictory conclusion to that which we drew from the clause limiting the uncovered notes to fifteen millions. For, if the authors of the Bank Act were so anxious that any lapsed issue of private banks should be made good by an increase in the issue of the Bank of England, it is impossible that they should have looked upon the notes as mere nuisances.

No new note-issuing bank is allowed to be established, but all those which were in existence in 1844 were allowed to continue their issue, but not to increase their circulation above that at about the time of the passing of the Bank Act. This clause means that if in a district there existed several note-issuing banks in 1844, it was a good thing that they should go on existing, however much the trade there might decline; and that in a new district which has developed ever so great a commercial activity since 1844, it is good that there should be no issuing banks at all. According to the authors and defenders of this Bank Act, what is good for one place is bad for another.

It also seems taken for granted that it was a very good thing for the banks to increase their issue up to 1844, but that to increase it after that mystic date was so perilous to the country, that, to prevent it, the sacred individual liberty had to be infringed.

No notes under five pounds are allowed to be issued at all. This clause suggests the idea that the authors of the Bank Act were anxious that the wear and tear of the circulating gold coin should be as large as possible, or that they were afraid that banking should become such a paying business that it might be extended to the poor and make them too well off and too independent; for the one-pound note in Scotland was known to contribute largely to the prosperity of the people. Why a five-pound note should be useful and a four-pound note be harmful, nobody has ever known, no one is ever likely to know, not even the defenders of this wonderful Bank Act.

Such are the leading features of the Bank Act which at present disgraces the Statute Books of the greatest commercial Empire of the world.

We have here pointed out the glaring want of logic, system, consistency, and respect for economic truth which characterises the Bank Act, in the hope of encouraging its present defenders to look into it and try to say a single word in its defence. But our object has not been to attack Sir Robert Peel, to whom its introduction was largely due. He could do, when he advocated it, what its defenders cannot do to-day—give reasons for its now obsolete clauses. And if these reasons in our days show themselves to be so many fallacies, Sir Robert is not so much to be blamed, because he was naturally the exponent of the prejudices of his age.

It is only just to give here some of Sir Robert Peel's motives, which we feel all the more inclined to do as we have never found any present defenders of the Bank Act attempt to explain them.

Sir Robert Peel was right in some things; wrong in others. He was right in perceiving that the country suffered enormously from the fabrication of paper-money which was going on in the issuing banks, and from the excessive cost of production and the high cost of living which resulted from the continuous and strenuous efforts to over-fill the country with paper-money. People who wanted to manufacture goods for export could not compete with the issuing bankers, who had plenty of margin so long as the general indebtedness could be extended; for the overflowing a country with paper-money, which has the same effect on the market as gold, is to place the country in the same position as a gold-mining district. There nothing pays, as we have shown in Chapter VI., except gold-mining, and in a paper-money manufacturing country, the producers have no chance to compete with those who make paper-money by the cheap agency of the printing press.

All this, no doubt, Sir Robert Peel saw in his own way, and his first concern was to raise coin to its natural value, which had been lowered by the concurrent circulation of paper-money; for only when this raising of the value of coin had been accomplished could the cost of production in England be in practical proportion to that abroad.

He also saw that the over-issuing of the bankers engendered a tendency to spurious business, general indebtedness, a total expulsion of all the metallic coin from the kingdom, and in due time a consequent general catastrophe. He was convinced that if the country did not go entirely to ruin, it would be harassed by short periods of over-issue, always ending in disasters.

The question was, how to put a stop to the deluge of paper-money, and bring prices to a normal condition which would allow of healthy production and export, and at the same time obviate the approaching collapse.

He was confronted by a Gordian knot. To untie it was not in his power—in no man's power in those days; and so he cut it.

Hence the arbitrary regulations and restrictions. The paper-money was the cause, and he forbade its increase. He looked upon the existing private notes as an evil, but counted on the increasing business of the country to correct the proportion between the circulating notes and the actual want of them. He wished to prevent the Bank of England from over-issuing, and pinned it down, as to uncovered notes, to the stipulated millions, caring little for either system or theories.

One great object he had in view, and this he accomplished. By leaving all the banks the volume of issue they had attained to, he warded off their opposition, and induced the Scotch banks to part with their freedom by flaunting the bait of a practical monopoly before their eyes. He saw the inconvenience of transporting large quantities of metals, and allowed the notes of the Bank of England to increase to any extent, so long as the Bank kept a corresponding sum of precious metals in their cellars, because in this way the extended issue would not drive the gold out of the country but into the vaults of the Bank, whence it could quickly reappear in case of a gold panic. He left the Bank effective means to protect its gold, for instance, by raising its rates of discount, and, from his point of view, he imagined that he had established a self-acting check on over-trading.

This is what Sir Robert Peel saw, and what he did. We shall now deal with what he did not see and what he ought to have done.

He did not see that the bank-note might be either a healthy, useful, wealth-producing credit-instrument, causing none of the evil consequences of an increasing quantity of circulating coin, and yet doing all the good work that cheques can do; or a mischievous piece of paper-money with none of the attributes of a good credit-instrument, but bound to produce all the pernicious effects of imported coin without the advantages of increased capital.

He did not understand that the usefulness of a credit-instrument is destroyed in exact proportion as it is subjected to State control, and that supervised notes do not affect the market for the better in the way credit-instruments do, for the simple reason that the facility with which they circulate under government control outside their natural markets, renders them to all intents and purposes coin. He did not see that notes, thus competing with coin, call forth none of the healthy and useful banking methods which free credit-instruments compel, but would simply expel from the country a quantity of gold exactly corresponding with their own aggregate. Though, to us now, it is evident, he does not seem to have perceived that if the mediums of exchange are to be increased in a country, it is absurd to attempt their increase by the introduction of one which expels another in exact proportion to its own quantity. In short, he did not see the totally different nature of free notes and State supervised notes, a difference which it would be out of place to explain here, but which will be fully elucidated in a later chapter.

In 1844, Great Britain afforded striking illustrations of these two diametrically opposed banknotes, namely those circulating in Scotland and those in England. Neither of them were extreme types of their kind, because the one was not absolutely free, and the other was imperfectly controlled. They, however, effectively tended towards opposite results. And this can be easily explained. When a government begins to interfere with a medium of exchange, it loses at once something of its effectiveness and usefulness, and this will be evident if we suppose that government were to gradually extend its supervision of cheques.

A certain amount of pernicious supervision can take place without conferring a coin-nature on a credit-instrument. But when government interference reaches a certain point, that at which the credit-instrument begins to circulate outside its own market, it has lost its nature as credit-instrument and has become coin. Now just before the Bank Act of 1844, though State interference with the notes in Scotland had reduced their usefulness, that point had not been reached at which it gives them a coin-nature or makes them paper-money; while in England, on the other hand, State interference with note-issuing had reached that fatal point, and the notes of the private banks, as well as those of the Bank of England, were doing all the mischief of paper-money and none of the good of credit-instruments.

The results of course were very different. While in England periods of over-issue and panic succeeded each other, and bank failures took place in alarming numbers, Scotland steadily progressed, bank failures were scarcely heard of, and whatever financial disturbance that country experienced was only the reaction from England. While now it is easily seen that under such circumstances things could not be otherwise, it is surprising to find that the different effects of note-issuing in Scotland and in England form the inexplicable puzzle they do to our economists. John Stuart Mill, and others, could explain to a certain extent the good economic effect of freedom in Scotland, and, on logical grounds, favoured such freedom, but, on the ground of experience, they condemned free note-issuing in England; and Mill dismisses the whole subject with the farcical conclusion that free note-issuing is very good north of the Tweed but very bad south of it.

The error of course was caused by taking for granted that note-issuing was actually free in England, while in reality government interference had destroyed the usefulness of the system. In England several legal formalities were required to start a note-issuing bank: a special charter was necessary, the amounts of the notes were regulated by law, certain clauses in their tenor were forbidden, and so on. These regulations in themselves were more than sufficient to give the notes a coin-prestige.

Even if these legal stipulations had not existed, it would have been absurd to say that note-issuing was ever free in this country after the establishment of the Bank of England monopoly. It is a well-known fact that the financial system of a country takes its key-note from the centre, and in the English centre Monopoly reigns supreme. The territory of sixty miles radius round the Bank of England is, geographically speaking, insignificant, but from a financial point of view it was one of the most important in the world. Here, where healthy issuing banking should have, not its market, but its origin, its supply of capital, its encouragement, and guidance for its extension, here private note-issuing was entirely forbidden as a local business, and consequently out of the question as an enterprise in distant places for the investment of surplus capital. Issuing methods fell into oblivion, and the word banking meant, in the city, deposit banking. Nothing was more natural than that the provincial banks should adopt the views and follow the example of the big London banks, if for no other reason than the advantage of working in harmony with them, and of leaning on them.

The provincial banks therefore tended to develop only as deposit banks, and when their notes, in face of the coin-prestige which government interference had given them and the constant demand for coin or notes, circulated to a considerable extent without much effort on the part of the bankers, these never exerted themselves to study the true methods of note-issuing, and naturally concentrated their attention on the development of their deposit business. It is evident that, had there been a total absence of government interference, note-issuing would have become the leading feature of banking in England as it was in Scotland, and that competition between the bankers would have compelled them to adopt the methods without which free note-issuing cannot succeed, and which render banking such a powerful lever for the economic and social elevation of a nation, as we shall prove later on.

Sir Robert Peel therefore had two different ways in which to accomplish his great object. He might have untied the Gordian knot without cutting it. To forbid the further issue of a single note by private banks, as he did, was one way of damming up the deluge of paper-money. But there was another more effective one still, namely, to deprive the notes of all power for evil, and to confer upon them immense power for good.

By withdrawing any kind of State interference with banking and thus leaving it entirely free, he would at one stroke have deprived the English notes of their mischievous coin-nature, and transformed them into healthy and useful credit-instruments; he would have achieved the object he aimed at in a far more radical way than he did, namely the re-establishment of a more natural value of coin, and prices more favourable to production and export; and he would have done this without inflicting on the British nation the prohibition of the only mediums of exchange which for our circumstances are suitable to the productive trades, without compelling a great importation of coin for each small development in business, without preventing co-operation between capital and labour by obstructing Free Trade in Credit and Capital.

When, for the sake of uniformity, it was resolved to extend the chief clauses of the Bank Act to Scotland, it might have been expected that it would dawn on Peel and his colleagues that freedom had in that country accomplished what he proposed to accomplish in England. He would have thus avoided a series of barbarous, arbitrary, and illogical prohibitions and limitations, the evil consequences of which were bound to affect the country, the Empire, and the whole world, and which in their evolutions will be felt through all time.

CHAPTER IX

HOW OUR BANKING SYSTEM DIVORCES CAPITAL AND LABOUR

BEFORE an opinion can be formed as to whether our banking system fulfils well or ill the objects of banking, we should first have a clear idea as to what those objects should be. Authors who say that the objects of banking are merely to store and deal in 'money,' no doubt find that our system attains this object. But such a definition of the aims of banking is not only meaningless but misleading.

The definition of the real objects of perfect banking should be based on the consideration of the following points: the origin of banking; the circumstances which compelled humanity to have recourse to it; the good it has accomplished when applied only partially; the evils which arise for want of it; and the benefits which it can be shown, by induction, it is capable of conferring on humanity.

We have seen that the exchanges by means of which our civilisation works, and by means of which alone prosperity can be attained, would be extremely hampered if they were to be worked directly without mediums of exchange; that direct credit, such as current accounts, are of extremely limited application; that indirect credit is absolutely necessary in every society where the economic activity is above the most primitive stage; and that the supply of indirect credit is banking.

From this then it is reasonable to conclude that the object of banking is to facilitate the production of wealth by the supply of indirect credit as a medium of exchange. From experience we know, that as circumstances have compelled or induced communities to have recourse to indirect credit as a medium of exchange, so their prosperity has advanced, and that they have attained to a volume of business, or—to use an economic term—an extension of the division of labour, which would be perfectly impossible without that medium of exchange, or with coin alone.

It follows from this that for a certain amount of

prosperity a certain amount of banking accommodation is indispensable. From both experience and theories we know that such individuals or classes as have enjoyed the advantage of indirect credit as a medium of exchange have been much benefited, and that such individuals and classes as are deprived of it, and whose exchanges and co-operation are limited to what can be accomplished with that small part of the universally coveted coin which they, through much sacrifice, can secure, have suffered enormously; and from this we may infer that when the benefit of banking is extended to the masses of the nation, their poverty may be changed into prosperity. The object of banking, then, may fairly be said to be, to supply indirect credit for all economically sound transactions according to demand on the cheapest possible terms, and with the use of the smallest amount of coin.

For the sake of clearness we may divide this function of banking into two parts: (1) the working of such exchanges as will transfer capital from those who possess it, and credit from those who can create it, to those who require capital for use in production; (2) the working of exchanges in general without the use of coin.

The first function, which we may call the supply of capital to labour, is of immense importance in our modern society. We have already dwelt on the vital part capital plays in production, and how ruinous it is for a modern worker to dispense with it. Work under such circumstances, if practicable at all, would not be production, but consumption, because the cost of living would by far exceed the product of the work. We also know that the productiveness of work depends upon the capital employed in it, and that those with little or no capital find it more advantageous to sell their work to those who have capital, than to work for their own account.

It is in human nature that a great amount of capital and the desire to be occupied energetically in a business, especially a productive one, seldom go hand in hand. People who are very well off find pleasanter occupations than business, healthier and more cheerful places than offices, mines, and mills, and therefore prefer to invest their capital and let others make it fructify for them. But those who have anything to gain in life through work, who wish to become wealthy instead of remaining poor, whose strong desire to rise in life has caused them to acquire knowledge and experience, they are the people who can best use capital, with good results to themselves and the community at large.

If we except some few cases where a large business has been inherited, it might fairly be said that the bulk of the nation's capital is in possession of those who cannot and do not wish to use it in productive work, and that the great majority of those who could best use capital in productive work do not possess it. Even those who work a business with a considerable capital can generally give a larger extension to their operations if they can add the capital of others to their own, and would not feel safe if they had not outside capital to fall back upon. If the productive work of this nation were limited to the capital in possession of the responsible leaders of the work, that is to say, the employers of labour, probably nine-tenths of our working classes would go unemployed, and the people would perish of starvation. That function of the banks, therefore, which consists in bringing about co-operation between capital and labour, is of the highest importance.

There are other financial mechanisms by which capital and labour are connected, such as sleeping partnerships, which are not very frequent, and limited liability companies, which are very numerous. But both firms with sleeping partners and limited liability companies generally stand in need of as much outside capital as anybody else. The latter owe their widespread and too often mischievous existence to our present banking system, as we shall show when we come to speak of the destruction of capital resulting from the Bank Monopoly Act of 1844. Here we shall only notice that the benefits which labour derives from limited companies is often of very limited duration, and that to capital liability companies often prove disastrous. Limited liability companies cannot be looked upon as adequately connecting capital with labour. Banks alone, then, remain the chief mediators between these two great factors in production.

We shall now proceed to examine how our present system accomplishes this mediatory work.

When the average Englishman speaks of banking, he means deposit banking. We have in England a number of provincial banks, which by the Act of 1844 hold an unjust, arbitrary, yet at the same time very limited, monopoly of issuing bank-notes, not under the amount of five pounds, fixed by Sir Robert Peel's crude expediency. But as government limitations and the absence of competition have, as we have already shown, deprived the business of these banks of all the characteristics of note-issuing banks, and as their deposit business grows constantly while their issuing business is stereotyped by law, note-issuing is gradually becoming less and less important to them. In fact, many private banks have renounced their privilege altogether.

It is therefore perfectly correct to say that all English banks are deposit banks. Not being what, for instance, the French *banquiers* are, or what for any better name we will call discount banks, and not being note-issuing banks, their interest entirely consists first in collecting as much capital as possible, second in getting as high interest, with as little risk, as possible. They naturally look out for wealthy clients, because these make large deposits, and when they borrow they take large loans with but little risk to the lender. The banks are quite willing to accept all the capital which small owners and struggling tradesmen are willing to deposit with them, nay, are often forced to deposit with them, owing to the absence of other safe deposit places, and the need of having cheques cashed. As depositors all are welcome. But as borrowers the wealthy have the preference in exact proportion to their wealth. There is no excuse for a bank manager, under our present system, accepting a worse security when he can have a better. Besides, the plan of favouring the wealthy works in two ways: it renders the business safe, and it attracts deposits, for a rich man will keep his capital only in a bank where he is allowed to overdraw largely when necessary.

The capital owned stands, in a successful bank, in very small proportion to the outside capital which has for the most part been received as deposits, or is held as balances of current accounts; a considerable portion of it may be called for; and a large part without any notice at all, another part at short or long notices. It is therefore necessary that all loans should be granted to customers who can without difficulty, on notice from the bank, repay them, and this comparatively wealthy people can do.

The security against which the bank advances must be of such a nature as to allow of immediate realisation, and such securities can only be afforded by people in a very large way of business. For these reasons bank accommodation is a privilege enjoyed only by the capitalist classes, and individuals and firms who are in a large way of business.

Does this kind of banking lead the immense capital manipulated by the banks into the channels of industry, and into the hands of workers or work-producers? To a very small extent, as we shall find when we come to consider the order of preference given to those who are supplied with capital, as well as the method of supplying it.

First on the list come the wealthy landowners who can command the capital in the banks, and then, in their turn, follow the owners of property, the wealthy gentry, the rich bankers and money lenders, the large investors, the speculators in goods, shares, and property, the cornerers of markets, the great sharebrokers, the company promoters, all those who invest largely abroad, successful professional men, and the bishops and rich clergy. All these present exactly the kind of securities which suit deposit banks to perfection.

Similar securities, or imitations of them, are

always at the disposal of the great army of over-traders, or workers of spurious business, whose whole activity results in destruction of capital, and therefore disposes of a very considerable part of the capital managed by the banks. Only the worst cases become known to the public.

Then we have the doubtful accounts in the banks, of which the now famous tannery supported by Greenway's Bank is a striking illustration. The holders of such accounts blackmail the banks, for if they are not supplied with capital they fail, and cause other failures, panics, and unpleasant disclosures. It is no uncommon occurrence for tottering firms to be kept up, at a fearful loss of capital, for fifteen to twenty years, though by adroit management, luck, or the final shifting of the loss on some one else, but very few of these cases become known to the public.

The whole import trade takes precedence of the productive trades, thanks to the securities it can offer in the shape of bills of lading, bonded warehouse and dock warrants, and adopted business methods. Down at the bottom of the list only can we place the employers of labour, and these again are served by the banks in exact proportion to their wealth or reputed wealth. The less rich the borrower is, the better must his security be, and he who cannot keep a considerable balance in the bank is excluded altogether.

For the hundreds of thousands of skilled working men who, with a little bank accommodation added to their own savings, would become successful employers of labour themselves, instead of a drug in the market, there is not a ghost of a chance.

Now, as to the methods, we know that the only way an average employer of labour could reach the capital in the banks is by a loan against a mortgage or by the discounting of bills. Those who have anything to mortgage have a natural reluctance to do so, as experience teaches them how difficult it is to shake off the burden a mortgage represents; and they therefore regard the step as the last desperate effort to keep afloat. As to bills, anyone acquainted with business in our manufacturing centres knows how exceptional it is for a manufacturer to draw a bill on his client. It is not done by one in a hundred. Bills are handy securities, encouraged by the banks, but they take them always as security for isolated, exceptional loans, because the system of carrying on the whole

K

exchange (or business) of the country through bills, as in France, is not and could not be in existence under our present bank legislation. There is among English business men a general disinclination to accept drafts at all, and all those presented for discount in the banks are the result of more or less special understandings. The bulk of them are accommodation bills in the wider sense of the word; a class of bills generally shunned by all manufacturers, farmers, and work-providers generally.

We have said enough, we hope, to show how small are the chances for capital to reach labour through our banks; but we must yet point out that a great part of that small amount of capital which reaches labour at all comes through the hands of the sweater. It is generally the arch-sweater who presents all the conditions which deposit banks require to give their capital on trust. The capital which reaches the working man through this channel is, as we shall show later on, to him not a blessing but a curse.

And how does capital fare under this system of divorce between capital and labour? What becomes of the yearly accumulation of capital, if only so small a proportion is invested in the productive trades of the country? Part of it is invested abroad and a larger part is lost. It is needless to dwell on the terrible sufferings of the working classes from the great loss of opportunity of work and of good wages through this investment abroad of a large amount of capital which is so much wanted in every corner of our Empire; but a word must be said on the actual destruction and loss of capital which has taken place and is now going on.

The severance of capital from labour in England and the consequent difficulty of finding lucrative investments have been the chief cause of the liberal credit, already referred to, which English capitalists have extended to foreign governments, a very large proportion of which has not been and never will be repaid. The amount of English capital lost through loans to foreign governments since 1844 is enormous.

But a much larger amount is likely to be lost in the same way yet. State loans are a modern development the end of which no one can foretell. As the resources of the borrowing States, though large, are limited, their credit must be so too, but most of them do not finance as if there were any limit to their borrowing. The debts of Turkey, Russia, Austria, Germany, France, and Italy, begin to acquire a fatal power of increase beyond the ability of any Finance Minister to control, and when no more can be borrowed, there will be no possibility of keeping up the large standing armies and enormous forces of police—the only guarantee the creditors have of getting the interest from the poor taxpayer. *Après moi le déluge* is evidently the motto of continental Finance Ministers, and when the deluge comes it will swamp a vast quantity of English capital.

Though the losses of English capital through loans to foreign governments represent so large an amount, it seems small compared with the losses by other investments abroad. To obtain statistics of such losses would probably be impossible, but could they be compiled they would certainly surprise us. For the last twenty years the speculators of every capital-wanting country have looked to England for capital for its undertakings. It is a cause of surprise to Englishmen travelling abroad to find in what a number of places, great and small, near and far, English capital has been sunk and lost, or is in process of disappearing.

But it would hardly be fair to deplore losses through investment abroad without mentioning at the same time losses—which probably exceed them—through investments at home. We need only recall the legion of defunct companies of all kinds in order to explain the enormous destruction of capital which is daily going on at home.

At this moment we have in this country an appalling number of companies whose dividends come out of plant account, and which, if they had to be wound up, could not pay their debts, far less their shareholders. To these losses must be added the commercial losses and the sacrifice of capital throughout the country during a state of trade such as the present. The sum-total of all these losses abroad and at home represents the amount of capital which is destroyed through the divorce of capital from labour; and this divorce is a necessary consequence of our present banking system.

CHAPTER X

HOW OUR BANKING SYSTEM DESTROYS PROFITS AND PROMOTES POVERTY

In the previous chapter we have shown how inadequately our present banking system fulfils one of the two great objects of banking, the mediation between capital and labour; and we have found that it does very little to further this object, and that this little is largely counteracted by what it does to sever capital from labour.

We have now to examine how our monopoly system fulfils the second object of banking, that is, to what extent it facilitates the working of the exchanges without the use of coin.

Our banks being all deposit banks, one striking feature of our system is the total absence of banks suitable for the productive trades, for employers of labour, for able but poor men, banks capable of existing in poor districts, banks calculated to connect capital with labour and to give banking facilities to the great bulk of the people—all such banks are forbidden by the Act of 1844.

The great masses which cannot avail themselves of the present banks have none of the facilities for their exchanges which the account-holders in the deposit banks have. They must use coin, the very best of value-measurers but the very worst of mediums of exchange. The result is the absolute necessity for tremendous quantities of coin in the country. Hence a constant tendency to high prices of production and low prices of sale, because the presence of a large quantity of coin in England affects those things which have been produced in the country very much and affects imported goods very little. Prices of sale must be low, not because they are kept down by foreign competition, but because we sell where coin is scarce.

It is evident that by barbarously keeping in this country a considerable portion of the world's gold, which should be distributed all over the world and should raise prices all round, we actually lower the cost of production for our competitors abroad while we raise our own. It is then clear that by prohibiting rational banking we drive up the cost of production of all British goods, and lower the cost of production of goods abroad which regulate our price of sale. Now can any method—barring actual violence—be more calculated to deprive the English producers of their profit?

Here we must reply to two very plausible objections. It may be remarked perhaps that in describing the English market as overstocked with coin, we contradict what we have said about the natural level of the supply of coin. But there is no contradiction, because we have spoken of the quantity of coin which a market holds as that which is natural to it, and this quantity is of course determined, as we have shown in a previous chapter, by many circumstances, of which the existing facilities of exchanges without the use of coin is one of the most important. A country with a hard-working, honest population, ready to suffer and to starve for its principles, and with a bad banking system, will be able to carry a far greater quantity of coin than a country populated with lazy people enjoying a perfect banking system; only the former nation must work for very low wages, and must be content with very little comfort and happiness.

The second objection which might be raised and which we are anxious to meet is this, that if everything goes up in price in a country in consequence of the presence of too much coin in proportion to the production carried on, wages must go up too.

We might reply to this objection by simply referring to many cases that exist in this city, and which demonstrate that high cost of production and high wages do not necessarily go together, but that high wages and low cost of production often do. But it will be useful to point out the fact that wages are the last thing to rise in price when a general rise in prices originates from such a cause as gold imported in excess. When wages are low it is because there is an excess of supply of labour over the demand. Before wages can go up the unemployed in each trade have first to be employed. As long as a few are out and are eager to get work, wages can be kept down. The rise in price of the other factors in production puts a stop to any promising improvement in productive business long before the improvement has caused any rise in wages. An improvement in wages can be produced only by such extraordinarily strong causes for trade inflation as we have witnessed several times since 1844, but which are not likely to occur again.

As examples of those things which rise in price through the presence of a great extra quantity of coin in a market before the price of labour rises, we may cite the following: land, rent, taxes, carriage, the services of middle-men, the profits of manufacturers, the profits of dealers and distributors, professional assistance, raw materials, food, and all articles imported from abroad, all comforts, pleasures, and enjoyments. The price of all these goes up before wages rise. General high prices cannot therefore be considered as the great boon to the working classes which they are generally believed to be. All depends on the cause of the high prices, because thereon depends the order of the rise.

High prices caused by too much coin hamper the production of wealth and damage the working man. But high prices produced by an increased demand for labour and good methods in the production will benefit the working man first and the whole community afterwards. When through any cause not strong enough to overrule entirely the effects of our vicious system, there is, however, a beginning in improvement of trade, the increased activity demands at once an increase in the circulating coin; and, as there is no supply of credit regulated by demand, as there is no note circulation which expands in response to the increased business, the result is necessarily that for a relatively small increase in business we have an enormous increase in the demand for coin. When the coin comes, and often before it comes, it produces the effect we have before described, that is, reduces production and exports, paralyses the impulse towards improvement, then quits the country and thus re-establishes the disturbed level.

Our banking system thus produces a terrible dead-lock, for we must be either short of mediums of exchange and short of capital, or we must get them in the shape of coin and give up our profit. From the dilemma there is, in the circumstances, but one escape, and this is by starvation wages. We cannot control the price of the other factors in production in face of a constant, never-ceasing tendency to swamp the country with coin; but thanks to reduced production and reduced export, to largely imported foreign goods, to continued improvement in labour-saving machines, we can sweat our work-people and our clerks, and that we succeed in doing thoroughly.

As long as the Act of 1844 is kept in force, there is no other alternative. The present prices leave the employer no margin for any reduction whatever in his profit; and to keep trade going the workers must be gradually driven into misery. Indeed, the profits of the employer must come from the privations of the poor.

Though the working people might suffer the most from the artificial raising of the cost of production which our banking system involves, employers of labour have heavy losses, especially of such profits as they ought to have realised. During the last fifteen years most business men and producers will have found that any beginning of improvement in trade has over and over again been checked by the impossibility to keep the cost of production within the universal prices.

It is of course the great and leading industries of the country which suffer most from this artificial vitiation of prices. Those may be unaffected by it who have secured some special advantages in their business, such for instance as good patents, extensively advertised specialities, secretly-improved methods, special facilities for keen buying, aptitude for utilising every favourable turn in the market, &c. But such industries as farming, spinning, sugar-refining, printing, tanning, &c., have had plenty of opportunities of convincing themselves of the correctness of our conclusions.

It is natural, when a legislative obstruction is placed against the production of a country, the leading industries should suffer most.

We have done our best to show how our banking system when considered from an economic point of view is bound to sever capital from labour, to lead capital into destructive channels, to raise the cost of production and cost of living, to lower the price of sale and wages, to reduce the consuming power of the people; and in the following chapters we shall show how completely the actual state of things confirms strikingly the correctness of those conclusions which true economic reasoning compels. This we shall do by tracing the connection between Bank monopoly and the evils from which our working classes suffer, as well as other troubles which engage the attention of our legislators.

CHAPTER XI

THE SWEATING SYSTEM

WERE the sweating system the only plague-spot in our social life, it would still call loudly for strict investigation and remedial measures. But it is indeed only one form in which a wide-spread and deeply-rooted evil manifests itself. To speak of the sweating system is therefore to speak of a great social problem which is steadily forcing itself forward for solution in every civilised country— a solution which must be more and more peremptorily demanded by the embittered masses as the knowledge of their power increases. The importance of settling the sweating system therefore cannot be exaggerated. The investigation is easy; the phenomena are close at hand; and its settlement is but the key to the whole Capital and Labour problem.

Does it not sometimes seem humiliating that

while we English display our love of freedom everywhere across the seas, indulging in our anti-slavery proclivities, lavishing our sixpence in the pound, and sacrificing good lives to suppress slavery in Arabia and Africa, we maintain a system of oppression at home in many features more objectionable than slavery in the East, without its compensations or its excuses? The condition of things such as the sweating system presents is not the necessary outcome of our civilisation, but altogether outside nature, and goes on contrary to the just expectations that might be founded on our progress and national wealth, and is irreconcilable with the teachings of Political Economy.

We have seen how labour is the most indispensable factor in the production of wealth, the inexhaustible store of raw material being supplied by nature—not gratis, but on very easy terms. How is it then that the demand for that which can alone produce wealth is, in London—the centre of craving for and consumption of wealth—so small that the supplier of labour, the worker, can be found to sell his work for next to nothing from sheer absence of competition in the demand for his wealth-producing power?

Were this anomaly set before intelligent men in the abstract, unprejudiced by surroundings, they would surely say, 'This is impossible unless brought about by brute force.' And they would be right. For it can be shown that this anomalous state of things has actually been brought about by brute force, sanctioned by selfishness, prejudice, and indifference, in fact by the might of Parliament.

Those trades in which the be-sweated victims are employed have a tendency to become more and more monopolised by large establishments in our commercially diseased London. What are the terms of the grand public advertisement which the proprietors of great establishments enact? 'Wanted brains, skill, and muscle.' But, read between the lines, this means, 'Disunion is weakness, capital is power. Wanted to convert ten thousand pounds into twenty, by means of glut of labour.'

The great merit of the be-sweated victims is that they prefer work to beggary, dry bread to dishonesty; it really amounts to Christian patience and self-abnegation! The employer gains the day; the milk and honey which should fatten the cheeks of the little children, which should animate the spirit of the mother, which should cheer the father over his work, turns into gold and fattens the pocket of the sweater.

The profits made in the modern large establishment are not fairly divided between capital and labour; capital is the master from the first, and as the business proceeds the power of capital increases in a ratio with the hopelessness of the workers.

Whenever the supply of labour is in excess of the demand, a starting-point for the sweating system is furnished. It allows the work-supplying capitalist to press down wages through competition among the work-seekers. He can wait until his terms are accepted; the starving people cannot wait. When he has conquered one, the rest must yield, because he pits the one against the other. The low wages he pays allow him to undersell his competitors, who in their turn are obliged to lower the wages paid by them, and the work-seeker has no escape from the tyranny of the employer. We ask, is it good that this sweating system should be the one under which so many English trades are carried on, their success depending on the amount of pressure that can be put upon the workers, the most heartless employer—the one who understands best how to apply the screw—being the one who will the soonest secure fortune and social distinction, even up to representative rank? The direct, and still more the indirect, moral consequences of all this are deplorable.

The system has not a germ of improvement in it, but on the contrary has a strong tendency to become worse and worse. A large number of the articles manufactured by the sweating system go to home consumption, and naturally the more ill-paid the workers (who are a large section of the people), the more difficult it becomes in the long run for the master to obtain remunerative prices for goods. Thus the effect of one turn of the screw in the sweating mechanism, instead of really benefiting the employer, only gives rise to competition in the trade, which means still lower prices and lower wages, or another turn of the screw.

Here we should note an anomaly in our trade policy in connection with our foreign markets, largely supplied by the sweating system. We hear a great deal of talk about extending our trade in distant, thinly-populated lands of small consuming power, while in our great home market, capable of immense consumption, we have established and maintain a system which tends to destroy it. We do more than that: we transplant this Upas-tree of sweating and usury in every colony we annex and in every country we take under our protection. It is said of the Turk that wherever the hoof of his horse treads no grass will grow; and it must be confessed that wherever the Union Jack flies the working man is the slave of the capitalist.

For the workers in East End slop-shops are not the only victims of our vicious economic system: other large bodies of workers are in the same plight, such as the chain-makers, the nail-makers, the scissor-grinders, the cabinet-makers, and now the miners. The agricultural labourer has had his miserable weekly wage reduced by about three shillings during the last three years. The wretched state of the labouring class of Ireland and the Crofters of Scotland is well known. In India the bulk of the population, owing to a system as irrational as our own, is obliged to live on a few shillings a month per family. Of course the depressed state of all these markets—affecting both customers and consumers—reacts on the London trades, and intensifies the evils of the sweating system.

The system, of which low wages are the essence, diminishes to a startling extent the purchasing power of the people—who are, after all, the great consumers—and in doing this it discounts the demand for labour, and with it increases competition in those trades which vainly attempt to extend their operations through low wages.

The presence of such ill-paid industries in London attracts the unemployed from the provinces, who, yielding to a stern necessity, prefer bad pay to none, as well as the famished labourers from abroad, who are equally determined to accept anything they can get, however little, for a living.

This latter effect of our wide-spread sweating system is mistaken by superficial observers for its chief cause, and the belief in a good result being produced by the prohibition of immigration is so general that it becomes necessary to explode this monstrous fallacy before attention can be secured to the real remedy.

Economics, confirmed by experience, teaches, as we have seen, that the aim of labour is best achieved, and most remuneratively, when under subdivision. The greater the number of labourers the more effective the subdivision becomes; the well-being of the community depending really on the amount of work done. Consequently the individuals who work hard and consume little are the benefactors of the others. This economic truth would never be disputed if a long experience under an unnatural system produced by State meddling had not blinded the people to it. But, in spite of the anti-economic system under which we live, a slight investigation will show that it holds good with respect to the poor foreign workers in London.

The in-coming foreigners—the persecuted Poles, the needy Germans, the cautious Jews—as representatives of cheap labour, form an important part of our present mechanism. On them depends the universal supply of cheap goods which dominates commerce, especially when times are bad; on them depends the very existence of masses of workers in departments that lie between themselves, the producers, and the retail markets. To prohibit the supply of cheap labour, therefore, means to ruin our trade in cheap goods, which is enormous, and so to deprive whole communities of hands of even the starvation wages they now so hardly earn.

Every business man knows that orders, especially those from abroad, do not represent a fixed quantity that can be counted on irrespective of circumstances, but depend entirely on the prices at which they can be undertaken. Merchants now execute orders from foreign countries for goods manufactured by sweating labour at the absurdly small profit of 1 to 2 per cent., and the quantity exported depends on how low the cost of production can be pressed. If the wages were to be raised for any article, competition from Germany, Belgium, and other places would at once carry off the orders.

What then would become of those vast British trades which depend largely on excessively cheap labour? They would at once collapse and widespread distress would follow. It is then evident that the more cheap labour is obtainable in London the more will business in cheap goods extend; and that the result of the parsimonious habits and the hard work of the foreigner in London—due to his own choice—is to keep up the demand for the raw materials as well as the products of the trades in which he is engaged. He helps to create work and profit for the spinners, the weavers, the dyers, &c.; the packers, the shippers, and the clerks; the makers of machines and tools: and while thus keeping the other trades going he supplies their workers with cheaper clothing than they could obtain without him.

For example, the woollen shirts which are exported to the Colonies represent two classes of labourers, the English in Manchester or Rochdale, and the Jewish labourers of the East End; and when it is granted that the selling price abroad is the highest obtainable, it must follow that the lower the price the Jew obtains for his part of the labour, the more there remains to the profit of collateral English industries. It is then evident that the abstemious and hard-working foreigner, far from being the cause of any want of work, promotes to a considerable extent the employment and welfare of the English workers. The shallow remedy, then, of destroying foreign labour, would be disturbing and disastrous.

If we compare the price at which articles manufactured under the sweating system are sold in distant markets—for example, Australia—with the price of production, the difference, comparatively speaking, is considerable. And why? A small part only of this difference represents freight and insurance ; but the bulk of it consists in profits for middle-men between the manufacturer in London and the consumer in Australia. The London manufacturer sells to the shipper, who is thus the exporter, and he in his turn sells to the wholesale importer in Australia, who again sells to another middle-man, and all this before the goods finally reach the shopkeeper in Melbourne or Sydney, who adds a further profit in supplying the consumer retail. The whole series of transactions would be interrupted if one of these intermediaries did not receive a profit.

All this is bad enough for the workers, but not the worst. We have yet to find that besides the series of middle-men between the manufacturer and the consumer, all of whom do no actual productive work, but who get a living and sometimes a fortune out of the be-sweated victims at home, there is yet another series of middle-men to be taken account of between the original working man and the manufacturer, namely, the sub-contractors and their sub-contractors who farm out the work from the one to the other, and, as intermediaries, have also a profit, and sometimes a very large profit.

It need scarcely be mentioned that the goods—such as tinned and frozen meats and other foodstuffs—which are supplied from Australia in return have to pass through a great many middle-men's hands—all involved in the same rotten system—before they reach the poor man's table in the East End. In fact his small means and the method of living from hand to mouth to which his poverty condemns him obliges him to obtain all his supplies from the very last man of a very long series of middle-men, who consequently also live on him. Thus he is under the pressure of two chains of middle-men, the one lowering his means of living by reducing his pay, the other raising the cost of his supplies.

The goods produced by one be-sweated man, and consumed by another, escape as little the tax of the middle-man as the goods exchanged through the channels of trade by the Londoner and the Australian, though producer and consumer be neighbours.

While poor producers who live in different parts of the Empire have all the advantages of their exchange of products intercepted by middle-men, those who live under the same roof in London are taxed by middle-men in the same way. If a poor shoemaker requires clothes, and a poor tailor, living in the next room, requires boots, they cannot exchange products or buy from each other at anything like the fabulously low prices they work for. They must go to the large establishments where the products of the sweating trades are sold, and pay a price which includes all the profits of all the middle-men. The reason is that they are too poor—they lack the capital—to procure raw materials with which to work on their own account, too poor even to complete one article entirely. They are generally reduced to one fragmentary, mechanical, monotonous kind of piece-work on material furnished to them by the sweaters.

Whether we examine individual cases in the east of London or whether we take a glance at the general condition of productive labour all over the world, we find abject poverty, or entire want of capital to carry on their work, to be the most active of the immediate causes for increasing the helplessness of the great masses of productive workers. This general want of capital must certainly produce the following effects, quite sufficient in themselves to account for the sweating system : it compels the workers to hire themselves out instead of working for themselves or for each other; it diminishes the number of employers and increases the number of work-seekers ; it enables the middlemen to tyrannise over them ; it intensifies competition for work and for the sale of products ; it reduces the consumption of goods to a small percentage of what it ought to be. The widespread scarcity of capital—or rather apparent scarcity of capital—then, is what we must inquire into.

It must strike every thinking man that there is a wonderful enigma afloat, at the solution of which Parliament has not yet made a guess, though it has been under their eyes during the whole of several sessions. It is the greatest enigma of the time, and they shall hear it, with its solution, for therein consists the cure of this sweating sickness.

It is the great enigma of our time that while the bulk of working humanity raises the bitter cry of scarcity of capital, the capitalists are equally complaining that their capital runs the risk of perishing for want of lucrative employment. Mr. Goschen was enabled and had the courage to achieve on the basis of plethora of capital his ever-memorable financial operation of conversion. What a singular contingency! Capital and Labour alike a glut in the market, capital crying aloud, labour crying aloud, 'O that I could find an employer!' Truly were it not that their dignity would be compromised, the capitalists would be justified in forming a procession of their unemployed to Trafalgar Square! This at any rate might lead to an advantageous understanding between the two unemployed classes, that is, between the capitalists and the labourers.

Surely it has occurred to many that the capitalist, against whose oppression the most opprobrious invectives are uttered by our Socialists, is subject, in our present system, to a tyranny as relentless as that which oppresses the labourer, and that he is really as innocent and helpless as the working man himself? Why is it, then, that capital does not offer itself where it is wanted, where it would be ever on the increase for the good of all, where it would fairly share with the myriads of oppressed workmen the large profits now pocketed and prevented by usurers sweaters and other middle-men?

For, while many a working man must give one half of his just due to that middle-man who stands nearest him—without counting the others—and thus virtually pay fifty per cent. usury for the use of his capital in raw material for a couple of days—or ten thousand per cent. per annum—any capitalist would be willing to accept five to ten per cent. per annum for the loan of his capital, and would even run some risk, which is more than the middle-man would do. But the only mechanism—rational banking—which would enable the capitalist to do so is forbidden by Parliament.

Now look at the unjust opinion which such a condition of things entails. The working classes have their own way of explaining things; they suppose that it is in the nature of capital to oppress labour, whereas it is simply in the nature of the sweater and his brother middle-men so to do. These they mistake for the real capitalists, and such they are in relation to them, and that suffices. This unjust view has led to an ever-growing animosity between capital and labour. The hatred borne by the poor classes towards capitalists is constantly on the increase, and the flame is carefully fanned by reckless agitators, many of them in the House of Commons itself.

This hatred is universal: it finds different expression according to the national character of the people. In France the oppressed people revive the 'Carmagnole' dance, now directing the verses once aimed at the aristocrats against the capitalists. In England we have our Christian Socialists, and highly respectable they are, who unceasingly reproach the rich classes with unchristian indifference towards the sufferings of their fellow men, and point to this indifference as the cause of all the misery which surrounds us, and broadly hint how good it would be for the souls of the rich were they compelled to work and undergo privation. Should religious fanaticism and Socialism succeed in establishing a compact league against the wealthy classes in England it would produce upheavals that would prove tantamount to the destruction of capital.

It takes more insight into Economy than the masses have to perceive that it is not the capitalists but the middle-men who tyrannise over them. To them the middle-man is the capitalist, and from this they wage unreasonable war against capital.

It is clear that neither the destruction of capital, as threatened by the Anarchists, nor its confiscation in part or entire, as advocated by the Socialists, can improve the position of the be-sweated victim, because free and private capital, far from being his enemy, is his natural ally and friend. It creates work; makes it easy and effective; and is the indispensable condition for the comfortable existence of the large populations of modern times.

While on the one hand capital is necessary to labour, on the other hand labour is indispensable to capital. The two depend on each other, and the more closely they co-operate the better for both. Everyone knows that when the workers have good terms the capitalists have good incomes; and that when bad times set in, both suffer together.

Why then are these two factors—labour and capital—separated and made to quarrel instead of to co-operate? We know that on the one hand capitalists are willing to take their share of risk in order to get an adequate yearly income from their investments, that is, for the chance of having their capital employed in labour so as to increase it or at least maintain it entire; on the other hand, we are aware how much the workers sacrifice to get hold of a fraction of capital, though only as wages. We have learned from the evidence before the Sweating Committee that women are glad to make trousers at eighteenpence per dozen, while the middle-man gets five shillings for the work, and thus clears three-and-sixpence profit, or 233 per cent. interest, for the one turn-over of his capital in a couple of days, or 35,000 per cent. per annum!

Under such circumstances, does it not appear amazing that the highly developed business ingenuity of our time should not be able to hit upon some plan for bringing capital and labour into closer co-operation, and so dispense with the army of middle-men? The fact that the workers themselves cannot be made to possess the capital cannot be an obstacle, for who holds the capital matters little so long as it is at the disposal of labour. The charge of a fair rate of interest, from five to eight per cent., by the capitalist, would be so insignificant, especially when compared with the monstrous usury we have shown is paid by be-sweated men to middle-men, that it could not be felt in the wages at all.

We have then any amount of capital seeking employment, any amount of labour looking for capital; willingness to run risks on the one hand, and willingness to pay good interest on the other, and an enormous margin of profit. From this we must conclude that there must be something wrong with the channels through which labour and capital should meet—namely, banking.

CHAPTER XII

THE EXCHANGED ATTITUDE OF PARTIES

THOSE evils from which the British Empire now actually suffers as inevitable consequences of our monopoly banking system, and of which the sweating system is a striking illustration, are surely bad enough; but the future evils that system threatens to bring upon us are far worse. The destruction of the right to private property, State interference with contract, land confiscation, Socialism, and finally the disintegration of the Empire, are among the evils which threaten us as a nation, and they are all of them fast coming within the range of practical legislation.

So far, it is evident that this work has been kept clear of party bias, but here it may be expedient to mention that our intention is to carry it out in the same impartial spirit, though we may be called upon to deal severely with mistaken aims and means. For what we have here denoted as future evils will by many be glorified as coming blessings, and it adds to our difficulty that these opinions are held on grounds which, certain economic mistakes once admitted, acquire a strong appearance of rationality, and that they are shared by men whose patriotism and philanthropy, whatever may be the accusation of their political opponents, are in our opinion beyond doubt, and whose motives even opponents must respect.

But herein lies the gravity of the danger. It is the sincere man who can best influence his fellow men; it is the devoted enthusiast who can carry the most far-reaching reforms; and when such men labour under a mistake the highest interests of humanity are in peril. Energetic men, full of hope and action, are only too apt to shun those long, laborious, logical inquiries in the search for real truth, without which zeal becomes fanaticism. They wish to achieve one great good, and, armed with courage, ability, and eloquence, they wait for the voice of some leader to tell them what means will bring about this good. The oracle speaks, points to the remedy, and the battle begins. Whether the remedy will lead to the desired result, is not inquired into by the rank and file. Unfortunately they are apt to be more fired by a spurious remedy, the plausibility of which lies on the surface, than by the real remedy, which like most scientific truths is to be found in the opposite direction of popular beliefs.

To carefully trace causes and effects, to constantly bear first principles in mind, is uncongenial to most natures, especially to the ardent and active; and so it generally happens that the remedy which was to bring about the great object acquires in the eyes of the masses more importance than the great object itself; and if it should be discovered that the remedy which has been fought for a long time is a spurious one, it becomes very difficult to impress this upon the rank and file of the militant reformers.

An illustration will make this clearer. If it be granted that the object of the Christian religion is to form Christ-like characters, we can understand that its earliest devotees, from the former experiences of humanity, should conclude that such a great work could best be performed by a complete religion, and the spreading of the new religion thus became the chief object of many. It was then assumed that the forming of churches and congregations was the best means of establishing the new religion, and this was zealously worked for. Churches required cathedrals; cathedrals were made attractive by ceremonies; processions were found among the most imposing ceremonies; processions without vestments were tame, and vestments represent now a burning question among many serious young curates. Thus by allowing the supposed means to become the real object, afterwards to be forgotten for the sake of another means, the high object of Christianity—the formation of Christ-like characters—has by many been left far behind.

Nothing is more common in political strife than to substitute the remedy for the real object, and the fact that all parties and all factions, as far as their sincere members are concerned, strive for the same object, does not prevent them from fighting furiously about the remedy.

How it has come to happen that so many sincere and noble-minded men are opposed in their endeavours to promote the well-being of their race and their country by another set of men equally sincere and noble-minded, will be explained by glancing at the development of political thought in

Great Britain during the last half century from the point of view of Political Economy.

A new departure was taken in British politics when Sir Robert Peel declared in favour of Free Trade. It was not the abolition of the corn laws and of protective duties alone which gave the Liberal party that immense prestige which kept them in office, with only short interruptions, for so considerable a period, and which even now secures them the hearty support of many logical and strong-minded men. The Free-Trade reform was only one of the outcomes of that adherence to scientific Economy which was the leading feature of their programme.

Never has a more hopeful spirit animated a political body than that which was imbued into the Liberal party by Villiers, Cobden, Bright, and afterwards Mr. Gladstone. That humanity suffered from anti-economic legislation had long been suspected by practical men. Those who traded with foreign countries were quick to perceive the impediments and annoyances to which trade and industry were exposed in countries where State interference and bureaucratic meddlings were more deeply rooted than in England; most men who had read Adam Smith's 'Wealth of Nations' were enthusiastically in favour of sound Economy, and such writers as Henry Buckle and others had exposed the glaring errors of state-craft in the past. Under such circumstances it was not surprising that the intelligence of the country should rally round a standard which bore the inscription of sound Political Economy. The first victory gained under it, Free Trade, brought such enormous advantages to the country that the Liberal party became irresistible, and faith in Political Economy almost general.

The Free-Trade agitation in England was simultaneous with a feverish agitation all over Europe for political freedom, and considering how few people are apt, even now, to make a distinction between political freedom and economic freedom, it can easily be conceived that no such distinctions were made forty years ago. As soon as economists had proved that the people suffered from the want of some special economic liberty, the advocates of political liberty at once added it to their programme, but in all cases taking it for granted that it was impossible to obtain such economic freedom under the existing form of government. They therefore demanded political reform, and especially that the power should be placed in the hands of the people.

The workers forming the bulk of the nation were expected to pass only such laws as would benefit themselves, and consequently the nation at large. There was some logic in this reasoning; because they had seen that when despots and dynasties had the power, they had legislated in their own favour; when the aristocracy had the power they had legislated in favour of the upper classes; and when the priests had the power they had legislated in favour of the Church. What, then, was more natural than that, when the masses got the power, they should legislate in favour of the masses?

Thus political liberties and economic liberties were mixed up on the programme of the reformers, and as the former appeared an indispensable condition to the latter, this secured the larger share of public attention. The spirit of reform and of revolution took possession of the masses all the more as the frightful economic misgovernment of the European States had engendered a deep sense of resentment and discontent. Where discontent prevails from any cause, it is always directed against those in power, and where whole nationalities were systematically misgoverned, overtaxed, and beggared, it was to be expected that the national cause should be identified in the minds of the people with the cause of prosperity.

There were, moreover, historical examples of small nations having improved both their social and economic position after having won their national independence. But what, perhaps, most encouraged the hope that democratic forms of government would produce prosperity, were the immense strides of progress made by the American Republic, which at that time did not indulge in the economic mistakes which now place the majority of its population under the heel of the capitalists.

In 1848 the national movements succeeded in several countries, and led to constitutional reforms in a national and democratic direction. In England that party which had gained the confidence of the people by showing their knowledge of the true theories of government and by increasing the prosperity of the country, added to their programme of economic reforms political reforms.

The example from continental States had

warned us against the danger of resisting popular demands, and the leaders of the Liberal party had easy triumphs. The resistance of the Conservatives became less and less active, and in 1867 they took the game out of the hands of the Liberals. This roused the spirit of emulation among their opponents, and it became to them a matter of political existence to outbid the Conservatives.

There was plenty of scope for reforms, especially in the domain of Economy, but it was political reforms which both parties most favoured, and this was natural, as the advocacy of these lent itself more readily to the methods of the platform, and did not demand the same careful and lucid exposition as that of economic measures. That prosperity would result from political reforms was taken on trust, and the correctness of this conclusion was never questioned.

When one extension of the franchise failed to bring about prosperity, it seemed so natural to recommend another. Behind the political reforms there always loomed, if not immediate prosperity, at least some economic reform which would lead to it, and which the Conservatives, for some reason or another, were expected to resist. The country had great confidence in Liberal promises, because so long as Cobden's programme was adhered to, as long as the party strove to break down such State interference as hampered economic liberty, their promises had been gloriously fulfilled. But after Cobden's death, Political Economy, the beneficent and potential element of his programme, by which the Liberal party had won such prestige, was gradually deserted. For a long period the reforms passed were mere political tamperings with the Parliamentary machine.

When the power became concentrated in the hands of the masses and the question arose as to how that power should be used, the idea continued to prevail that the new legislation should be specially in favour of the masses. It was then found that certain misgivings of the Conservatives with respect to the ability of the masses to master those sociological and economic problems on which prosperity depends, were not so entirely unfounded as the believers in the *vox populi, vox Dei* dogma had intimated.

It was hardly politic for Parliamentary candidates and politicians in general to warn the masses against committing the error of their predecessors in power, namely, to legislate for their own class exclusively. Expediency, the existing animosity, and the spiciness of political aggression naturally tempted Liberal candidates to favour such measures as would lead to a good party fight. The measures which seemed to rouse the strongest opposition from the Conservative side were such as interfered with property and with private contract. It is only fair to say that this was due perhaps more to their instinct of self-preservation than to their knowledge of scientific principles.

But there were more powerful motives than tactical ones for favouring measures which ran counter to the principles of Political Economy.

Though the Free-Trade reform had enormously increased the business of the country, and had benefited largely the trading classes and skilled workmen, there remained a considerable residue of poor people whom the benefits of Free Trade did not seem to have touched, not only in the slums of the cities but also in the rural districts, and the agricultural population of Ireland remained in a deplorable state.

Perhaps the increasing prosperity of the other

classes made them more tender-hearted towards the poor, or perhaps the misery of so large a number of British subjects was used by partisans as political capital. In any case public attention was vigorously called to the existing poverty.

The followers of Cobden, convinced that Free Trade was sound Political Economy, forgot that sound Political Economy does not consist merely of Free Trade. They had rashly prophesied great improvement for even the lowest grades of workers, and when their prophecies were not fulfilled in this respect a very large number of the weak-kneed disciples of Economy wavered in their faith. Eager philanthropists, benevolent clergymen, and a host of well-meaning people who had not been able to master the close reasoning of the economists, called upon Parliament and the government for charitable legislation, for paternal protection, and other measures of ever-growing State-socialistic tendencies; and when they met with a galling opposition from the devotees of Political Economy, who proved that such legislation was incapable of good and pregnant with evil, there began, as described in our Introduction, to grow up that hatred of what they called 'the dismal science.'

Later on, when several of the great causes of trade inflation, of which we have already spoken, ceased to act, and a trade depression which threatened to become permanent had set in, the jeering against Political Economy gained in vehemence. At that time the belief in bank monopoly being in full force, and the importance of Free Trade in Capital not being understood, the economists became crestfallen, for in face of a clamour from their adversaries for more miracles, they stood without a constructive programme.

As Political Economy seemed to desert the Liberals, the Liberals deserted Political Economy. The whole party embraced the State-socialistic principles of their extreme wing, and the Liberal party became the Radical party. The great truths of Henry Buckle were forgotten; Cobden's programme of resistance against State interference in the affairs of individuals was abandoned; the teachings of Herbert Spencer, though never disproved, were disregarded; and since 1878 alone, no less than three hundred State-socialistic measures have been passed. Though the host of anti-economic measures which have been carried are claimed by the Liberals as part and parcel of their programme, it is only fair to say that the Conservatives are as responsible as the Liberals in this respect. For not only have they themselves passed many, but the opposition against others they have offered has been lame and of a kind which has often suggested that their opposition was interested. If anybody should be blamed, both parties should be blamed alike; but it would be obviously unjust to expect any legislative body to apply principles of Political Economy before they are known.

It is only lately, since the Radical party have placed on their programme measures which threaten to destroy the right of private property, and to disintegrate the Empire, that the Conservative party, with the exception of some erratic members, have paused in the socialistic race, and taken up a position really antagonistic to the other party; and as they now begin to draw their best arguments from the arsenal of Political Economy, it is becoming an historical fact that the two great parties of the State have within thirty years changed ground.

The position the Liberals held thirty years ago the Conservatives are gradually taking up, and that which the Conservatives occupied is being taken by the Liberals. The Conservatives begin to stand up for individual liberty and scientific methods of government, while the Liberals have adopted State tyranny as their goal, and a class legislation reckless enough to destroy even those which it is intended to benefit. The Conservatives show trust in the working man, and a desire to protect his liberty and dignity. The Radicals would make of him an irresponsible dependent on a superior class, the new aristocracy, the bureaucrats; and as far as sound economic measures are beneficial and State interference destructive to prosperity, the Conservatives promise to be the working man's friend and the Liberals his persecutor.

Through these evolutions of ideas the two great parties have almost exchanged places and remained opponents. Since the settlement of the great question which had divided them for centuries—namely, whether the power should remain in the hands of the upper classes or the masses—had through the wide extension of the franchise been settled in favour of the masses, the great parties have, however, managed to find bones of contention enough to keep up their existence, and though their objects have changed their tactics remain virtually the same. These tactics may be described as an energetic pushing of reform on the part of the Liberals, and a slow yielding on the part of the Conservatives.

As long as this pushing of reforms on the one part and yielding on the other tended to advance our nation and our race towards that glorious goal of individual liberty, and that high degree of prosperity for all, which alone institutions in harmony with sound Political Economy can secure—as long as that goal was aimed at, the result of the tactics of the parties was steady progress.

But by the inter-exchange of programmes the result will be the contrary, namely, retrogression. The advance from complete slavery of the individual under the State which characterised the dawn of civilisation towards that noble individual freedom which alone can give free scope to the higher nature of man is being arrested, and the return to barbarism is slowly beginning. Cobden and his followers took us near the goal, but Mr. Gladstone and his followers threaten to take us back to the Egyptian slavery after allowing us but a glance at the promised land. It is this retrogression which at every cost must be stopped if Great Britain is to maintain her position as the pioneer of civilisation.

CHAPTER XIII

STATE SOCIALISM AND TRADE

To stay the new retrograde movement, to induce the nation to take up Cobden's programme at the point where it was abandoned by the Liberal party, to encourage the dissolution of the now obsolete party division and to promote the formation of a new party to govern for the benefit of the people instead of for the benefit of parties—to do all this it does not suffice to show what splendid results would ensue from governing according to the science of government.

It is also necessary to demonstrate that the methods suggested by party expediency, popular prejudices, and thoughtless applications of Domestic Economy in domains where Political Economy should reign supreme, can only lead to the very opposite of the results hoped for.

Herbert Spencer, in his 'Introduction to Sociology,' points out the generally prevailing *naïve* idea that the government can do things better for the people than the people can do them for themselves, and how the best logic and thousands of years of experience to the contrary have left but very little impression. There is no doubt that the further the individual in his social position is removed from government circles, the less his knowledge of what government means, the greater his belief in the omnipotence and omniscience of the government.

Those who themselves have had experience of government know best what folly it is to overload it with innumerable functions and responsibilities; and how necessarily every additional task with which it is encumbered hampers the fulfilment of the aggregate of its duties. It cannot be otherwise, because, though new tasks imposed upon government may often appear to be well accomplished, and executed without detracting from the fulfilment of other tasks, it should be remembered that the way in which government is carried on depends on one man.

In Great Britain this man is the Prime Minister. He appoints his Cabinet; each Cabinet Minister selects his officials, the officials select inspectors and managers, and these supervise all those who work for the government. How complete the chain of responsibility is has over and over again been illustrated by incidents. Not long ago a Cabinet Minister felt unsafe in his seat because a policeman had molested a girl in the street. This gives an idea what the position of a Prime Minister will be when the management of the bulk of the economic activity of the nation is in his hands—when the grievances of every individual of an Empire with hundreds of millions of inhabitants must reach him before they can be abated.

What will happen when individuality becomes levelled down to one type we can learn from Germany where the whole national life is manipulated by one Minister. However much the Prime Minister of a country works, the time he can add to his working hours is ludicrously short compared with the enormous labours heaped upon him. What is he to do? He achieves the most important part, and leaves the rest undone, or delegates it to officials with the severe injunction that he is not to be pestered. He must trust to his subordinates in matters the most grave, and if they have capacity enough to help him to remain in power, he is obliged to shut his eyes to those mistakes, corruptions, and petty tyrannies which they, like most subordinates, are apt to indulge in. They on their part have to delegate power to screen their subordinates in their turn, and thus are laid the foundations of an all-powerful bureaucracy.

To trust to the government is therefore to trust to the bureaucrats.

In a coming chapter devoted to Socialism we shall show how the centralisation of power, the multiplication of government officials, and the creation of an omnipotent bureaucracy—all indispensable features of a socialistic form of government—prevent the expected benefits and add to the misery of the masses.

Here we shall deal with another batch of evil effects from State Socialism which are the direct outcome of that serious mistake of applying the principles of Domestic Economy to a nation whose institutions still retain some elements of individual liberty.

The fundamental fact on which all true Political Economy is based—the solidarity of humanity—is far from being recognised. Its economic consequences have never been permitted to develop. Civilisation began by government, and governments always disregarded the principle of the solidarity of all. Ambition, dynastic aspirations, the spirit of class and caste, religious fanaticism, the short-sightedness of civic corporations and trade guilds, have unremittingly created artificial antagonism instead of amity; competition instead of co-operation.

We now live under many artificial regulations and restrictions, the results of which make it difficult to believe that the advantage of one man is also the advantage of all. But, despite all that has been done to obscure this truth, we find it asserting itself whenever it has a chance. The doctor who cures his patients best has the best practice; the merchant who sells the best and cheapest goods has the largest business; every man who wishes to gain a living has to find some way of making himself useful to others. In spite, then, of State interference and the anomalies it brings about, we find that the great truth of the solidarity of mankind underlies the whole commercial system of the world.

Even the exceptions point in the same direction. The capture of slaves in Africa and their compulsion to work on the American plantations, appeared to be an advantage to the slave-owner and a disadvantage to the slave; but recent experience has shown it to be a disadvantage to both, for free labour has been proved to pay better than slave labour. The immense difference in the social advantages of the wealthiest classes and the great masses of the poor has induced many a reformer to preach the redistribution of wealth; if such preachings have had no effect in those countries where the masses hold the power, it is because they have recognised that an attack on the property of others, that is to say, on the capital which finds them the work, would do them more harm than the capitalists.

The universal evils which flow from usury cannot be cited as evidence against human solidarity until it has been proved that the destructive usurer would make more money as a usurer than as a useful banker working without State restrictions. The grasping middle-man has recourse to oppression because it increases his profit under a system which makes the demand for labour far less than the supply. Under a system which would make the demand for labour great the man who is now a sweater would have to exercise all his ingenuity for the good of the working people, who are indispensable factors in his business. The fact that even under a most perfect system men would be found who would try to profit at the expense of others, does not disprove the solidarity of humanity, because they might belong to that large proportion of people who do not understand their own interests.

London, or any other great city, illustrates how the solidarity of all tends to increase the comfort of each individual. In London you can probably obtain more easily than anywhere else the products of every clime, every industry, and every art. It is to the interest and advantage of thousands to hold these things at your disposal for the least possible return on your part of goods or services. Four and a half millions of people are daily provided, not only with ordinary necessaries of life, but with the best results of which art and science are capable, and everybody's interest is to serve others well.

With this wonderful example of a huge free economic mechanism before us, it will be understood why the natural and free result of human solidarity may be likened to the works of a watch. The more perfect such works are the more destructive would it be if a pin, or any other clumsy instrument, were from time to time crushed into them with the object of accelerating the movement of the wheels.

Socialistic measures are violently introduced obstacles into the mechanism of free division of labour, in the vain hope of improving its working. When the velocity of one wheel is thus, from abnormal causes, accelerated or slackened, it is out of gear with the other wheels and the whole mechanism is affected. The entire movement becomes irregular, and all its various parts seem to call for abnormal tamperings.

One crude piece of Domestic Economy violently introduced into the delicate mechanism of free division of labour will in this way mischievously affect the whole system, and in order to obtain any visible result from the innovation, as well as to counteract the general disorder, more interfering measures are suggested and often carried, without attaining the original object.

An abstract consideration of the two systems of economy—Political Economy and Domestic

Economy—leads irresistibly to the above conclusions, and our experience during the last decade confirms them in a most striking manner.

The chief result of the mass of modern State-socialistic legislation is a growing demand for more.

And it could not be otherwise. Those who dream of benefiting the people through State-socialistic measures hardly ever consider the full bearing of the Bills they advocate on the general conditions under which they have to be applied. They usually overlook the fact that the remedy they propose only applies while the existing conditions remain unchanged, and ignore that these very measures bring about a change in the conditions which reverses the effects.

For example, if a community is suffering from drunkenness, and finds that most of the drinking is done in a public-house, it might be suggested to close the public-house as a means of preventing drunkenness. While the public-house was open there was little or no inducement for home drinking or secret unlicensed drink traffic. But by forbidding public-houses this condition of things is entirely changed, and there is a strong temptation to encourage these and even worse evils. Far from being an absolute remedy, the closing of the public-house will only produce that much good which forms a difference between the old conditions with the public-house and the new conditions without it. If the conditions remain the same with closed public-houses as the teetotallers generally take for granted, it would be very easy to render a nation sober.

It will be useful here to look into some of the State-socialistic measures which have been passed in Great Britain with the view to improving the condition of the working man, in order to make it clear why they have failed and why they are bound to fail.

To be perfectly fair, we will first take some measures which have been popularly regarded as successes, and which are generally defended by politicians who have achieved popularity, namely, the Factory Acts.

Richard Cobden and John Bright, the two greatest and most practical benefactors of the working classes in England, have frequently been held up by their opponents as the secret champions of capitalists against the working classes because they opposed the Factory Acts.

Nothing proves more their thoroughness as both democrats and economists. They saw what the uneducated could not see, that by arbitrarily fixed rules for labour in a free country they would harm the country at large and the working classes in particular. They struggled to bring about short hours, and easy and highly-paid work for all, in the most effective and direct way, namely, by increasing the prosperity of the country until short working hours would suffice for a working man to provide for himself and his family. They wished to leave it to each man's option to work longer and harder when such extra application was demanded by circumstances. They knew that prosperity could not be brought about by Act of Parliament, but only by entire respect for economic laws.

Their opponents, on the contrary, finding a certain amount of trade going on in England, took for granted that by some mysterious ordinance of Providence the same amount of trade would continue to exist, irrespective of the conditions under which it was carried on. They did not see that, by compulsorily limiting the hours of work, they facilitated competition abroad, paralysed the employer in his enterprise, raised the cost of production in England, and, thus reducing the demand for British goods, strongly favoured a decrease in wages.

It is evident that the reduction of the working hours accompanied by a reduction of wages is not progress—not what the working classes aim at. The absurdity of the proposition to compulsorily curtail the working hours without diminishing wages—all other conditions remaining the same—is easily demonstrated by the inevitable corollary—that no work at all produces the highest state of prosperity! The above economic reservation, 'all other conditions remaining the same,' was of course overlooked by the advocates of the Factory Acts, as it always is by the advocates of State Socialism. But it was not overlooked by Bright and Cobden.

The Factory Acts were never accused of having produced those bad results towards which they tend, because everything else did not remain the same. Simultaneously with the passing of those Acts, British trade experienced an extraordinary inflation from the Free-Trade reform and other powerful causes. The tendency of the Factory Acts to lower wages was, by the leaps and bounds of trade in general, reduced to a check on a rise in wages.

The working man was, through the Factory Acts, legally deprived of the right of earning all he could; but as he earned more than ever, as short hours agreed with him, and as in many trades overtime was practicable, the working man never made a grievance out of this prohibition. On the contrary, the flourishing state of trade was by many of them, and especially by their leaders, attributed to the short hours—with such effect that even now many of the working classes remain under the impression that the more the working hours are reduced the greater the chances of work and the better the pay.

Similar opinions have been adopted, either sincerely or out of diplomacy, by certain prominent politicians. Lord Randolph Churchill, for instance, advocates an official reduction of the working hours as a means of increasing wages and opportunities of work. Such a measure can only be recommended by starting from the fallacious supposition that the work to be done is a fixed quantity, a stable factor in the problem.

Far from being a stable factor, the quantity of work to be done is one which varies most sensitively with the conditions under which it is accomplished. It is only too evident that, under a system of competition between many countries for the sale of goods in neutral markets, the quantity of exported goods depends entirely on the cost of production. It might be disastrous to whole industries, as it has been to parts of such, to be tied down to fixed working hours and similar regulations at a juncture when competition compels us to put forth all our power. In such cases the reduction of wages might not suffice, especially when expensive machinery, expensive moulds, rollers, and patterns are required for goods which are subject to all the fluctuations of fashion. Apart from cost of production, quick, and especially exact, delivery is a condition which often determines the orders. By rigidly fixed hours not only might large present business be lost, but our specialities might be permanently secured by foreign competitors.

There are other points to be considered. Lost business means not increased but reduced capital, which certainly results in fewer chances of employment. The employer who knows that, however able he may be to pay high wages, he is deprived of making a free contract with his labourers, must be very circumspect with regard to the contract he accepts from foreign customers, or he must stereotype his activity in a way which places British industry at a disadvantage.

In this and many other ways the Factory Acts tend to reduce wages and to deprive the working man of opportunities of work. Besides, it should be specially noted that the benefits which these Acts are expected to confer on the working classes are only attainable when business is good enough to keep wages up and employment plentiful—that is to say, when the working man is in a position to make the best terms for himself without Factory Acts. They only prevent him from earning more if such should be his desire. When employment is scarce and many workers compete for it and would willingly work extra hours to tide over the bad times, then the Factory Acts cannot help the working man at all. On the contrary, they can only prevent the return of those good times, which bring with them high wages, and freedom for the workers to live by short hours of work or to work hard for future independence.

No man can defend the Factory Acts from the accusation of being worse than useless when times are bad and ridiculously superfluous when times are good.

So far, we have only considered the effect of the Factory Acts on those working people who have remained within the circle of their direct influence, that is to say, the workers in industries which continue to be carried on in factories. But among the general economic effects which the Factory Acts have contributed to produce is the gigantic development of the sweating system.

Such industries which foreign and home competition did not allow to be carried on with certainty of continuity and a fair chance of profit in State-regulated factories were relegated to the homes of the poor people. Apart from the unhealthiness and discomfort, home-work for large industrials involves necessarily the agency of a great number of middle-men, whose considerable profits are all taken out of the wages of the workers, and render that state of slavery possible which we have described—a state under which the starving

o

and pinching of the poor bring about the inevitable result of less demand for goods, and a consequent diminution of the chances of employment.

Such is the real nature of one of the most popular State-socialistic measures, and it is unfortunate that the working classes should look upon those who wish to free them from this ruinous bondage as their sworn enemies. But on the other hand it is gratifying that the Factory Acts need not be repealed. All that is required is to convince the working classes that there is a direct and short road to high wages and short hours, viz. the removal of other older and more pernicious State impediments to prosperity. When this is done, the Factory Acts, like so many other pernicious Acts, will become obsolete.

It is a hopeful sign that the labour congresses are sufficiently aware of the fallacy of the eight hours' reform to resist it as a new burden which well-meaning ignorance or cynical ambition would foist upon them. It is amazing that political leaders do not perceive what the majority of the labour congresses are no doubt aware of, namely, that if they reduce the working hours, the working men will suffer unless they fix the wages at the same time. If they fix the wages without having a guarantee that the employers will not dismiss any of their men, they might bring about an alarming want of employment. We thus see that the introduction of one piece of domestic legislation into our free system interferes with its entire working, and that before a compulsory shortening of hours can be beneficial, the whole productive trade of the country must be State-organised.

Another popular socialistic enactment is the one which purports to prevent a landlord from seizing the chattels of a tenant under the value of 5l. sterling. This Act was certainly well intended, was easily carried, and generally looked upon as legislation in favour of the working man.

But what are the results? The usual and inevitable ones. The conditions under which the Act was to be applied have been changed by the Act, and the result is reversed. If before the Act a landlord let tenements to a man, or a family, owning chattels under 5l., and the Act had been put in force, while the tenants were in possession of the place, the goods would have been safe against a harsh landlord. But under the new Act, a working man is not permitted to take possession of a dwelling of a harsh landlord except his chattels exceed the value of 5*l*. by one week's or one month's rent, as the case may be, or he must pay his rent in advance.

We thus find that while this Act was not required in the case of considerate landlords, it has aggravated the position of the working man in his relations with a harsh landlord. The Act deprives the working man of credit to the extent of 5*l*., prevents him from using his property in the way circumstances require, and places him in the disadvantageous position of a minor without the compensation of having any single one of his wants provided for.

The benevolent socialistic measures of the two staunch friends of the working man—Her Majesty's Government and Her Majesty's Opposition—do not always meet with an enthusiastic reception from those in whose favour they are framed.

Very creditable sympathies with the hard-worked and under-paid pit-girls moved their State-socialistic friends in Parliament to take their work from their shoulders by that easy and simple method, so dear to State Socialists, namely, prohibition. The girls were to be forbidden to work at the pit-mouth. Those acquainted with this class of work will be surprised that it could ever be supposed to possess such irresistible attractions as to render a Parliamentary prohibition necessary to prevent the girls from doing it, and thereby neglect such womanly occupations as ornamenting their homes and devoting themselves to the culinary art. That they were driven to this rough work from sheer necessity, and that, when deprived of it, they would have no work to fall back upon, never struck our State Socialists until a deputation of pit-girls sued for protection against their undiscriminating friends.

But it is not often that the bad effect of socialistic measures lies so much on the surface as in the case of the pit-girls. The contrary is usually the case: the advantages appear plausible while the disastrous effects can only be arrived at by exact economic reasoning or by a dearly bought experience.

The Merchandise Marks Act is a case in point. It was hailed with general approval, except by those whose business suffered directly from it. Since the Act has come into force, some few instances have been pointed out in which the Act is supposed to have benefited British trade, but on closer examination it has generally been found that the cases which have called forth these eulogies of the Act have been entirely isolated, and of a nature to gratify the sentiment of jealousy and retribution rather than to further British industry. But the bad effects it has produced on many branches of British trade, and especially on our shipping, are both numerous and far-reaching.

The object of the Act was to prevent the names of British manufacturers from being placed fraudulently on British goods, to prevent British manufacturers or dealers from having their own names placed on foreign goods, except accompanied by the express declaration that the goods were not manufactured in Great Britain. This enactment was supposed to benefit British manufactures by protecting them from foreign imitators of goods and labels, and from having the reputation of their products discredited abroad by spurious imitations. It was supposed to benefit the working men of Great Britain by increasing the sale of the goods in the manufacturing of which they were engaged, and in preventing employers from having part of their goods made abroad.

How have these expectations been fulfilled? First as to the spurious imitation of British goods and labels abroad, the British government have no power to interfere with it. All they can do is to stop such goods when they come to this country to be consumed here, or to be trans-shipped in British vessels. The huge trade that is carried on abroad in the manufacturing countries themselves, or with other countries, in goods labelled with spurious British labels, cannot be interfered with by our government. That the prohibition of the importation into Great Britain of such goods would benefit British industry was based on the patriotic bias that British goods are good and foreign goods are bad, and that the public would always give preference to British goods if they could only distinguish them from foreign ones.

This supposition was much truer before the Act than after it was passed, because the public, not being the helpless fool the State Socialists always suppose it to be, selected their goods according to quality, and the foreign imitator, requiring a profit on his fraud, manufactured bad qualities with intent to make a large profit. By natural selection the British thus sold the most.

This is now altered. The Act has put a stop to the importation of foreign imitations, and the foreign manufacturer being thus rudely reminded of the fact that honesty is the best policy, has only one way of getting his goods accepted in Great Britain, that is by establishing a reputation for his own trade-mark in this country. This is now an object on which many foreign manufacturers are seriously intent, and as they become more successful the competition which they offer to British manufacturers will be more formidable than before.

In preventing the trans-shipment of imitation goods in the British ports the Act in no way diminishes the sale of such goods in foreign countries: all it does is to deprive British ships and steamers of freight, and encourage a direct trade between Germany and the neutral markets.

The prohibition to British firms to label unconditionally their goods manufactured abroad in the same way as they label their goods manufactured in Great Britain is a serious blow to British commerce. One of the great advantages of Free Trade is that English business men and manufacturers can avail themselves, with great advantage to their own trade, of all the best results of foreign industry.

Free Trade allows, or rather did allow, a British producer or merchant to make up his range of samples from both British and foreign manufactures, and thereby present a complete collection which could defy competition both as to assortment and as to price—an advantage which business men can well appreciate. These facilities made Great Britain the market of the world, and brought customers for a far larger quantity of goods than Great Britain alone could produce. They tended to render British ports the chief shipping places of European goods to neutral markets, and British steamers the carriers of the world. It has not infrequently been the case, that French merchants in a French colony have bought all their continental goods, including those from France, through English merchants, and had them shipped by our vessels.

This great advantage for English manufacturers, merchants, and shippers is considerably diminished by the Merchandise Marks Act. The goods must either not be shipped at all for British account, or shipped without any label, or with a label indicating their origin. All three ways are bad. The loss of sale of some qualities might lead to the loss of the sale of all, and reduced business means reduced profits, reduced shipping, reduced capital. No label will indicate that the goods are not British, and raise the buyer's desire to ascertain the first source. A label indicating foreign origin would more effectively wean the customer from British trade.

The result is now that colonies founded by the English people buy from Germany goods introduced into the colony by English merchants, manufactured according to English ideas, and perhaps invented by English genius. Foreign cheap labour, instead of swelling the bulk of English trade and shipping, becomes the basis of a new buying market; foreign industry, instead of being the handmaid of English enterprise, is converted into a formidable rival.

When to this is added that, since we have thus encouraged a direct German shipping trade to the neutral markets, the German manufacturers take good care to place their own labels only on their best qualities, and when they use English labels reserve them for the worst, we can form an idea of the amount of good the Merchandise Marks Act has done for the English manufacturer and the English working man.

And when we remember that British manufacturers—with the exception of a few advertising makers of specialities—never raise any objections to placing the labels of their customers, British or foreign, even on the very best qualities, and that just now in the extending colonial trade of the Germans an immense importance is attached to labels, it is evident that the Merchandise Marks Act tends effectively to give our foreign competitors that lead in the export of manufactured goods which England hitherto has held.

Such an Act would never have been called for had banking been free and trade prosperous. It is intensity of competition, caused by restricted supply of capital and mediums of exchange, which tempts British traders to clutch at such plausibly protective but really destructive measures.

CHAPTER XIV

THE PERSECUTION OF THE CHILD BY THE STATE

WHILE our Parliament, under the influence of the modern State-socialistic spirit, aims at emulating Prince Bismarck's bureaucratic system, its zeal, as we have seen in the case of the pit-girls, sometimes receives a check. A certain circumspection is therefore made necessary in the case of legislation for adults.

But the children of the poor cannot form deputations, cannot sign petitions: they therefore become easy victims of well-meaning and pragmatical philanthropists.

The importance of the task we have undertaken demands that State Socialism should be proved fallacious even and especially in the case of those institutions which are regarded by its votaries as complete successes, and which are constantly pointed to as so many inducements to a further development of the socialistic system. These institutions are the Post Office and the National School system. In a coming chapter on complete Socialism we shall deal with the Post Office, and devote this one to the consideration of State-socialistic enactments regarding children.

It must be clearly understood that in pointing out the failure of State Socialism to solve the problem of National Education, we are not advocating an instantaneous abolition of the present system, nor deprecating its introduction under the circumstances existing at the time, nor its usefulness under present circumstances. Those who criticise our National School system are often exposed to the accusation of being in favour of ignorance and of a degraded state for the masses. Let us therefore at once explain that we are well aware of the immense value of education, and believe that the duty of every government is to place no obstacle in the way of a good education for every individual in the country.

Nowadays most people would say that it is the duty of the government not only to remove obstacles in the way of education, but to promote it with all its power. Our contention is that when the government has removed all the obstacles that stand in the way of popular education it has done all that is in its power to do, because it will then have established a system under which the laws of Political Economy and Sociology have free play. Should the government introduce socialistic measures into such a perfect system they would not favour national education, but vitiate it. And this because State interference always produces mischief so long as it is not complete, and to really promote popular education by State interference would mean to introduce a complete socialistic system. But, as we shall show in the following chapter, a complete socialistic system is degrading to the individual and consequently destructive to education in its best sense. Far then from being the opponents of education, we wish to demonstrate that popular education can be made far more effective and more genuine than it now is.

As the franchise was extended, the want of education in the classes destined to hold the balance of power in the country caused some alarm among the upper classes. The cry was, 'Let us educate our future masters.' But there were other influences at work in favour of improved education of the masses.

When, in spite of the expansion of trade and the rise in wages, such a large proportion of the people remained in chronic misery, it was surmised that the lowest classes were too ignorant to take advantage of the flourishing condition of trade. Drunkenness, vice, thriftlessness, were attributed to ignorance, and philanthropists became fervent advocates of education. The success of popular schools in other countries, such as Switzerland, Denmark, and Sweden, inspired British patriots with the desire to emulate their systems.

These examples set by other nations had a great deal to do with the form the national education system in England took: for without them it would not have been so rashly decided that education was identical with cramming.

A good education, in its best sense, is the greatest boon that can be conferred on a human being, and it is no wonder that the English people should gladly accept the offer of our politicians to confer this boon on every English child. Parliament spoke of education, but meant cramming. Nothing is more difficult to give than a good education, and the State is wholly incompetent to give it. But any power, anyone in authority, is equal to cramming.

This was the way in which the mere storing of the memories of the children, and the teaching of reading, writing, and arithmetic, were confounded with education. The educational system which had succeeded in the above-mentioned countries consisted merely of schools where these three subjects were taught, and the memories of the children were stocked. It was supposed that as schools had produced so much good abroad, they ought to produce the same effect in England.

The vast difference in circumstances was entirely disregarded. The good effect abroad was experienced mostly among the children of the peasantry; these children were poor—extremely poor—but they lived in the pure air of the country, in close contact with nature, and though their food was coarse, it was sufficient and regularly supplied. They lived in rustic but scrupulously clean homes. Their parents were ignorant, but moral, religious, proud, and strictly honest; bent on setting their children as perfect an example as possible. These peasant children had, therefore, all that goes to make up an education, except schooling. It was no wonder, then, that, when this want was supplied, the result was satisfactory.

Here it might be remarked that the effect of public schools in the country districts of Great Britain should be the same as among the peasantry abroad. But there are marked differences which should not be overlooked. There is no peasantry in England at all. The population is divided into landlords, farmers, and labourers. The two former classes educate their children themselves, and the children of the farm-labourers are certainly not so well provided with regard to food, clothing, and homes as the peasantry of the countries we have named. In Ireland, there is a peasantry, but their position is hardly better than that of the labourers in England; and in Scotland the education of the country lads has for a century stood uncommonly high, thanks, as we shall show later on, to the absence of State interference in other directions.

But when national education was advocated, it was not so much the country districts that were uppermost in the reformers' minds, or referred to as frightful examples of neglected education. I was in the courts and alleys of the large towns swarming with children, that it was expected to achieve the greatest triumphs. The children o the lower middle class, or of the superior working class, were not the objects of our legislators solicitude, for these had already some home education and attended some kind of schools.

The aim of Parliament was to confer education on the children of the great mass of poor people who could ill afford school-money, and whose desperate circumstances made them indifferent to the future of their offspring. If we compare the position of these children with that of the continental peasant's children, we shall find it widely different: instead of plenty of food, starvation instead of healthy and seasonable clothing, rags instead of country air and contact with nature the slum and the gutter; instead of good examples, corrupt surroundings. The educational requirements of children living under conditions so different must necessarily be of an almost opposite nature; and it was vain to hope that effects such as were produced in Sweden, Switzerland, and other countries, should follow from cramming.

If our legislators intended to educate the children of the poor, they should first have provided them with wholesome food, then good clothing, then healthy and pure homes, and so on, placing cramming at the end of the list. The Spartans, two thousand years ago, understood that if the State has to educate the child it must take entire charge of it. This is why we have said that national education, to be successful, presupposes complete socialistic institutions.

And what results can logically be expected from a system which consists in giving children instruction without any other educational care; in sharpening the mind without elevating the character; in developing faculties for the gratification of passions and instincts, without religion, morality, or even philosophy; in arousing desires and yearnings that cannot be satisfied; in overcramming underfed brains, and overtaxing feeble and starved bodies?

The results to be expected are weak bodies, weak minds, weak morals, premature corruption, abnormal cunning, lessened self-respect, false pride, contempt for honest work, gambling propensities, love of literary trash, and inordinate selfishness. If these results have not been more apparent than they are, it is because many of even the poorest children have for parents religious and respectable people, and not the monsters which the advocates of State interference with children seem to suppose; because there is in the English character a considerable element of independence and self-respect, traits which here have been developed, thanks to more individual freedom than that enjoyed by any other people.

That the deplorable consequences of our one-sided educational system are not wanting, will, however, not be denied by anybody. Children of twelve to fourteen years, who have already seen the inside of a great many prisons, are modern products. Our Reformatories and Industrial Schools contain now about twenty-two thousand juvenile law-breakers, and if we consider how many juvenile crimes remain undetected, owing to a highly developed cunning, and what a very small percentage of actually detected crime leads to the Reformatory or the Industrial School, the given statistics of juvenile criminals are, to say the least, alarming.

Apart from the influence on the child, there are

other hardships to be endured by the poorest children in our Board Schools. Some have to learn hard lessons on empty stomachs; some have to walk a long distance in cold weather, half-naked; and the occasional inability to bring the school pence is a cause of humiliation and moral suffering which all who remember childhood can readily conceive.

As to the parents of the children, the school laws seem to be framed on the supposition that the well-to-do have the monopoly of fine feeling. How would a member of Parliament or his lady like to send their children to a school to be crammed even when the child is unfit for it; to have them associate with children to whom they object, to be taught by people they dislike, to be exposed to ophthalmia and other contagious diseases; to have their homes invaded by inspectors, and not to be allowed to instruct their own children without being called upon for the proof of results?

This is what the parents have to submit to because they are poor. We shall not dwell upon the numerous and very painful cases in which parents have been summoned before the courts, fined and imprisoned, because from sheer poverty they have been unable to conform to the official regulations; for we should be met with the usual reply, that it is the parents' own fault, though in thousands of instances a good defence could be set up for them. It is a slow and thankless task to bring home to bureaucrats that the poor under their power should have any rights or liberties.

The advocates of our present system will here probably ask if it has not produced good and great results, and what would be the state of things if the instruction supplied by Board Schools had been wanting? The reply to this is that the question is not whether the present system of instruction is better than no instruction at all, but how far it can favourably compare with that education which would have been supplied to the children if this country had not suffered from State interference. If State education, even so one-sided and defective as that afforded to English poor children, were the only kind of education that could be had it might be expedient to submit to the evils it involves in order to escape greater evils. This fortunately we have not to discuss. We have simply to show that State interference exercises a baneful influence over the people in every respect, State education not excepted.

We shall presently make clear what kind of education would have taken place if State education, if State interference, had not prevented it, but we must first say a few words about the results claimed by the advocates of the present system, namely, that it has reduced mendicity, crime, and drunkenness.

There is happily a considerable diminution of these evils, but it will be very difficult to determine the relative potency of the factors that have produced it. The Sunday School teachers claim the improvement as a result of their exertions; the teetotallers declare that it is entirely due to the sobriety they have inculcated; the clergy affirm that it is traceable to Church-work; and the Salvation Army boast that it is due to the safety-valve of excitement they have supplied.

All these may have had a share in the good work, but there are many and powerful causes that alone are sufficient to explain our social improvements. There are, in the first place, all the enormous causes for trade inflation already referred to, such as Free Trade, Joint-Stock banks, development of the Colonies, locomotion by steam, &c., whereby the condition of the working classes has been immensely improved. For prosperity stimulates self-respect—*noblesse oblige*. Then we have a more humane administration of our laws, improved workhouse organisation, more stringent poor laws, an increased and improved police force, a more elevated tone and a greater supply of public amusements, Trades Unions, Provident and Benefit Societies, and the unprecedented and immense efforts on the part of the wealthy classes to influence the lower for the better.

It is, therefore, unreasonable to claim for national education the moral improvement among the masses when so many other potent causes have been simultaneously at work. The fact is that the increased depravity among the young, in face of a general social improvement, does not point to a healthy influence of the School Board system.

To educate adequately the children of a nation by the agency of the State would, as we have pointed out, only be possible under complete Socialism. Apart from the degrading influences of Socialism, it still remains an open question whether State education can ever excel education by the parent.

When we consider that all parents in this country who can afford it, as a rule, strive hard to give their children as good an education as they possibly can, it is only fair and reasonable to conclude that it is only poverty and misery which prevent the poor from giving their children the benefits of education.

We have already shown how State interference with banking inflicts poverty on the majority of our working classes, and if it be granted that prosperity would enable and induce them to give a good education to their children, it becomes evident that State interference is the original cause of the gross neglect of children which we have witnessed and still witness in this country. What we deplore is that one piece of State Socialism—State education—should have been introduced in order to remedy the effects of another piece of State Socialism—bank monopoly.

Had bank monopoly not prevailed, and Free Trade in Capital had accompanied Free Trade in foreign goods, the people would have enjoyed a degree of prosperity which would have rendered compulsory education entirely unnecessary. We should have had all the advantages of parent-supervised education, without the many evils of State education, and there can be no doubt that both the moral and physical condition of the children would have reached a higher standard than under our present State-produced poverty and compulsory cramming.

What is here stated is strikingly confirmed by experience in Scotland. In a coming chapter, we shall fully explain how Free Trade in Capital there produced, despite the many obstacles which prevailed at the time, a remarkable degree of prosperity; and there, as in all countries where production has flourished, special attention was paid to education. It is a well-known fact, that the poor children in Scotland enjoyed, during the last century and the beginning of this, a degree of education far above that of the poor of any other country. There are no doubt people who will say that education in Scotland was not the effect of prosperity, but prosperity the effect of education. But here again experience is on our side: for though education is generally good in countries where production flourishes and the lowest ranks of the working classes are well off, in the countries in Europe where instruction by State interference has been brought to a high standard, there is very little prosperity among the masses.

In face of the economic and political situation produced by State interference, we would not advocate the abolition of what now are inaccurately called the educational laws: for, unfortunately, one State-socialistic enactment renders others necessary.

When Free Trade in Capital is introduced, the prosperity among the working classes will stimulate in the parents the desire to give a good education to their children, and they will be able to escape the tyranny of the school laws in the same way as the upper classes escape them now. The present educational laws will, like thousands of other Parliamentary Acts, become obsolete without being repealed. They will remain on our Statute Books to be quoted by future students of history as results of the strange socialistic mania which possessed the British nation in the latter half of this nineteenth century.

While there are many excuses for the school laws, there are other examples of Parliamentary persecution of children which are entirely without excuse. One of these is the recently passed Act which prohibits the employment of children in theatres. It may seem strange that our State Socialists evinced such strong sympathies for theatrical children, while they remained indifferent to a hundred times the number of neglected children in the purlieus of great cities, to whom the employment in theatres would have meant several hours of comfort, warmth, amusement, healthy exercise, useful training and discipline, and, above all, the means of better nourishment and personal care.

There are probably only two reasons. The first of them is that by paying a few shillings the theatrical children could be comfortably inspected from an opera-box, while the condition of the other children would only strike those who take sufficient interest in them to visit their wretched homes. The second, that doing good by prohibition costs nothing.

With some the prejudice against theatres, for which managers are to a certain extent responsible, was the incentive to voting for the measure. It would be to credit the advocates of this measure with too much Machiavellianism to suggest that they had it in their minds to still more demoralise the stage in order to destroy it altogether; and we must therefore attribute their action to mere thoughtless animosity against the stage, when they deprived it of its purest element.

If the employment of children on the stage exercises a demoralising influence upon them, the witnessing of performances would be still more so for children; and if morality is made a plea, the theatre-haters should have begun their meddling work by prohibiting the children of the rich from visiting theatres. This would not have deprived them of the necessaries of life, and the influential position which many of these children are destined to hold would have furnished a more reasonable excuse than did the case of the theatrical children.

If the children of the poor have good parents, that is to say, parents who consider the interests of their offspring before their own, such parents would understand much better than Parliament whether it is better for their children to have such additional supplies as their work in the theatres brings in, or suffer from want. In such cases Parliament has taken upon itself to condemn the children to want. If, on the other hand, these poor children have bad parents, that is to say, parents who would sacrifice the true interests of their children to gratify their own tastes, the inability of the children to contribute to the household expenses would certainly not add to their happiness. On the contrary, in such cases Parliament has deprived these little ones of the only means of securing kind treatment.

It is indeed surprising that members of Parliament should be unable to understand, or unwilling to concede, that to prevent the child from being useful to selfish parents, without taking it out of their hands altogether, is to place it in the dreadful position of a slave forbidden by government to work for his master, but condemned to depend on him for his sustenance. This Theatrical Bill therefore illustrates the vanity of hoping for improvement from State-socialistic measures before complete Socialism is introduced.

As the only merit of State-socialistic measures is that they pave the way, accelerate, and finally compel entire Socialism, the false economic system from which we suffer cannot be logically condemned until the true nature and results of Socialism are explained. We shall therefore in the next chapter examine into what complete Socialism means.

CHAPTER XV

THE SOCIALISTIC MIRAGE

WHEN a State-socialistic measure fails to produce its expected results, the lesson is always lost on our State Socialists, and they remain as numb as ever to the teachings of our Sociologists which supply the reasons why State-socialistic measures must fail. The excuse they usually take refuge in is that the failing measures were not strong enough, not compulsory enough, not comprehensive enough; and they are ever ready to introduce another batch of State-socialistic remedies of a more stringent nature.

The legislation for the protection of life at sea may be selected as an example. It is a fair one, because the object it has in view is one with which every Englishman must sympathise. When Mr. Plimsoll, some years ago, allowed his feelings to get the better of him in the House of Commons, he uttered words of righteous indignation which (though he had to apologise for them) secured him so great an amount of public sympathy that he was enabled to carry—at least to a great extent—those measures of State supervision over shipping which he considered favourable to the protection of life at sea.

But how far has this object been attained? Only lately, it seems, first one steamer and then another left a British port in conditions which caused Mr. Plimsoll to foretell their loss; and his prophecy was only too truly fulfilled. A greater proof of the ineffectiveness of State supervision of shipping, as far as it has been tried, it is scarcely possible to imagine.

The cry now will go up for more stringent measures. A government official must fix the load-line and take other steps to prevent overloading. But when that is done more disappointments are in store for us. Over-legislation always generates subterfuge. For the sake of economy ship-owners will so change the construction of their ships as to overload despite the official load-line. Then the whole shape of the ships will have to be regulated by Parliament. Ship-builders—under the lash of competition—will try to economise on the materials, and every plate will have to be examined by a government official. The shipbuilder's wages, in order to reduce cost, must be cut down, riveters will scamp their piecework, and government inspection of every rivet will be demanded.

Similar inspections and stringent regulations in every possible direction will be absolutely necessary before any good results can be logically expected from government supervision. Indeed, if the most perfect system of government control were established, an indispensable condition for its success would be a staff of government officials, each of perfect efficiency and perfect honesty. A single exception would be a serious matter: for it is a well-known fact that the less educated people are the greater their confidence in government. What government has guaranteed or supervised is generally taken entirely on trust, without inquiry or personal investigation. The more regulations we have about shipping the less will crews and passengers exercise their own judgment in the selection of a ship. Here, as in all cases of State supervision, the responsibility which the government undertakes is enormously disproportionate to the miserable and inadequate means it can bring to its fulfilment.

But there is another drawback which powerfully counteracts the object in view, namely, the increased difficulty which each government regulation places in the way of British shipowners in their keen competition with foreigners. The augmented expenses and the loss of freight which government regulations impose have to be made up for in some way—generally by a reduction in the pay of captain and crew. This reduction, again, is accomplished by working British ships to a great extent with foreign crews and inefficient captains. While thus we strive to benefit British sailors by bureaucratic supervision—which, as we see from the Continent, tends to degenerate into sham and bribery—we actually protect them out of existence.

We need not say that the only true way of protecting our seamen is to keep our shipping so flourishing that a lively demand for their services will enable them to give bad firms, bad ships and bad captains a wide berth. But when this is not recognised or considered possible, and when prohibition and compulsion continue to be regarded as the only means, it is not difficult to foresee that British shipowners will have to be protected from foreign competition. This would be the beginning of socialistic regulations, not only of our shipping but of all the commerce and industry which depend upon cheap freight and upon the ability to compete with foreigners. All work would have to be carried on by government regulation, and even the Colonies would be drawn into the socialistic vortex, because, under a State-managed production and trade, it would be absurd to count on any other markets than those we can keep open by force of arms.

In this way every rash interference with the immutable laws which Economy and Sociology have revealed to us produces a constantly increasing demand for more interference until a complete socialistic system has been established, or till some catastrophe gives an entirely new course to events.

There are plenty of State Socialists who will not discard their hobby and yet disclaim any intention to work for the establishment of a complete socialistic system. These would, in the case of the sailors, no doubt consider their duty fulfilled after having carried their pet measures, and then leave British sailors and British shipping to struggle as best they may under the unnatural and awkward conditions they have created, little heeding what becomes of their victims.

But there are examples of State interference which absolutely compel a progressive movement towards complete Socialism. For instance, enactments intended to enforce suitable dwellings. It is evident that to regulate the size of rooms would simply be pernicious, if we do not also regulate the number of inmates. There is no sort of advantage in large rooms if they are each occupied by several families. A small room for each family would be far more preferable. If therefore we regulate the size of the rooms, we must arrange a system of supervision to prevent overcrowding. This involves a nightly inspection of every house in the kingdom, for in a country where the working classes have the power, it would be absurd to have one law for the poor and one for the rich. The frequent cases of overcrowding in small rooms among well-to-do people which all of us have met with, and the unsuitable bedrooms which are given to servants, as the law courts sometimes reveal, would very soon supply sufficient pretext for a general inspection.

The mere demolition of rookeries has not proved itself an efficient remedy for overcrowding, but has simply widened the circle of the evil and infected new districts. The building of new houses by the agency of government does not augment the supply of cheap dwellings, because if the government houses are let cheaply they prevent private builders from competing with the government and the supply of dwellings diminishes instead of increasing. Only by undertaking to build all the houses required by the working classes could the government hope to do any good, and this can be done only by a complete socialistic system.

While the many State-socialistic measures already passed induce and compel other measures of a still more socialistic nature, there are other agencies at work to accelerate the advent of complete socialism. Politicians eager for popularity proclaim themselves Socialists; a section of the press speaks about the retrograde movement towards State despotism as if it were progress; philanthropic clergymen identify Socialism with the Christian religion; and a great many charitably disposed people with better hearts than heads work for the advent of Socialism as if it were the beginning of the millennium. All this has its origin in want of knowledge of what Socialism really means, and tends to impress the majority of the nation with the idea that Socialism must after all be a good thing.

Under such circumstances it becomes a duty to show up Socialism in its true colours, and divest it of the seductive glamour thrown upon it by Utopian dreamers—and this all the more because all that energy which now is wasted in luring the nation towards an abyss is needed for the inauguration of a truly economic system.

It should be first borne in mind that of all the enthusiasts who have been anxious to draw up a practical scheme for Socialism none has succeeded in establishing a plan which would bear the slightest test. The very attempt to systematise Socialism has led thousands of logical people to reject Socialism altogether, as a curse instead of a blessing. We have any number of fanciful and flowery pictures of impossible Socialism, of attractive Utopias, belonging to an imaginary world. Their authors have generally started from some absurd supposition, ignored human nature altogether, remained blind to all historical experience, and displayed a lofty contempt for the laws of nature, Political Economy, and arithmetic.

An indispensable condition for the success of practical Socialism is an ideally perfect government, but Socialists do not perceive that, by taking such a government for granted, they have supposed a better state of things than they strive to establish.

And the socialist government need be perfect indeed, for it would have to organise and superintend that immense division of labour, with its almost illimitable ramifications, which has made modern production so wonderfully easy. It is evident that such work and such responsibility could not be undertaken by men with the slightest knowledge of the duties before them, without the most absolute, unlimited, and undisputed power over everything and everybody.

A government that has to provide food, clothing, shelter, education, defences, and public amusements to forty millions of people; that has to carry on the entire agriculture, the entire industry of the country with a result favourable enough to compete with foreigners—such a government must necessarily have the power to compel work. It requires but little reflection to understand that the whole system would break down ignominiously if individuals were allowed to work or be lazy at their option, to pick and choose their work, to object to tasks allotted to them, or to lose time in executing orders.

In the absence of those severe overseers which Political Economy can point to in a free system— namely, self-preservation, the care for home and family, the desire to rise in the world—in the absence of these upholders of discipline, socialistic society would be a helpless chaos if the governing authority had not absolute power. It would be like a huge ship in a gale without officers, or like an army without discipline.

However unpleasant absolute slavery might be to the individual, it would go terribly against his interests to object to it: for, as we know, not everybody can be such an enthusiastic Socialist as to put forth his best powers in the accomplishment of an uncongenial task. There will always be people of a lazy disposition who will not do more work than they are compelled to do. Those who were anxious to work hard and do their best would have no other option than either to do duty for the lazy ones or give the government full power to compel the individual to work. The slightest opposition to this power would recoil in the shape of extra drudgery on the good Socialist, and would at once threaten to destroy the whole State.

Practical Socialism is therefore exactly the same thing as slavery. And it could not be otherwise. As we have already pointed out, there are only two ways in which division of labour can work: under individual freedom regulated by the laws of Political Economy, or under compulsion regulated by some authority on the principle of Domestic Economy.

Socialism is the principle of Domestic Economy applied to the State. In all Domestic Economy compulsion is paramount. The husbandman or the employer of labour does not flog his servants or employés, but he has means as powerful as corporal punishment by which he can compel work: to dismiss a working man, in these days, who has a wife and family and who is sensible of his duties to them, may to him be tantamount to the severest bodily punishment; a bad character to a servant girl might be the ruin of her life,

Thus, wherever we see the principles of Domestic Economy applied we find the principles of compulsion prevailing, and in the State we can as little afford to dispense with it as in the factory and the home, if we are rash enough to manage the State on the same principle as a house or a factory. This undeniable truth is further illustrated by the demand for compulsion which accompanies the introduction of State-socialistic legislation.

Compulsion, or slavery under the State, being then a characteristic feature of Socialism, it remains to be examined under what conditions it would be exercised. It should first be remembered that State-managed production is expensive, if not ruinous. Without referring to the ironclads built by our government at twice the natural cost, every undertaking all over the world carried on by government management proves that it is anything but economical. Then we must consider that compulsory labour has a very small commercial value, and can only be executed under very expensive supervision. The production of wealth in the country would therefore be enormously reduced.

A socialistic government must either refrain from all trade with foreign countries, or carry it on on a commercial principle, that is, produce more cheaply at home than it sells abroad. If it elected the former alternative it would reduce the people to an almost barbarous state, compelling them to produce goods and articles with a fearful amount of work and at enormous expense which could be bought cheaply abroad. In the case of the second alternative, it would have to compel the people to work for very long hours and to live on the smallest possible consumption, in order to compete with countries where the work was carried on on a sound economic principle.

In the case of all governments being socialistic—a far-fetched supposition, which, however, must be faced, because Socialists, like bi-metallists, quickly take refuge in a cosmopolitan application of their theories when they have been proved impracticable for one country—the situation would be still worse, for the total production of wealth would be so much more reduced, international exchanges would be insignificant in consequence of the extremely reduced consumption, and the competition between the nations would be fought with the savage intensity of war, and would degenerate into war.

While thus the produced wealth would be small, the expenses to be met by the government would be gigantic. Apart from the industrial and social expenses there would be a necessity for many other considerable outlays. The number of government officials, inspectors, and overseers, not to say slave-drivers, would be appalling. The fractiousness of the indolent and discontented would compel the maintenance of a powerful police-force and a standing army as large at least as that of Germany, without which Prince Bismarck's socialistic measures would be impossible.

The expenses for the police and army would have to be heavy because such compulsion as is exercised in Germany for recruiting purposes would not be possible in a socialistic State. The rank and file would fraternise with the discontented and would form a dangerous majority. In Germany a million and a half of rank and file can be kept in subjection because in that country there exists, thanks to the absence of complete Socialism, energetic and courageous upper and middle classes, a large peace-loving peasant class, an immense amount of capital in private hands, time-honoured traditions of loyalty to the reigning house, and an intense fear of foreign invasion. While thus in Germany the best educated, the wealthiest, the most courageous, and the most thrifty portion of the nation combine with the officers of the army to maintain discipline and make the army a means to coerce the destitute and discontented classes, in a socialistic State the army would have to coerce the whole people and would have to be paid very highly to remain loyal. Those who have to do the work in a socialistic State will therefore have to labour very hard and to live on miserable fare.

One inevitable consequence of complete Socialism is a sharp division of the nation into two castes, the labouring caste and the bureaucratic caste—slaves and slave-drivers. The condition of a working man, that is to say, of anyone who does not hold the post of inspector or superintendent, would be so hard that everybody would be anxious to become one of the bureaucrats. These again, having very extensive powers, would do their utmost to secure appointments for their friends and kinsmen, and thus prevent them from becoming labourers.

The central government, holding absolute power, would make all appointments in the most arbitrary manner, and where such a system prevails we know that favouritism, not to say corruption, at once sets in. The United States is an example of this, and if it were not for the frequent changes of Presidents, the bureaucratic class there would rapidly grow into a powerful body, though they possess only a fraction of the influence which they would have if America were a socialistic State.

It is therefore certain that the bureaucrats would combine to keep the good appointments for themselves and their friends and would soon develop into an all-powerful caste, because they would hold in their hands all the capital of the nation, all the appointments, and the power to mete out misery or happiness to the whole non-official classes. They would, of course, have command of the police, and would probably league themselves with the military caste. We should thus find that Domestic Economy applied to the State would in modern England produce the same effect as it produced in the ancient States, the division of the people into patricians and serfs.

If a socialistic State could be established in this country it would prove the greatest calamity that could befall the working classes, because they would have no chance of being members of the government caste. This would certainly be recruited entirely from the upper classes. Even if it were recruited partially from the working class, the number benefited at the price of the misery and degradation of the rest would be small.

The advocates of complete Socialism are aware of and regret the necessity for compulsory labour as part of their programme, but consider it a gain for the working classes to escape the tyranny of capital by submitting to the tyranny of the State. In face of the prevailing destitution, it is no wonder that they should hold such views, especially when it is considered that they do not see that labour can be enfranchised from the despotism of capital by sound Political Economy.

They cling to the hope that the government on which they would confer such immense power would be elected by the people themselves, and that consequently the coercion exercised by it would be regulated by public opinion. In other words, this means that the government and the bureaucratic class would consist of men actuated by such perfect patriotism and self-abnegation that they could be trusted to wield absolute power over all the resources of the community, to dispose of all the working-power, and to preside over the distribution of all the necessaries of life, and yet not yield to the temptation to follow out their own ideas and retain a power which none could dispute.

This is of course an empty dream. Even the very best set of men might easily, under such circumstances, deem their retention of power an absolute necessity for the salvation of the country, and would pay little heed to the clamours of men destined to live under chronic coercion. Nay, they would find it their duty to summarily suppress all opposition in its earliest stage, lest discipline, on which the whole community would depend, should entirely break down. In fact, public opinion would have no existence. How could it exist in a country in which the newspaper press would be managed, all books published, and all instruction supplied by officials? Any successful attempt on the part of the people to check the government would amount to a revolution and involve the destruction of the whole system.

The results of complete Socialism have been dwelt upon here, not because they are likely to be inflicted upon us, but because our State Socialists recommend government interference on the ground that it represents progress. They thus convey the idea that a complete socialistic system is a goal worthy of our national aspirations—a step in advance in the march of humanity towards that high destiny of which we may dimly dream, but which is only known to the Creator.

It is therefore incumbent upon us to endeavour to popularise the knowledge which now only a limited number of thinking men possess, that complete Socialism, far from being a step in advance, is a return to the primitive institutions of State despotism which characterised the dawn of civilisation.

Our Socialists would, by thus interrupting our progress towards complete individualism, bring us back into the vicious circle of alternating progress and retrogression, in which, as history shows us, so many Empires have struggled into existence, held together for a term, and perished.

Our nation is now confronted by the mighty problem of Capital and Labour, the rock on which so many States have suffered shipwreck, and if we do not solve it by means of continuous progress towards individualism—in other words, by elevating and liberating man—and, repeating the old mistakes of vanished Empires, subject the individual to State tyranny, then shall we be engulfed in the back-currents of retrogression, lose the result of centuries of toil and suffering, and resign the standard of progress to future nations.

What the present State-socialistic tendencies will lead to is not complete Socialism but the tyranny of bureaucrats. As government supervision and government administration increase in geometrical ratio, so State officials must increase. Apart from the baneful influence of State interference on trade and industry, the appointment of a vast army of officials will in itself constitute an increasing burden on the people. By constantly diminishing the number of tax-producers and increasing the number of tax-consumers, the position of the working classes will become worse. By concentrating all management and the disposal of all resources in the hands of the bureaucrats, we give them almost plenary powers over the individual. When they dispose of all the revenues, all the land, all the railways, all the banks, all the mines, large government factories, artisans' dwellings, public places of entertainment, all schools and academies, water-works, gas-works, tramways, railways and canals—when the bureaucrats dispose of all these, administration would be impossible if opposition were allowed.

The country would be like one vast factory or army, where one single breach of discipline would jeopardise the whole. Such a mighty government class would soon find it necessary and extremely easy to monopolise the press and fabricate public opinion. Legislation would soon be entirely in the hands of the government officials, who would understand how to absorb into their enormous police force and into a huge standing army the most strong-minded among the working classes, and the rest would gradually sink down to the lowest depths of dependency.

State despotism, exercised by the people themselves, is a paradox impossible of realisation. Once State supremacy is established the people will be excluded from the government, and the only question will be whether it should be held by a despot, a military, or a bureaucratic class. The condition of things which now exists in Germany and Russia is the goal for which our extreme Socialists in their thoughtlessness strive.

They will attain to all the evils of Socialism; class division, oppression, decay of industry, loss of the Colonies, stagnation and moral degradation; but not to the only miserable advantage they hope for, namely, the regular supply of the necessaries of life.

Our only reason for dealing with Socialism being that it constitutes the only alternative to Free Trade in Capital, we have regarded Socialism chiefly in its administrative and economic aspects. As to its moral consequences, they are very vast, not to say infinite, and may be easily evolved from what we have already said as well as from historical examples. It should be above all remembered, however, that the marvellous progress which has taken place in the world is due entirely to the extension of individual liberty, individual initiative, and free competition. Socialistic institutions necessarily destroy the incentive to personal exertion, daring, adventure, invention, self-control, abnegation, heroism, and must result in a moral slothfulness which can best be studied in the workhouse.

One institution there is in Great Britain which is largely responsible for the prevailing anti-individualist proclivities, and which is constantly quoted as a successful realisation of socialistic principles—we mean the Post Office.

The fact is, it proves the contrary, for the success of the Postal Department is due to what yet remains of individualism in this country. Let us, for the sake of argument, suppose that the Post Office is administered in a satisfactory way, and let us say nothing about the penny rate being twice as high as it ought to be, about the high charges for parcels, about the low wages paid to the poor employés, the large amounts paid to the wealthy steamboat companies, the danger of sending valuables in unregistered letters, the time it takes—four hours—to send a letter from the City to the West End, the disappearance of illustrated papers posted to the Colonies, &c.

But in recognising that all short-comings of the Post Office administration are pardonable, and that its merits are considerable, we must not forget that all modern improvements in this department of government grew out of the introduction of the penny postage. This reform, far from originating from within the department, was not only suggested but carried by an outsider (Sir

Rowland Hill), in the teeth of official opposition. It was through that powerful and free public opinion which only exists in a State where individualistic principles predominate, that Rowland Hill was able to carry his reform. In a socialistic State the government officials would have gained the day, and the reform never would have been accomplished.

Socialistic administration fails because the officials dominate the public and do not allow the public to check them. In England—thanks to our individualist principles and the fractional power officialism has so far acquired—the Post-Office authorities and employés are under the control of every individual who writes or receives a letter.

The simple function which the Post Office has to fulfil—namely, the collecting of letters in some places and delivering them in others—being vigilantly inspected by the Argus-eyed public, has no chance of being seriously tainted with red-tapism. Matters would be very different if the position were reversed, and the Post-Office officials were the inspectors of the public instead of the public being the inspectors of the officials.

The opponents of individualism often seem to

take for granted that it excludes the principle of co-operation. Nothing could be further from the truth. The very success of individualism depends on the boundless extension it gives to universal co-operation. Several individuals can co-operate, a whole community can co-operate, and a whole nation can co-operate, without the slightest taint of Socialism.

The postal arrangement is one of those undertakings in which the whole Empire—indeed, the whole of humanity—should co-operate, but such co-operation does not constitute Socialism. The reason why the Post Office has been looked upon as a socialistic institution is because all national co-operation presided over by government has in every country a tendency to become socialistic, thanks to the pragmatical proclivities of officials. Thus, the Post Office in Great Britain has not escaped the socialistic taint.

What we find is that this institution illustrates the two principles of co-operation and Socialism. Whatever is good is due to the one, whatever is bad is due to the other. The advantages of co-operation are evident when we see one postman deliver many letters in many houses in the same street. But we get a taste of Socialism when we are fined for risking our own valuables in unregistered letters.

All petty tyrannies or interference with private rights exercised, and all the monopolies maintained by the Post Office—not severely felt in Great Britain, the most individualist country in the world, but creating much annoyance in many continental States where officialism is paramount—are so many samples of Socialism.

What the Post Office teaches us is to exercise the greatest vigilance to prevent such co-operation, which, for expediency's sake, is presided over by government, from degenerating into socialistic oppression, but the success of the Post Office cannot be used as a plea for Socialism, nor be set up as an example of socialistic triumph.

CHAPTER XVI

THE SOLUTION OF THE CAPITAL AND LABOUR PROBLEM FOUND

THE many evils which characterise our civilisation in its present stage, and which, as we have seen, it is hopeless to try to remedy by socialistic measures, cannot be regarded as inherent in the individualistic system of division of labour, for the simple reason that we have not attained to a complete individualistic system. The most vital organs of that system, the mechanisms of exchange, have been obstructed by a gross piece of State Socialism, bank monopoly, to which we have already traced some of the most glaring anomalies in modern society.

While hoping that the conclusions which we have drawn with regard to the evil consequences of the Bank Act of 1844 will be amply confirmed and illustrated when in coming chapters some of the burning questions of the day are dealt with, it is now important to demonstrate that Free Trade in Capital, or in other words entirely Free Banking, produces results opposite to those produced by our present monopoly system.

The purpose of banking is to supply a mechanism for exchanges. As the leading feature of our civilisation is an extreme, minute, and universal division of labour operating entirely through free and voluntary exchanges, it may easily be understood that if the mechanism of banking is defective the production of wealth may become extremely difficult though there be plenty of raw material and workers and the most intense demand.

An immense benefit would therefore accrue to the world if a mechanism for the operation of exchanges could be established so wide-spread and so complete that all exchanges favourable to the production of wealth could be accomplished without loss of time and without economic sacrifice.

Important steps towards the realisation of this desideratum were taken when the value-measurer, coin, was introduced, and when credit, that is exchanges through accounts, was invented. The impossibility of procuring coin in quantities in any kind of relation to the number of exchanges, the economic law which compels coin to find its level in the markets of the world, and the many inconveniences which come of the handling of large quantities of coin—all this has caused indirect credit, or banking, to become the chief and indispensable medium of exchange in all countries which have emerged from the most primitive state of civilisation.

What consequently is required in order to arrive at prosperity is a good banking system, or banks in as many places as possible, and that those banks should be so organised as to give the greatest possible facilities to all exchanges tending to produce wealth.

When we remember that so many economic problems have been solved by liberty, and that free competition has been found the only means of supplying adequately the great general wants, it is only natural to come to the conclusion that the best way, the only practical way, of supplying the world with that enormous amount of banking which an universal prosperity would demand, is to leave it free—free to suit itself to circumstances, free to adopt the best methods that can be invented, free to expand or contract according to demand.

If no State interference hampered banking, it is certain that it would be taken up widely, and by people capable of conducting it successfully, and consequently there would be no lack of banks. Deposit banking has been free in England, and we find that since 1844, when an important legal obstacle to joint-stock banking in the banking centre of the country, London, was removed, deposit banking expanded and improved to an extraordinary extent. Though this deposit banking is the most difficult and most dangerous of all banking, both to the banks and to the public, disasters have seldom occurred. When note-issuing banking is made free we shall witness a far more remarkable extension, because such banks, for reasons which we shall give, do not require, as deposit banks do, to start in districts where wealth is already created, but can and will select poor districts for their operations, and there realise good profits. As poor districts abound in this Empire, there can be little doubt that the number of issuing banks and branches of issuing banks would grow apace.

Free issuing banks would succeed because issuing banking is a paying business. By issuing notes, a small working capital can be multiplied, a large turn-over may be arrived at, and consequently large commissions earned. Moreover, the issuing banker can charge a high interest for his capital, for capital entrusted to him, and for the credit he can create, because he works in a comparatively poor district, where his customers, through his assistance, can save much and considerably increase their profits.

For want of banking accommodation and such financial assistance as an issuing bank can supply, many manufacturers, employers of labour, and producers of all degrees are compelled to buy their supplies from middle-men, to pay extra prices, to sacrifice discounts and miss good opportunities, to sell to middle-men and to allow heavy discounts for cash.

Let us instance the discounts alone. A small manufacturer turns over his trading capital ten times a year; each time he sacrifices $2\frac{1}{2}$ per cent. discount because he cannot pay cash, and allows $2\frac{1}{2}$ per cent. because he requires the capital in order to go on with his production. He thus sacrifices an amount equal to 50 per cent. of his trading capital.

If now a bank offered him a credit equal to his trading capital, and asked him 10 per cent. interest, the manufacturer would thankfully accept the offer; for he would gain yearly an amount equal to 40 per cent. of his trading capital. If prices, opportunities, extended production, &c., are taken into consideration, his gains through such a credit would be far more considerable; in many cases it would mean a paying business instead of a ruinous one.

For such reasons the issuing banker would be able to charge a high interest, and yet enormously enhance the prosperity of his market. To begin with, he would have no competitors other than the usurers, who not only charge a ruinous rate of interest, but aim at embarrassing and plundering their victims, not at increasing their profits, as the banker does.

In Italy the new banks established on the Schulze-Delitzsche principle generally charge 10 per cent., not for regular banking accommodation such as an issuing banker would afford, but for ordinary loans, and yet the people look upon these banks as great benefactors. The profits on issuing banking would therefore be sufficiently large to cause the establishment of banks or branches wherever profitable production is possible.

By inquiring into the methods a free issuing banker would be compelled by circumstances, by the natural economic laws, to adopt, we shall be able to form an idea of the extent to which free note-issuing furthers the interests of the poorer classes, and what a potent remedy Free Banking would be against stagnation, scarcity of work, low wages, and the manifold miseries which grow out of vitiated Economy.

The profits of an issuing banker depend largely on the amount of circulation he can arrive at, and a successful issue is the first step towards forming a profitable connection and laying the foundations of that prosperity of the neighbourhood which will secure to him a large income. The issuing banker's chief aim, therefore, is a large circulation.

One of the curious fallacies which for centuries have stood in the way of rational banking is the belief that note-issuing is a business which can be taken up by anybody, and that a note circulation can be established in almost any way. The public, our legislators, and even some economists of repute, evidently hold the opinion that by printing a certain formula on a piece of paper this paper acquires, as by a magic stroke, all the attributes of coin, especially the power of circulating from hand to hand all over the country for any length of time. This opinion is based on the wide, varied, and not very pleasant experience the world has had of Government notes and State-supervised notes, but not on experience of private free notes. The two kinds of notes have been treated as equivalents, and the conclusions which have been drawn from the experience of the former have led to dread of the latter. Government notes and private free notes, far from being similar in their nature and their economic effect, differ to such an extent in every respect that they must be considered as extreme opposites.

Government notes and State-supervised notes circulate, exactly as coin does, indiscriminately all over the country; they drive from the market an amount of coin exactly corresponding to the amount of coin they represent, they affect prices as coin, they affect credit and banking as coin, they do not compel any special banking methods, any observance of economic laws, on the part of the issuer—in short, to all intents and purposes they are coin.

When we are better acquainted with private free notes we shall find that in all those points they differ entirely from State-supervised notes, and are in relation to their effect on the market, on business, credit, and banking, similar to cheques.

The popular idea of the facility of note-issuing is an absurd delusion, as we shall show. If note-issuing were perfectly free and everybody were at liberty to issue promises to pay on demand, hardly any persons who do not carry on a regular banking business would issue notes. The belief that the dishonest might issue large quantities of notes and then decamp is preposterous, because no one would accept in payment the notes of a man whose integrity and ability to fulfil his obligations were not well-established. The very fact that an unknown man tendered his own notes in payment, say for goods, would surely suffice to rouse the suspicion of the most credulous. We know that the respectable-looking man in the possession of a cheque-book of a good bank cannot buy goods for his cheque if he is entirely unknown. Swindling by means of cheques and other documents is so much easier than by notes, that no dishonest man would go to the expense of engraving notes. If by any chance such a note were accepted in payment by any one, it would at once be presented for payment, and the deceiver would have gained but a brief respite by issuing it. Note-issuing by dishonest people for swindling purposes under a free system may be discarded as perfectly impossible.

Even the wealthiest and most respectable man could not circulate notes by purchasing goods for them. His notes would be taken as his cheques would; but they would not remain in circulation. They would not be paid out again, but changed into cash as soon as possible, because, being issued by a private individual or firm not known as bankers, everybody would not know the value of the signature, and they would be charged with a banker's commission; the fear of a possible forgery and many other similar considerations would cause every holder to cash the notes or to send them to a bank. In either of those two cases the notes would speedily be presented for payment, and the rich man who bought goods for them would have incurred a large expense in having them manufactured, but would not have had any advantage in issuing them. Wealthy men can obtain goods and services in many other less troublesome and less expensive ways than by note-issuing, and would not attempt such a foolish method. For a rich man who is not a banker to have a number of small amounts called for irregularly would be a nuisance not to be sought for, but on the contrary to be avoided as far as possible.

Consequently, bankers alone would issue notes. There are, however, instances of experiences which to superficial observers appear to run counter to this conclusion. In remote districts in a thinly populated country, where change is scarce, traders and others have sometimes found it convenient to give their I O U's for small amounts when small coin was not available, in order to square accounts, and those I O U's have been known to circulate as coin for a considerable time and for a considerable amount. Now, this can hardly be called note-issuing by private parties. It is simply a kind of primitive book-keeping employed amid extraordinary circumstances not likely to appear often in civilised countries. Where such transactions have taken place they have had no objectionable consequences;

on the contrary, they have facilitated trade and progress.

Some apparently strange experiences in Scotland will be explained in our chapter on Free Trade in Capital in Scotland before 1844.

The construction of the Market in Jersey without any financial transaction other than the issue of notes is, on the one hand, an interesting example of the facility with which productive work is accomplished when credit is allowed to be used in the fashion most suitable for each case; and, on the other hand, the complete success of this operation might be quoted as an instance of notes being successfully issued by a non-banking issuer. Though the story of the Jersey Market notes has been told often, especially by advocates of fantastical note-issuing schemes, it may be worth while to give the outlines of it here, as it illustrates some important economic laws.

A Market was badly wanted in Jersey, and careful calculation demonstrated that its cost of construction would soon be covered by rents. The energetic governor, having no funds for the enterprise, and being unwilling to load the undertaking with heavy interests, commissions, &c., which the calling in of a financier would have involved, determined to finance it by issuing notes. All the contractors and workmen to be engaged on the building agreed to take notes in payment. In this way the governor was enabled to pay for the whole building by notes of his own manufacture, and when the Market was finished the rents which it produced were applied to the withdrawal of the notes from circulation. This was easily accomplished, as there was no interest to pay.

From the point of view of the Bank Act, this financial operation, though eminently sound, and useful to everybody concerned, would be unlawful, and would be punished as a crime throughout the civilised parts of the British Empire. This simple way of allowing a good building transaction, so to say, to finance itself, is not allowed, howsoever great the want of the building, howsoever plentiful the materials, howsoever numerous the unemployed. To accomplish any such work amid such circumstances, a lion's share must be given to a capitalist or financier. All over the Empire instances may be found where such free and natural financing, carried out by individuals or by issuing banks, would supply work and create wealth. But, thanks to prejudices and the now prevailing protective spirit, those millions of undertakings must not be attempted if the capitalist does not get an unnaturally large share of the profit.

But it is absolutely necessary to point out that the success in Jersey in no way justifies the many wild conclusions which have been drawn from it, not in favour of Free Trade in Capital, but of unlimited note-issuing by the State and by communities; and also that it does not prove the possibility of issuing notes without banking.

Let us first remember that the governor of Jersey in this transaction stood in the place of a Government, and that the experiment was not one of private issue at all, but of Government issue. Then, the issue was limited to a fixed sum, and the repayment of the notes was guaranteed by a valuable property, the Market. Had the issue been unlimited, and extended for less wise production, the value of the notes would have been affected, and have tended to fall to zero if over-issue had continued.

As it was, the notes filled the place of coin in an isolated district where a large undertaking created an increased demand for mediums of exchange. The notes no doubt drove out a certain amount of coin from the island; but, as the issue was small, not all the coin was driven out, and consequently the notes were not subjected to any discount. The notes were *not* payable on demand, and partook, therefore, of the nature of shares. All those who worked on the Market had pledged themselves to treat the notes as coin, and not to present them for payment until the funds were ready; and finally the whole of the community had an interest in the success of the undertaking.

It is evident, then, that in the Jersey case there were a great many factors at work, all of which would be absent in the case of a non-banker issuing notes for his own use. In the very best case such notes would be treated as cheques and become a source of great inconvenience to the issuer.

A banker who aims at establishing a good note-circulation cannot, more than any one else, circulate his notes by purchasing goods or services, for the notes would at once come back directly from some other bank or clearing house. The goods he purchases, or which are purchased by those for whose services he pays, cause an extra demand for such goods. This demand is filled from districts where the banker's notes are not known, and they consequently come back to be exchanged for gold. The banker would thus receive his notes back and be minus his gold. If he gave his notes away, the same thing would happen. He would soon find that he had parted with his gold.

There is only one way, then, of working up a circulation, namely, by carrying on a banking business, and by that means circulating notes.

But even in lending and discounting the banker must carefully respect the laws of Political Economy, or his notes will not circulate.

He will soon find it impossible to circulate his notes by lending or discounting outside his own market. If he were to lend his notes to a customer living, or working his business, in any part of the country where his bank was not known and where the people were not used to his notes, he would find himself in the disagreeable and dangerous position of receiving his notes back again by return of post with a request to pay them at once in gold. No reasonable banker would expose himself to this, but would quietly cultivate his own market.

Private notes would never circulate outside

their own market. The banker himself would certainly not send them outside, and other people would not be credited with such remittances until the notes were paid: they would therefore prefer to send bank drafts or cheques, which would be much cheaper too. If any private free notes were to stray outside the market in parts where they were not known, or into the territory of other banks, they would at once require an endorsement as a cheque does, and would be charged with a banker's commission, which is more than sufficient to send them home.

Many mistakes would have been avoided if economists had remembered that private bank-notes do not circulate outside their own market, for it would have explained to them how wide is the difference between the economic effects of private notes and State-supervised notes. Experience in England might have pointed out this tendency of private notes to circulate in their own market only. There are more than one hundred private note-issuing banks in England; yet people who do not live within the markets of those banks hardly ever handle a private note, and this is in spite of the State-supervision exercised over the banks and the monopoly the banks possess, which renders new issuing banks impossible,—all circumstances which should tend to cause notes to stray beyond their natural market.

Even within his own market, the issuing banker cannot lend his notes indiscriminately if a good circulation be his object. If he lends his notes to consumers, people of wealth who do not use the notes in production but give them out for purchases of such objects and services as represent pleasure and enjoyment, the notes will come back at once for payment in gold as if the banker himself had made purchases with his notes. Goods are consumed which are replaced by goods from other markets, which are paid for, not with notes, but gold. The only chance the banker has to circulate his notes is to work with people whose business consists in production, or in furthering production, because in this way the increased production causes, not an extra import into the district, but an extra export, from which naturally results a tendency of gold to come into the district, which will increase the banker's gold stock.

Consequently, the issuing banker must be careful not to have among his customers producers who work at a loss, or who over-trade, or carry on a spurious business, because any production resulting in loss is equivalent to consumption.

To sum up, then, we find that, in order to keep his notes in circulation, the issuing banker must only lend his notes to, and discount for, producers in his own district who work at a profit. Any deviation from this rule will tend to diminish his circulation and his metallic cash.

Now, it is a well-known fact that people who are most apt to succeed in productive business are not the wealthiest, but those possessed of the required ability, the experience, the industry and frugality. Such people are not generally capitalists, and to them an ordinary deposit banking account is of little use. But, as they cannot circulate the notes without having an account, the issuing banker is obliged to grant a 'cash-credit account'—that is, a banking account without deposit, a pure credit for a certain fixed amount. The economic conditions the issuing banker must look out for are such that the bank must be satisfied with much poorer securities than a deposit bank would demand. The guarantee of two or more respectable friends might be considered sufficient. The issuing banker, making far larger profits than a deposit bank, is satisfied to take a somewhat greater risk, especially as he risks only a small amount in each case and finds his safety in numbers.

The cash-credit holders, being thus generally people who are not offered credit from deposit banks, and to whom a small credit is of the utmost importance, will gladly take the trouble to fetch the notes from the banks instead of drawing cheques. Moreover, as they are mostly people in a small way of business, or mostly employers of labour whose chief disbursements consist of wages, it suits them better to use the notes than to draw cheques. When note-issuing is entirely free, it will assist the bankers, in creating a circulation, to issue small notes suitable to wage-paying trades.

The natural economic laws which regulate free note-issuing that we have just explained, compel the issuing banker to select his customers in the very opposite way to that which a deposit bank must adopt. While a deposit bank must give preference to customers according to their wealth, the issuing banker must give preference to those who can best employ labour and best further the prosperity of his own market, and must shun customers who have nothing but wealth to recommend them.

The deposit banker need not consider the interest either of his market or of the country so long as he holds good securities for advances; but the issuing banker has his interest intimately bound up in that of his district, and every loss which he, by mistakes, causes to the district means to him loss, inconvenience, or risk. His interest is that the production of his market should be as flourishing as possible, that no source of raw material should be neglected, that no ground should remain uncultivated, and that nobody who can work should be idle. In order to protect himself against losses, he must carefully avoid over-issuing. Every note he issues affects his market, *and his market only*, as coin would affect it. It tends to increase the demand for raw materials and for the workers in the district, and consequently to raise the cost of production within his district.

If the banker were to issue too many notes he would encourage over-production, and his customers would find that, instead of a profit on their production, they would have a loss. Loss on a production means that the capital which is consumed is greater than that which has been produced; and, consequently, there would be a deficiency of capital in the district, which, in the face of plentiful supplies of mediums of exchange, would at once be made good from other districts. Those imported goods could not be paid for, as we have seen, in the notes of the over-issuing banker. The notes would therefore be presented for gold or—which is as unwelcome to the issuing banker—for drafts on other places, and the banker would find his metallic cash dwindling fast. This would at once compel him to curtail his business and his profits, and, if his over-issue were considerable, many of his weaker customers would be incapable of repaying him their loans, and his losses might become serious.

In this way the issuing banker would be warned by the state of his metallic cash, so soon as he had exceeded the note-holding capacity of his market, that he must not attempt to issue another single note. Thus, the dullest of bankers could, by regulating his issue on the state of his metallic cash, keep his market in a constantly healthy condition, and the clue to the nature of his customers' business which his account books afforded him would always enable him to weed out any bad accounts.

The existence in every district all over the country, not to say all over the Empire, of at least one institution which has both the strongest interest and the most powerful means to supply capital to those who can best use it, to encourage poor but able and honest workers, to facilitate every possible production of wealth and at the same time effectively check over-production and nip in the bud every cause of bad trade, stagnation, or panic—the network of such institutions would certainly produce a state of prosperity altogether undreamed of.

By the great advantage it would confer on the working classes it would enormously increase the consuming power of our big centres, and thus transform them from over-producing and under-consuming districts into insatiable markets. The difference from the now prevailing state of things would be extremely striking, because, as we have seen, while our present banking system severs capital from labour, causes capital to be destroyed and exported, and enforces a deplorable under-consumption all over the Empire, the Free-Banking system establishes the closest possible co-operation between capital and labour, accelerates enormously the production of capital, and increases considerably the consuming power of the masses.

We have, in a preceding chapter, shown that the Bank Monopoly Act of 1844 destroys the prosperity of the working classes, not only by severing capital from labour, but also *by raising the cost of production and the cost of living and lowering the price of sale.*

From what we have said regarding the methods the issuing banker is compelled to adopt, it is easy to conclude that even in this respect the effects of the Free-Banking system would be exactly opposite to those of our present deposit system.

When such large masses of business people are supplied with banking accommodation (as we have seen to be the case under a free system), the greater part of such business as is now cleared by cash (coin and Bank of England notes) would be cleared by banking, without the use of coin. The bulk of the remainder would be cleared by free notes, not by coin. A very small proportion would have to be settled by metallic coin, or by such notes as replace coin in this country—that is,

Bank of England notes, or such notes as Government may issue as a substitute for sovereigns and half-sovereigns. The free system would therefore allow a very material increase in production without importation of extra coin. The rise in the cost of production, which would consequently be small in this country, would not be lowered abroad. While the desire for gain on the part of the bankers would induce them to keep the production as flourishing as possible, and consequently wages high, their prudence would prevent them, in self-protection, from encouraging so high a rise in wages and cost of production as to destroy profits. A healthy and happy medium would thus be attained, which no other system could effect.

When in every part of the country unhealthy competition is checked by the bank, and when all the working classes are in a position to consume normally (not to say largely), production, in the hands of the most suitable people, would be carried on on a large scale, according to the very best methods, with the best machinery and cheapest raw materials. The goods produced would therefore be of good quality and cheap. Every good system of banking ought to produce low cost of production and high wages. As we shall see later, the French *banquier* system tends strongly in this direction.

We have in this chapter striven to show that correct reasoning from the natural laws of Economy alone—without reference to experience—leads inevitably to the conclusion that entirely Free Banking is the true solution of the problem of Division of Labour and the most effective means of bringing about national prosperity. In the two following chapters we shall demonstrate how the conclusions we have arrived at are completely borne out by experience.

CHAPTER XVII

FREE TRADE IN CAPITAL IN SCOTLAND BEFORE 1844

So general and so strong are the prejudices against free note-issuing that, in spite of any amount of unimpeachable reasoning to prove it to be the only kind of rational banking, it would be hopeless to attempt to introduce it into England (and the authors of this work would certainly not have thrown themselves into so uneven a struggle) were it not for the one hundred and twenty-eight years' successful experience of free note-issuing in Scotland. With such an experience to fall back upon, it should be easy to rivet the attention of so commercial a nation as England to the explanation of this experience and to arguments in favour of economic freedom and of the abolition of an obsolete monopoly.

The first bank in Scotland was established in 1695, and was not a free bank. It had a Government charter for twenty-one years; but when, in 1716, the charter expired, nobody proposed its renewal, and from that date banking was free in Scotland. If we except some of the cantons in Switzerland, where banking was unhampered by Government interference and where industry and thrift consequently progressed marvellously, the period between 1716 and 1844 in Scotland is in modern times the only example of Free Banking the world possesses.

Of the beneficial effects of the Scotch banking system there cannot be two opinions. All writers on banking, all economists, and all historians throughout the world, who deal with it, are unanimous in its praise. Dunning Macleod likens its beneficial effects to those of the fertilising waters of the Nile. Had the economic theories which underlie free note-issuing been known at the time, banking would have been free in Scotland to this day. With those theories in our possession, the rapid economic development in Scotland ceases to be a wonder.

What we find in the history of Scotland is that up to about 1690 this country was, as regards economic development, security to life and property, and, in fact, civilisation in general, in a most deplorable state.

But from that period we note a marked and marvellous change, a steady progress in every direction—a progress, considering the almost semi-barbarous state from which it emerged, entirely unrivalled by that of any other European nation. One hundred and twenty years later—that is, in the middle of this nineteenth century—Scotland could boast good communications, splendid ports, a large commercial fleet, an extensive trade, various and world-famed manufactures, a system of agriculture which served as a model to the rest of the world, developed mines, flourishing fisheries, some 30,000,000*l.* sterling deposited in the banks, and a loyal population characterised by business habits and a spirit of thrift from which England and the Colonies have largely benefited.

And all this progress was achieved in the teeth of formidable obstacles. The climate was hard, the soil mostly poor, protective duties weighed down trade and industry, political and religious animosities were smouldering; in England Government interference produced financial distress and panics, which reacted on Scotland; but the greatest difficulty the banks had to encounter was the total absence of the true theories of note-issuing. All their progress in banking, all their good methods, were the result of experience, sometimes very dearly bought. The history of banking in Scotland makes this evident. This history has been too well told to need repetition here, and we shall therefore only glance at those passages of it which are interesting from a politico-economic point of view.

From 1716 there was no legal obstacle to the establishment of note-issuing banks in any number, nor to the issuing of notes by anyone to any extent and of any amount. Anyone was allowed to issue notes, if he could, from a penny to thousands of pounds. During the first part of the eighteenth century this liberty was but little used, for the number of issuing banks was small and the establishment of branches had not been tried. The first experiments with branch offices were not successful and had to be abandoned. Thus we find that there was none of that swamping the country with notes which is so generally supposed to be the immediate consequence of free note-issuing.

The banks did not find it easy work to extend their issue. They made it, however, more difficult than it need have been by striving for a bad and impossible object, namely, over-issue. They seem to have been under the very general delusion that bank-notes are coin, and that coin is wealth, for they manufactured large quantities and devised every dodge to circulate them.

We say tried, for that was all they could do. Experience in Scotland between 1716 and 1757 confirms in the most striking manner the truth, we might say the economic axiom, that *free notes* cannot be over-issued. The Scotch banks, eager to circulate their notes, granted new credits when their markets were choked full of notes; and the result, of course, was that prices rose, consumption increased, and capital was imported from other markets, especially from England, and the notes rushed back on the bank to be exchanged for gold. Instead of restricting their issue, the banks continued their vain attempts to over-issue; and, in order to meet the notes which came back, they ordered gold from London.

This gold had to be paid for, and the payment was made in drafts on London which the banks bought in Scotland at a premium, or the gold was obtained from London by a system of drafts and return-drafts between the banks and their agents in London. Each way entailed a heavy loss on the banks. It is recorded that at one time it was a paying business to sell one-month or two-months drafts on London at a premium for notes, then to present the notes for payment in gold and send the gold to London to meet the drafts. In any case the gold which was brought from London returned thither in obedience to the economic laws which compel coin to find its level, and it was quite a usual thing that the stage coaches which met on the road from London and Edinburgh were both laden with gold.

All this expense and all this trouble would have been avoided if the bankers had understood that every market will hold only that amount of notes which is natural to it, and that over-issue is impossible when the notes are deprived of all Government prestige.

Had the Government interfered a little with the note-issuing in Scotland, the attempts of the banks to over-issue would probably have succeeded. Their notes would have permeated the whole country, cash payment might have been suspended; the notes would then have circulated with a discount, might have lost their value gradually, and finally become valueless. When Government interferes with banking, the people suffer from the mistakes of the banks; but when the banks are free the consequences of their mistakes fall on themselves.

Another great cause of loss to the banks was their attempt to ruin one another. One bank collected secretly a large amount of notes of another bank, and presented them all at once, hoping thus to cause a run on its rival, and compel it to stop payment. This attempt, however, never brought about the catastrophe aimed at.

It can easily be conceived how those mistakes of the banks must have prevented the free system from working out the splendid results of which it is capable, and when we try to gauge the effect of Free Banking in England, Ireland, India, and the Colonies, we must remember that such mistakes would now be entirely out of the question.

In the year 1756 the attempts of the banks to over-issue were most strenuous; and, as at the time there was a brisk demand in England for coin, the banks felt severely the consequences of their folly. Smaller banks had been established, especially in the north, which issued notes of very small amounts; and, as the great scarcity which resulted both from the financial stress in England and from the mismanagement of the Scotch banks, caused a good demand for small notes, those small banks followed the example of the big ones and did their best to over-issue. The scarcity of change-coin and the small use which was made of book-keeping induced many private firms to issue their own notes, especially in places where no banker had taken up this business; and in this way the country really seemed inundated with notes.

Some of the large banks, in order to protect themselves from the surprises of their rivals, had quietly added to the text of their notes (generally in very small print) reservation clauses whereby the payment of the notes might be made on presentation, or six months after, at the option of the issuing bank. As those clauses were not taken advantage of against ordinary holders, but only against intriguing rivals, the public did not mind them: in fact, the people did not study the text at all so long as they knew the bank to be safe.

This example of the large banks was followed by the smaller ones and by private issuers, and notes soon appeared with very singular reservations indeed. But, as they were very rarely taken advantage of, and the people were perfectly free to take the notes or not, no harm was done. Perhaps the most curious examples of the notes of those days were some issued by an innkeeper for very small amounts, in which the issuer reserves himself the right to pay either in coin or in beer. On the back of some of these notes might be found receipts for so many jugs paid on account. 'What an awful thing for a country to have its currency in such a state!' currency theorists and opponents to Free Banking will probably exclaim.

In this work we have, as most of our readers will have observed, tried to supply the most plausible arguments against Free Banking, in order to meet them and thus remove as many doubts as possible. Now, we have mentioned these shocking specimens of free notes to show the futility of objections which at first sight appear serious enough. The exclamation of the currency theorists has no meaning at all, because the word 'currency' has no meaning and is not defined. If currency means legal tender such notes cannot possibly be reckoned currency, for they were simply pieces of paper on which the people recorded their transactions, for want of book-keeping and small change. If the innkeeper had been forbidden to maintain order in his business by means of such papers, he would have used his shutter and a piece of chalk. Would not this piece of currency have been just as shocking?

The fact was that not one note, howsoever absurd in nature and tenor, was issued which did not constitute a convenience for the people amid the circumstances in which they lived. The country had received a strong impulse onwards by the easy supply of capital and of mediums of exchange which Free Banking involves; and when the people, eager to produce and to trade, had to face an extraordinary scarcity of coin caused by Government mistakes in England and by the mismanagement of the banks, and when, in the absence of theoretical knowledge and correct theories, banks did not come forward in proportion to the demand for mediums of exchange, the people helped themselves as well as they could without proper account books.

Slight reflection will at once make it clear that no free note will circulate an hour after it has ceased to be useful, and that clumsy, troublesome notes will, under a free system, soon have to give way to better ones which competition is sure to supply.

Here is perhaps the place to show that the so-called 'nuisance' of notes of very small amounts is entirely imaginary; for the amount of each note will be regulated, exactly as the tenor, by the convenience of the public as long as there is no State interference. Small notes cost as much to print and check as large notes, and no banker would, therefore, circulate notes smaller than the public require. The very moment small notes ceased to be useful to the public, and long before they became a nuisance, they would cease to yield profit and would consequently be withdrawn.

There is in all free notes a tendency to make room for better mediums of exchange by disappearance from circulation. This was clearly demonstrated when the London banking houses who possessed an old privilege of issuing notes gave it up voluntarily. They did so because their notes did not circulate any longer, or at least not with enough facility to yield a profit. The reason of this was that their customers became too wealthy to use so primitive a medium as notes. They gradually all became deposit-account holders, and the natural mediums of exchange in connection with deposit accounts are cheques, not notes. Consequently, notes made room for cheques. Notes will circulate only where the people are poor enough to wish and willing to pay for cash-credits. If note-issuing is made free in England, the day will come when free notes will cease to circulate. England and most parts of the Empire are beyond that stage which allows such notes to be used as those of the innkeeper who promised to pay in money or in beer at his own option.

Those who objected to the many small notes were not the people, but the larger bankers, who could not make small notes pay in the wealthy centres where they worked, and who were short-sighted enough to believe that they were injured by the success of the smaller banks through small notes in the poorer district. Had they understood their business better, they would have encouraged such small banks instead of intriguing against them.

When the over-issuing attempts of the larger banks continued to fail, these raised a cry against the inundation of the country by small notes which drove the coin away. They saw the mote in the eyes of the small banks, but did not see the beam in their own. In the year 1756 a Royal Commission was got together in order to inquire into the scarcity of coin in Scotland and the causes of the troubles of the banks. It seems strange to us now that a Royal Commission should be required to find out why people got into trouble because they promised to pay more than they could.

The recommendation of the Commission was twofold. They told the bankers not to issue more notes than their respective markets would carry, which was very sensible; and they asked Government to forbid the small notes, which was very foolish.

It is not surprising that people in the year 1756 should deem it wise to forbid mediums of exchange which circulate only on the strength of their usefulness with a view to improving trade; but it is strange, to say the least, that modern writers on Banking should endorse such views. Some English authorities on Banking have not hesitated to declare that the Government, in adopting the recommendation of the Commission to forbid all notes under one pound, acted wisely, and thereby removed the banking troubles in Scotland.

The fact was that the scarcity of coin was caused by the banks' own mistakes in trying to over-issue; and when, after 1756, they saw the error of their ways, and began to work in a rational way, their difficulties of course disappeared. When a cause is removed the effect is bound to go too. Why the small notes have been associated with the evil and their abolition with the remedy is impossible to explain except by the somewhat general weakness in favour of State interference.

Far from being an advantage to the country, the prohibition of the small notes obliged the banks in the poor districts to shut their doors, and the consequences of this may be seen now in the Highlands and Islands. Just as now many of the Scotch branch offices would have to be closed if the issuing of one-pound notes were forbidden, so the small banks could not make their expenses when they were not allowed to supply mediums of exchange suitable to the condition of the country. In a poor country a small coin or a small note goes a long way, and this is the secret of cheap living and cheap production.

When the mediums of exchange which it is the business of banks to supply were no longer allowed to regulate themselves on the requirements of the country, and when the arbitrary amount of one pound was fixed as the lowest limit of a note, the Free Banking system was maimed and deprived of its great pioneering power. When we study the effects of Free Banking in Scotland in order to form an opinion of what it would do for other countries, we should remember that the very year the banks began to work in a rational manner, when they at last gave up their attempts to over-issue, that very same year the first blow was struck at the free system. Had this blow not been struck we should have seen results in Scotland far exceeding those which followed.

When the first branch offices of the Scotch banks were established, this was done with a view to force their notes on the market. Having after long experience come to the conclusion that there was a natural limit to the note-holding capacity of every market which could not be exceeded, and that the notes had a tendency to remain in the place where they were issued, the bankers hit upon the idea of opening a branch in another part of the country where notes might be issued while they paid them only at the head office. It was expected that the notes would gradually percolate from the issuing place to the head office, thus saturating the intervening district.

What happened? A certain quantity of notes circulated round the new office as round the old one, but any notes that were issued above that quantity came straight back to the head office for payment in gold, and very few of them strayed into the intervening districts.

When the banks realised that such were the results of a new branch they had at last discovered the right way of extending their circulation and their business. As each branch gave them a new market capable of holding a certain quantity of notes, they had only to increase the number of their branches in order to extend their business. And this they did so energetically that at the end of the free period there were about three hundred bank offices in Scotland. The banks also found that the offices which they started in poor districts circulated more notes in proportion to the metallic cash required, and though the average business in such places was small, it paid well because it was done chiefly with notes. When this discovery was made, the poverty of a district was never looked upon as an obstacle to the success of a branch; all that was wanted was a population willing to work.

The securities the bank obtained for cash-credits in poor districts were generally only such as poor people can give, usually the guarantee of two friends. If the branches could, under such circumstances and with such guarantees, arrive at a large turn-over without suffering losses from bad debts worth mentioning, the explanation is to be found in the thorough healthiness of the whole system. With Free Banking, production pays well and there is nothing to cause loss to anybody. The most dishonestly inclined find honesty the best policy, and a good character and punctuality in business become indispensable conditions for a cash-credit.

The more the workings and the effect of the Scotch system are studied the more clearly will it be seen how they confirm in every way the conclusions we arrived at by induction in the previous chapter. Had the freedom not been curtailed in 1765, the whole system would probably not have suffered destruction in 1844, when Peel's Act created a monopoly for the then existing banks in

Scotland and limited their issue to the amount which they had in circulation at that time.

As Free Trade, that indispensable condition for real prosperity, was not introduced into Scotland until the very time at which Free Banking was abolished, we have no example of a country enjoying these two blessings simultaneously. It is certain that the effects of the one would greatly enhance the effects of the other, and as we know that the prosperity of one country reacts favourably on that of another, there can be little doubt that the introduction of Free Banking into Great Britain and Ireland, India and our free-trading Colonies, would produce results far exceeding those which followed the adoption of Free Trade.

CHAPTER XVIII

THE FRENCH BANQUIER SYSTEM

THE Scotch free banking system is not the only one which brings about co-operation between capital and labour and furthers production. The French *banquier* system accomplishes the same beneficial results. Though these two systems appear so different in methods and organisation, it is an interesting and instructive fact that the benefits arising out of each of these systems spring from their compliance with the same economic laws.

By the French *banquiers* we do not mean the few large loan offices which advance cash on shares and other securities, but the thousands of private *banquiers* who everywhere in France, in small centres as in large towns and villages, compete with each other in supplying capital to labour. The nature of their business is to favour, not the richest consumers, but the best employers of labour, thus facilitating work and production in every corner of the land.

The chief medium of exchange in the French *banquier* system is the draft. When a French producer or merchant has sold a parcel of goods and made out his invoice, he at once draws a draft on the buyer. This draft he takes to his banker, who makes out a *bordereau*, or a statement in which the net value of the draft or the drafts paid in that day is arrived at by the deduction of interest, differences of rates of exchange and banker's commission. The banker credits the drawer for the net amount of each *bordereau* in account current, and allows either the full amount or part of it to be drawn at once. As a keen competition exists between the bankers, producers or merchants whose drafts as a rule in due time meet with a prompt acceptance and payment can generally draw the full amount, and are often allowed an overdraft.

The business of the mass of *banquiers*, who are spread like the meshes of a net all over the country, consists chiefly in discounting such drafts. It is easy to understand that this method of banking is to the banker more profitable than money lending, even at a very high interest, for it allows him to turn over large amounts with a very small capital. The drafts the banker discounts for his customers are generally drawn on some place outside the banker's market, and he always gives preference to such outside drafts before drafts on his own place or promissory notes. As soon as a banker, let us say in Valence, has received the drafts on other places, he sends them each to a banker in the place on which they are drawn, or if he has no connection with any banker in small places, to a banker in the nearest centre. Drafts on foreign places he sends to Paris or to a foreign banker.

On receipt of the drafts these corresponding bankers credit the Valence banker with the net amount, and send him in return drafts drawn on Valence and its neighbourhood from other places which have collected in their hands. These the Valence banker presents for payment, and thus supplies himself with cash which he holds at the disposal of his customers.

If the Valence banker has only a small working capital he cannot do very well with return remittances consisting of drafts which have a long time to run, and as some bankers in minor places may be in the same position, the Valence banker sends such of the longer drafts as he or his corresponding smaller bankers cannot keep until maturity to the wealthier bankers in the large centres. These credit him with the net amount, and he can draw at sight on them, or their Paris banker, for the amount.

In this way the Valence banker can always renew his cash supply, and as drafts on places outside his own district give him the greatest facilities for so doing in the ordinary routine of business, he gives preference to these kind of documents.

Those who can draw them are not the wealthiest, but those who can sell local products outside the district, that is to say, those who can best employ labour, best utilise the resources of the country, and those who have the greatest ability for business. The rich people who require cash for consumption purposes are not suitable customers for the local banker, because any capital which he advances to them he cannot replace, except by borrowing himself.

We find then that the business of the French *banquier* encourages thrift, enterprise, and production by holding capital at the disposal of those who can best use it, and tends to keep cost of production low and price of sale high. Consequently it benefits the country in the same way as free note-issuing would, though not to the same extent.

The present deposit banking methods in England, the French *banquier* system, and the old Scotch Free Banking, are not necessarily three distinct systems of banking, but rather different stages of development of banking, in the form it would take if government could be induced to leave it free.

Under entire freedom, banking would take the form of note-issuing in any district replete with workers, virgin soil, or raw materials. The notes would gradually diminish as compared with the business transacted, and though a certain number might continue for a long time as change mediums, the bulk of the business on the spot would be done by cheques, and the business with other districts would be done by drafts in the French way. The immense advantage of freedom would therefore be that we should in this Empire enjoy all the advantages of all the best methods.

The results of the French *banquier* system are low cost of production and of living, high price of sale, great demand for labour, well-distributed property, general prosperity, and a growth of capital and wealth, the rapidity of which—in the face of great financial and political disasters and of economic misgovernment in France—forms a standing object of universal wonder.

Here we shall refer to France only so far as to reply to the objection which probably presents itself on reading the above, namely, that the economic circumstances in France do not just now bear out such an opinion as to the effects of the French *banquier* system. But if we take circumstances into consideration we shall find that they do.

In the first place, France, like England, is hampered by a central monopoly Bank, and all the good effects come from the traditional methods of private firms. Then only look at the powerful causes for trade depression and suffering among the working classes which are at work in that country, such as an unsettled government, an enormous national debt, a gigantic army, a great navy, a ruinous protective system which renders nine-tenths of the industries a burden on the rest, sugar bounties, ship bounties, octrois in all the towns, bureaucratic interference in everything, economic misgovernment of the colonies, &c.

While thus French legislators seem determined to ruin their country and to drive their working classes to desperation, some of the most important industries in the richest parts of the country, the Southern, have received heavy blows from other causes. The vine has been attacked by 'phylloxera,' which is still raging; the cultivation of the madder-root is dying out, owing to the discovery of the aniline colours; and silk-growing is far from being what it was before the silkworm was attacked by disease. If the fact that France, spite of all these causes of ruin, can find 8,000,000*l.* for M. de Lesseps's daring engineering enterprise in Central America, is due to the French *banquier* system, as we contend it is, this system has certainly a wonderful wealth-producing power.

But we can better appreciate the great advantages of this *banquier* system in Germany, for there it is comparatively new, and our English commerce has been immensely influenced by the results it has produced. Economic science teaches us that protective duties tend to destroy the export of manufactured goods, and experience universally confirms this fact. But the exception to this rule which Germany seems to form has puzzled both economists and commercial men in England. For while the German government, as continental governments are wont to do, endeavours to prevent prosperity and industry by legislating in defiance of the plainest truths of Political Economy, the export of German manufactured goods does not seem to decrease, for it is the general complaint of our Fair Traders that England is becoming swamped by German goods.

The explanation is simple enough. Prince Bismarck's mistaken Economy produces in Germany the same dreary results that similar mistakes produce in all other countries. At the same time there is a great silent reform going on in Germany, unassisted by government and unnoticed by economists, namely, the gradual adoption of the French *banquier* system; and this reform has so vivifying an influence on the industries of Germany that it counteracts—at least to a considerable extent—even the pernicious effect of the government's mistaken Economy.

The new method, coming from France, entered Germany by the eastern border, as well as from Belgium and Switzerland, where it had been earlier introduced, and is now spreading all over the country. The Germans take little heed of it themselves because the change has been slow and gradual; but the older inhabitants of Germany will tell you, if you ask them, that in places where they had not a single *banquier* thirty years ago, they have now several competing for business, while in large centres *banquiers'* establishments abound in ever-increasing numbers.

By simply comparing the method of financing productive business in Germany now and formerly, we can at once form an idea of the importance of the change now going on in that country. Under the old *régime* a manufacturer had to limit his business to the small amount of capital he actually possessed or could borrow from some one against mortgages or other securities. His purchases of raw material consequently had to be small, and generally from some middle-man at a pretty high price. When he had manufactured goods up to the extent of his means, he had to restrict his production until his goods were sold and paid for; and as he generally wanted cash quickly, he had to sell to another middle-man, often at a low price. Dear raw material, low price of sale, small production, and heavy expenses—these were the conditions under which the manufacturer in Germany used to work.

It is very different now. The *banquiers* there are ever on the look-out for genuine commercial drafts to discount. The manufacturer can now buy very largely and in the best markets—free of the middle-man—for the *banquier* will at once discount the seller's draft upon him. He can manufacture largely, because as soon as his goods are out of the works, he can draw drafts on his customers, and against these his *banquier* renews his capital at once. If he has only made his calculations aright, and if he has got the orders, there is now very little trouble about financing.

All commercial men will understand the enormous advantages this system gives to the German manufacturer. We shall pass over the benefits he derives from buying wholesale in the best market, on terms which for the seller are nearly as good as cash terms, and merely point out the great benefit he derives from a large turn-over. In all business, and especially in a manufacturing business, there are large expenses which remain the same whether the turn-over be large or small

—such as rent, interest on machinery, living expenses, clerks, foremen, models, patterns, moulds, travellers, advertising, experiments, samples, artistic assistance, dies, stamps, &c. There are small factories where these expenses amount to as much as raw material and wages; and in many crafts carried on on a small scale, these are the chief expenses, while raw material and wages are insignificant. If a man has 70 per cent. such expenses and a small turn-over, and can, by better financing, produce ten times more, his goods cost him 63 per cent. less, and he will easily beat those who work in a small way.

The great benefit produced by improved financing does not affect the manufacturer alone; it extends naturally to the working people. A larger production means a greater demand for hands, which sends up wages; and cheaper production means lower living expenses and more enjoyment for the workers. The *banquier* system thus brings about a result which a good system should produce, namely, *higher wages with lower cost of production.*

To many this seems an impossibility and a contradiction, but we have now seen that this is not the case. Under such circumstances it is not surprising that German manufacturers should look out for large customers, and that they should strain their utmost to extend their connection among large English import firms or among even large English shops, and among English exporters to the Colonies and neutral markets.

Now the question obviously arises, Does the system under which our manufacturers work resemble the old system fast becoming obsolete in Germany or the new *banquier* system? There is no denying the fact, the conditions under which the English manufacturers work—in spite of many advantages in other respects—are, as far as finance goes, very similar to those in Germany thirty years ago. What wonder, then, that the English manufacturers feel themselves handicapped, and that they have to strain every nerve and sweat their work-people, in order to compete with the Germans!

If we suppose that the *banquier* system were introduced all over our Empire, it will not be difficult to imagine its beneficial effects. Here, in the Colonies and in India, we should see the same results as in Germany; capital and labour united, greater demand for hands, low cost of production, high wages, great power of consumption, an immense demand for goods, and high selling prices. In fact, in free-trading England the effect would be very marked, and the reaction between a prosperous Great Britain, prosperous Colonies, and a prosperous Indian Empire would certainly result in such competition for the working man that no sweating system would be possible.

But it will no doubt be said that the Bank Act of 1844 does not prohibit the *banquier* system from being introduced into England, India, and the Colonies; it simply prohibits private note-issuing; and this is forbidden even more strictly in both Germany and France. True: there is nothing in our law to directly prohibit the *banquier* system in the British Empire; yet it can be shown that this Act of 1844 is the only obstacle to the practical introduction into the British Empire of the *banquier* system, or at least a system which would include all its advantages and a great many more.

The *banquier* system in France is the natural product of an historical evolution which we have not experienced. We would not undertake to explain how it arose and was developed; but it is pretty certain that great troubles had something to do with its growth. Government oppression, unreliable coin, official dishonesty, scarcity of precious metals, bad paper money—these were probably the evils which impelled the development of the French financial methods. Whatever the causes which called the system into existence, they must be looked for far back in history. In Germany, where the system has been imported ready-made from France, its adoption has been very slow and gradual, and this in spite of the unbroken line of contact of German commerce with that of France, Belgium, and Switzerland.

From this we may conclude that it would be a very long time before the system, under present circumstances, were adopted in England generally enough to confer the same benefits on the English trades as it has conferred on the French and German. Nor must our reluctance to adopt anything foreign, as well as the peculiarity of our geographical position, be forgotten. Besides all this, our existing methods present special obstacles to the working of the French system among us. Of these we will, by way of illustration, point out only two, namely, our own banking methods, which from the banks' point of view are profitable ; and the general objection on the part of the commercial and trading classes to drawing and accepting drafts —which are the indispensable instruments of credit in the French system. When, thus, both the banks and the public are prejudiced against the system, what hope is there that it will be ever introduced?

None under the present circumstances. But Parliament has it in its power to change these circumstances, and to sow at once the seed which will speedily grow up into the most perfect banking system the world has ever seen. For it is a fact that all the good methods of the French *banquiers* which Parliament itself could not persuade, coax, or force the British public to adopt, would naturally develop out of the free Scotch banking system, as it existed in Scotland before 1844. The example of England, with its palpable result, would cause the Colonies to follow suit.

If Parliament introduced Free Trade in Capital, we should not only reap the unprecedented advantages which Scotland derived from it, but that system would prepare the way for the adoption of all the best methods of French *banquiers*. We contend that freedom of banking would very soon overcome the prejudice against acceptances, on the ground of the great advantages drafts and acceptances would offer both to banker and his customers, such as larger turn-over, larger credit, greater regularity, cheaper cost of production, higher price of sale, &c. Some of these advantages would accrue without note-issuing, but the inconveniences which may arise from acceptances would not be guarded against without a free note-issuing. Besides, it is evident that a *banquier* system could not exist without *banquiers*, but the many small bank offices, which freedom would call forth everywhere, would all take the place of the *banquiers* and would have the greatest interest in developing in that direction.

CHAPTER XIX

ABUSE OF FREE NOTE-ISSUING AN ECONOMIC IMPOSSIBILITY

WE should have to indorse the opinion of Monsieur de Voltaire, and declare that our globe is the madhouse of the universe, were there not weighty excuses for the maintenance of a system of pernicious monopolies and irrational prohibitions, such as the bank legislation of all civilised countries involves. Everywhere we find Free Banking forbidden. This is perfectly on a par with the rest of the economic legislation of many continental powers, whose Ministers of Finance seem to have entered into a secret conspiracy in order to destroy the prosperity of their countries, bring their governments to bankruptcy, and drive the people through poverty and misery to regicide.

But how is it possible that rational banking should be forbidden in England, where we have at least some respect for Political Economy; or in Scotland, where it once produced world-famed blessings? Why should every new colony where the absence of State interference at first allows a quick development, be in such a hurry to taste the miseries which spring from that automatic prosperity-destroying mechanism—a Bank monopoly Act.

The explanation of the enigma is that a strong prejudice has for centuries prevailed, and still prevails, against free note-issuing. This prejudice, one of the most distressing of all the nightmares that have tormented poor humanity, derives much of its extraordinary strength from misunderstood experience, false but plausible reasoning, and spurious Political Economy.

The general belief is that if note-issuing were left free it would be appallingly abused. Everybody would issue large quantities of notes; a short but intense inflation would be the consequence, then reaction would follow and everybody would fail and everybody be ruined.

Such opinions have acquired an appearance of reasonableness in many ways. The coinage had of old been considered one of the attributes of kings, and as in most countries the first regular issuing bank was more or less connected with the government, its notes consequently circulating all over the country in the same fashion as coin, the people came to look upon notes as a kind of paper-coin. The terms 'money' and 'currency' were indiscriminately applied to both coin and notes. The relations of the governments with the banks resulted in over-issue, suspension of payment, depreciation of the notes, and other irregularities which proved disastrous to the community both in their direct effects and the reactions which followed.

Such catastrophes as were produced by John Law's wild experiment in France, by the French assignats, and by the South Sea Bubble in England, deeply impressed business people with the danger of excessive note-issuing. It was never understood that all the mischief came from government interference with the notes, nor that entirely free note-issuing, however mismanaged and distorted by ignorance and surrounding anomalies, could never produce the mischief which so spontaneously sprang from notes transmuted into paper-coin by government supervision.

No distinction was made between documents so different as supervised notes and free notes, and the bad results produced by paper-coin were expected to follow from free notes.

It might have been expected that the success in Scotland would have induced the economists to make a distinction between notes and notes; but the improvement which followed after adopting the recommendations of the Royal Commission of 1765, and which was in reality the result, as we have seen, of the more rational way of working which the banks entered upon, was attributed to government interference in forbidding small notes, and did much to upset the faith in freedom.

It is amusing to read the explanations of the success of freedom in Scotland which many writers on banking attempt to supply. Any cause for this success seems to them good enough except the real one, freedom.

Two financial disasters contributed specially to strengthen the fear of free note-issuing, namely, the failures of banks in England in 1825 and the bank panic in the United States in 1837. Both these disasters were attributed to abuse of free note-issuing, while in reality both were due to government interference. In England, as we have already pointed out, the business of note-issuing was never entirely free after the creation of the monopoly of the Bank of England—never free enough to induce the banks to work rationally. There was just enough of government meddling to deprive the private notes of their cheque nature and give them that coin prestige without which abuse becomes an economic impossibility.

In the United States the banks were far from free. There were certain general Congress regulations as to Reserves, Inspection, &c.; besides, the separate States had their own stipulations. The result of course was that the notes circulated indiscriminately all over the United States. The banks had no inducement to adopt the methods of real issuing banks, but carried on ordinary deposit banking, using the notes as coin and employing all kinds of dodges in order to swell their circulation. The government inspection was worthless as a safeguard, but it deceived the people into security.

The quantity of circulating notes swelled rapidly and prices went up apace, import became excessive and export diminished, gold soon began to leave the country, and when more was wanted than could be had, in order to pay for more imported goods, the banks of course could not produce it. Their attempt to realise their securities depressed prices, making matters worse, and so the bubble burst.

If anyone should doubt that this was the way in which the great crisis of 1837 came about, he may ask those who lived in America at the time whether it was not a fact that, when the banks began to fail, lists were published to show daily which banks had failed and which were yet standing, so that the public would know which notes to refuse. Now the publication of such lists proves that the notes did not circulate as free notes, each within their own market, but that government supervision had given them a coin nature and sent them circulating all over the country.

An excellent stricture on such misleading government supervision was at the time contained in a caricature in an American comic paper, 'Puck,' in which a bank director tells the cashier to go out and borrow twenty dollars because the government inspector is coming.

If we regard the financial and economic experience of the world in the light of sound Political Economy, or (failing that) of correct logic, we shall find no instance which can be quoted in favour of the existing popular prejudice. On the contrary, every transaction—large or small—since the dawn of civilisation proves the correctness of those economic theories on which our advocacy of Free Banking is based, and points to its freedom from danger.

But the fears founded on misunderstood experience are not the only ones we have to combat; those springing entirely from imagination are just as strong, and must be met.

What we have already said about the conditions which a free issuing banker must observe if he is to establish a paying circulation, will no doubt have convinced most readers that note-issuing by others than bankers or banks is under normal circumstances out of the question. The abnormal ones, which may (at least apparently) allow an exception from this rule, so seldom occur, and with the progress of civilisation tend to disappear so rapidly, that the temporary consequences they would produce need hardly be discussed. It may suffice to point out that any document issued by a non-banker, but partaking of the nature of a banknote, would be subjected to the same economic laws as promissory notes and I O U's, which (as many people have experienced) have a very limited circulation.

But could not (it is often asked) an issuing banker, taking advantage of the credit his bank enjoys, issue an immense quantity of notes, and then fail or decamp? When our opponents wish to demonstrate the possibility of abusing free note-issuing, they generally start from the supposition that a fraudulent banker has succeeded in exchanging some millions of his notes for coin. With such a supposition it is not difficult to prove that there is danger in the case. What should have been proved has, in fact, been assumed as granted.

There is nothing to prevent a banker from failing or running away once he has got the gold for his notes in his pocket, but it would be impossible to obtain a large amount of gold in exchange for his notes. Who would take notes to the amount of a million, or any other amount—even one single pound—give the banker gold, and keep the notes locked up? It would be a senseless transaction that could not take place between rational beings. A man might give his gold for a small amount in notes when he desires to make a remittance and cannot do it in a better way, but all notes thus bought for gold would at once come into circulation; and, as the amount of notes thus issued without a corresponding economic need for them in the banker's market would be in excess of the quantity which the market was capable of holding, a similar quantity of notes would at once be presented for payment. The banker would thus have exactly as much gold as he had before.

When banks, even State banks, wish to increase their gold reserve by buying gold, they do not buy it for notes, for they would thereby do more to lessen their metallic cash than to increase it, especially when the gold is wanted to meet notes coming back. They therefore buy the gold for promises to pay at a future date, or for other securities they wish, or are compelled, to realise. The fact that they may sell such security for notes and then buy the gold for notes, or *vice versâ*, would only be selling securities for gold in an indirect way.

The only chance a free note-issuing banker has of circulating his notes is by carrying on a banking business such as we have described, and as enabled the Scotch banks to succeed; that is to say, the granting of cash-credits liberally but intelligently.

Now such a business does not increase the banker's gold stock by a single pound. On the contrary, though he can strongly influence his customers to take notes, they require a certain amount of gold too for payments outside the district, and, moreover, a portion of the notes he issues comes back to the bank to be exchanged for gold in the ordinary course of business. The position of the banker is then this: he has lent a certain number of notes plus a certain amount of gold to his customers, and, in exchange, he has obtained nothing but claims against them, backed by more or less innegotiable securities. If a banker in this position were to run away he would run away from his own capital. It is, therefore, evident that an issuing banker, as such, is the creditor not the debtor of the public, and that while his customers can deceive him by not paying their loans back, he cannot deceive his customers because he holds no trust from them. When this is borne in mind, the absence of disasters through free note-issuing in Scotland ceases to be the great wonder which it has been hitherto.

While thus our present deposit banking, the capital-absorbing system, is a trusting of the banks by the public, free note-issuing, the capital-distributing system, is a trusting of the public by the banks. Consequently, if government interference is required at all, it certainly ought to begin with deposit banks.

Still, it is quite possible that a note-issuing bank might fail. It is extremely unlikely that the note-issuing would be the cause of such a failure, because when, as we have seen, the circulation depends on the prosperity of the account-holders, these are not the people to cause a bank to fail with a large quantity of notes in circulation. But the issuing banker, like everybody else, might ruin himself through speculation, cornering, or gambling. We must, therefore, contemplate the possibility of a note-issuing bank failing with a considerable quantity of notes in circulation.

Not even under the worst circumstances could the loss to the note-holders be material. If the circulation of an issuing banker is considerable, so must that amount be which he has advanced to the holders of cash-credit accounts, because, as we have seen, the circulation depends on that amount. Any one with practical experience of note-issuing would not for a moment suppose that the circulating notes could ever reach the aggregate amount of the granted cash-credits. From reasons which we have given, each market will hold only a limited amount of notes, which tend to decrease as compared with the business done. A large increase in the business does therefore not imply a large increase in the circulation. At the end of the free period in Scotland, the total amount of the circulating notes was only about 10 per cent. of the deposits. We are sorry that no statistics are available showing the proportion of the granted cash-credits to the circulation in Scotland at the end of the free period; but there can be no doubt that the granted credits by far exceeded the circulation. The same will always be the case with any issuing bank working under a free system.

If this be granted it is evident that in case the banker stops payment, and even if he is incapable of paying a penny in the pound, the note-holders would run no great risk, because each cash-credit holder would be able to cash the notes up to the amount of his debt to the bank. This they would probably do against a small commission. When the bank failed the cash-credit holder would be called on to refund the notes advanced to him, and if he presented that amount in the bank's own notes, he and the bank would be quits. Under a system of State supervision no cash-credits are granted, and the holders of the notes of a bankrupt bank would have to submit to the same loss as the other creditors.

And this naturally leads us to reply to the question whether free note-issuing would not further the creation of fictitious capital, an immense circulation, and sudden panics.

We have seen that each banker has a keen interest and great power of nipping every cause for inflation in the bud, and also that the circulating notes can never reach those enormous amounts which imagination, unchecked by a knowledge of facts, is prone to conjure up. To these reassuring circumstances should be added, that, under a free system the creditors and the debtors of the banks, at least as far as the note-issuing is concerned, are often the same people, or at least the same class of people. Those people who mostly handle the notes

Y

are cash-credit holders. The bank owes them the amount of the notes, but they owe to the bank the amount of their cash accounts. In the case of a crisis the one class of debts is squared against the other, and when that is done the notes have been withdrawn. They have only been documents for the recording of business relations between two sets of people. When we consider that free note-issuing is simply liberty for people to co-operate and keep account of their co-operation, it will be possible to form an idea of the injustice and the cruelty of an Act which compels the workers either to limit their co-operation to the small extent which can be financed by the means of the naturally scarce value-measurer, or pay a ruinous tribute to middle-men.

Our present system does not offer the same solid guarantees against commercial panics as the free system does. At present an immense quantity of promises to pay gold are based on the small reserve which is lodged in the Bank of England. The creditors of the banks are not the same people nor the same class as its debtors. When the next panic comes the creditors of the banks will claim every penny from the banks and the banks will claim every penny from their creditors. There will be no natural squaring, but as soon as faith in banking is shaken every holder of a promise to pay will demand every penny in coin.

Then the unsoundness of the present system will come out, and we shall be punished for having so long violated the laws of Political Economy. The value of the securities deposited in the banks will vanish; the shares in all our precious companies will be thrown on the market by the Bankruptcy Court in quantities sufficiently large to drive their value down to that of waste paper. The folly of raising capital to be repaid after three months' notice on shares in African land, requiring ten years' development before it yields a profit, will then be patent. The amount of real capital, produced by English hard work, wasted abroad, and now represented by mere scrip of more or less imaginary value, will then be missed. The large fortunes now figuring in ledgers and on paper will vainly strive to take a palpable form, and must be sacrificed to meet one of those small documents beginning 'Accepted, payable at,' or 'I promise to pay.'

The bank panics which we have experienced

since 1847 were mostly caused by the Act itself; the mere artificial disturbances in an otherwise healthy situation. When, therefore, the cause of these panics was removed—when the Bank Act was suspended—the disturbance subsided. Though the Bank of England now manages to defend its gold supply by the manipulation of the rate of exchange, whereby any beginning of real reversal in trade is speedily checked, we have no guarantee at all that the Bank Act will not again produce panics as it has done before. For a long time we have been protected by a protracted dulness, but the reaction from any somewhat strong inflation of business would be a critical juncture.

In consequence of its nature our present monopoly system always tends towards a crisis. And will the next one be so easily allayed as the former ones, simply by suspending the Bank Act? This is not probable. The superstructure of bank credit which is based on the metallic reserve and the notes of the Bank of England has during the last twenty years developed enormously, and as the inverted cone is becoming out of proportion to its base, the equilibrium will the more easily be shaken.

During the depression of trade which has so long

prevailed, much real capital has been lost while immense quantities of factitious commercial capital have been created. It is therefore to be feared that in case of a bank panic the suspension of the Bank Act, the mere knowledge that the Bank of England could issue an unlimited amount of notes, might not suffice to restore confidence; the notes might be actually wanted, and if an immense quantity were to be issued and circulated, large payments abroad might cause a considerable part of them to be presented for gold. When over-issue had practically been resorted to, the inevitable result would follow, namely, a heavy drain on the gold. As soon as the notes ceased to be paid promptly they would fall in value, and a gold premium would make its appearance. We all know what that means! Gold would at once be hoarded in order to be sold at a profit, and a gold panic would grow out of the bank panic.

Such are the dangers to which our present system exposes us. The large amount of real wealth in English hands, as well as the able and careful management of our large banks, has done much to counteract the fatal tendency of our monopoly system, and consequently there is little risk of a bank crisis in the immediate future. But the danger exists, and as the knowledge of the existence and origin of a danger are necessary to ward it off successfully, we have not hesitated to point out how much more perilous is our present monopoly system as compared with a system of rational Free Banking.

It is to be hoped that our bankers and business men will do their best to induce Parliament to suspend the Bank Act once more, and this time for ever.

The prosperity and the rapid increase of real wealth which would follow the introduction of Free Trade in Capital in England would soon consolidate the economic position throughout, so that all danger of a crisis would be averted. All securities, such as landed property, works, ships, bonds, shares, &c., would certainly rise, and the phantom fortunes which now haunt the ledgers of our capitalists would gradually assimilate substance and again become tangible wealth.

The chief reasons why the free system presents greater stability than our present system may be summarised as follows.

That great part of existing liabilities represented by the relations between the issuing banks and the people in their districts can easily be balanced, the creditors and debtors being to a large extent the same parties. A very large majority of the created credit-instruments represents real transactions and real capital. The real capital advanced is invested in the country in profitable trade, and can easily be realised or transferred. Capital would not be invested abroad except in close connection with home business, in the very safest undertakings, and would follow or go out simultaneously with—not precede—emigration from England. The large banks would find a great and growing business coming to them through the smaller banks, especially the issuing banks, and all paper discounted for account of the smaller banks would represent real capital. As they would bear the endorsements of at least one good seller, one good buyer, and one good bank, this business would be eminently safe, the small local banks acting as buffers against any ordinary loss. With such safe and large business within their reach the great banks would have little inducement to grant risky credits, lock up capital in permanent loans, lend against unbusinesslike securities, or to carry on their business on the money-lending principle.

The large banks would thus take a more leading part in the mechanism of exchange of the nation, have a larger stake in the country, and more interest in keeping the business of the nation in a healthy condition.

Instead of a single gold reserve in the country, there would be thousands. As matters stand now, a clique of financiers, or even one wealthy firm, can manipulate prices and create a panic at any time by demanding gold from the Bank of England for a large portion of its notes. In case of a war this would be part of the tactics of our enemies, and would paralyse the country. In case of a riot the rioters could easily barricade the streets leading to the Bank of England, and take possession of the gold before sufficient military force could be brought together to protect the Bank. With the only gold reserve for the whole of the country in the cellars of the Bank of England, such a riot would result in a general breakdown of the economy of the country, and immensely favour the rioters and facilitate their escape from punishment. All such abuses and dangers arising out of the centralisation of the gold stock would be considerably reduced, if not disappear, under a free system.

The only way the Bank of England now can protect its gold stock is by raising the rate of discount. It is certainly not realised what this means to business people in Great Britain, otherwise such an absolute obstacle to a healthy state of trade would not be maintained.

We shall not revert to the immense amounts which are extracted from those engaged in trades and industries in favour of capitalists every day the discount is abnormally high. The evil is a great one and often complained of, but it pales before others more formidable emanating from the same cause, as we shall see by simply tracing the cause and effect of the raising of the discount by the Bank of England.

A drain on the gold stock of the Bank of England may be produced in many ways besides the one we have already considered, a panic. A foreign country may suddenly require a large quantity of gold, a syndicate may create a demand in order to send prices down and secure land, buildings, steamers, shares and bonds, at a very low price, and so on; but besides these more or less artificial causes for a drain on the Bank gold stock, there is a more natural cause which always tends to assert itself, namely, a greater demand for coin in consequence of increased prosperity, and this cause deserves special attention.

When through any circumstances business takes a healthy turn and the demand for goods increases, the activity all over the country extends. All producers and traders are anxious to take advantage of the good times. Everybody buys and sells more, and consequently there is a great demand for mediums of exchange. Our legislation does not allow any suitable ones for the productive trades except the value-measurer itself, gold. The demand for gold thus becomes intense, and the stock at the Bank begins to go down. The replenishing from abroad is not easy. The regular influx from the gold-mining countries is soon absorbed by the demand for coin, and the flush times make holders of goods unwilling to sell abroad; brisk import of raw materials is going on whereby the foreign rates of exchange remain unfavourable to the importation of gold. If the impulse towards good trade is a strong one the drain on the gold stock of the Bank of England becomes severe, and the directors, who are placed in their positions for the purpose of keeping the gold stock up, are obliged to raise the discount.

Under a monopoly and centralisation system like ours, it is natural that the rate of interest of the central monopoly bank should influence the rate of interest all over the country. When the Bank rate is raised credit becomes dearer for everybody. This naturally produces a great variety of wide-felt consequences. Prices fall and bargains are declined, usual credits are refused, buyers become sellers, securities lose part of their value, and the loans are called in; a general disinclination to business is abroad, discounting becomes difficult, and impossible in millions of cases; all weak firms, or firms who happen to be in a difficult juncture, find themselves embarrassed, and have to sacrifice the result of previous success, of lifelong work perhaps, to keep afloat. Now all production must be reduced, hands be dismissed, cheap offers from abroad accepted for English products which in many cases are exported at a fearful loss, while there is a general stagnation in healthy business, slaughtering is going on, and usurers and moneylenders make fortunes.

The object which the Bank directors were

supposed to have in view, the replenishing of their gold stock, is certainly effected; the reduced import of raw material, the increased export of slaughtered goods, turn the rates of exchange in favour of gold importation, and the gold comes in from abroad and is lodged in the Bank of England; the reduced activity on lowered wages demands less mediums of exchange, and the coin goes back to the Bank; there is less demand for capital, and surplus quantities find their way to the reserve stock in the cellars of Threadneedle Street. The object is accomplished, but at what price! The Bank directors might quote the young doctor who reported that the operation succeeded but the patient died.

Who can wonder that trade is bad, that profits are small, that losses are frequent, enterprise a curse to the active man and his family, and poverty rampant, when we have rendered prosperity impossible by such a self-acting check.

It has been objected that if note-issuing were entirely free, forgers would be able to circulate spurious notes. In reply to this we need only refer to such countries where private note-issuing is carried on by a great number of banks under government supervision, such as Sweden for example. When the government supervises the notes the people do not stop to look what bank has issued the notes which are received and receipted as coin. The notes of the banks in the south of the country are circulating in the north, and *vice versâ*, and when the note of a new bank is presented in a part of the country where nothing is known of the new bank, no one refuses it.

Here then are facilities for forgeries which a free system does not present, and yet the forgeries of notes in Sweden are of rare occurrence. Under a free system the public would refuse any notes issued outside the immediate neighbourhood, and, as we have seen, the circulation of each bank would be kept within its market through unfailing economic causes. A forged note would have so little scope and would appear so often in the issuing bank, that the forger would not be able to realise enough profit to cover his expenses.

Besides, a man who would inspire confidence enough to buy goods for notes unknown by the seller, would also have credit enough to deceive through other forged documents, less expensive, less risky, and less difficult to pass. Under a free system strange notes would always be regarded with suspicion, and as the possession of a cheque book always inspires a certain confidence, it is incomparably more easy to deceive by means of cheques. If therefore the protective spirit of our age demands government supervision of mediums of exchange in order to protect foolish people from spurious documents, the beginning should certainly be made by forbidding cheques and not bank-notes.

The hollowness of this last objection to Free Trade in Capital is not more striking than that of all others. The more the real facts in connection with free note-issuing are studied, the more will it be manifest that were there none of the overwhelming reasons for entire freedom from State meddling which we have dwelt upon, this branch of business is by its very nature so unamenable to abuse that it ought to be the very last to be interfered with by the State.

CHAPTER XX

THE IRISH QUESTION

THE Irish question at present occupies so prominent a position in the public mind that any project of reform which is not understood to have a bearing on it would hardly be declared urgent by the nation. The solution of the Irish problem and the Capital and Labour problem would be furthered by demonstrating the intimate connection between them.

We know by experience only too well that when the Economy of a country is vitiated by bad legislation the discontent which ensues in consequence of State-produced poverty is generally directed, and not unjustly, against those in power. It would be unreasonable to expect the suffering masses to point out the exact economic mistake which has been committed. The masses are ready to clamour for reform, but to formulate the new programme is left to their leaders. These are generally chosen from among men of action, eloquence, and pronounced political views. Such men seldom have the time, the patience, the taste for the study of economic and sociological questions. They are generally tempted to seize on some startling political reform the advocacy of which requires no special training, and which in itself is of a kind to capture the imagination of the masses. Political reforms appear all the more promising because the way in which they are to benefit the people cannot be expected to be clearly defined. The process by which they are to be attained is left in a hazy and immature state which affords a wide scope for the imagination.

Such has been the course of events in Ireland as in many other misgoverned countries. The demand there is for a far-reaching political reform which has sprung from economic difficulties, and which is supposed to bring about in some mysterious way the great desideratum—prosperity. Home Rule is the only item of the Irish programme, and, though it is so far merely a word for which a definition is still wanting, the imaginative and long-suffering Irish have centred upon it all their hopes both as a down-trodden race and as poverty-stricken individuals.

The task we have is to show that logic and prudence demand alike that the removal of the chief cause of the misery in Ireland should replace, or at least precede, an irretrievable leap into the dark abyss of political experimentalism.

Such being the case we must first consider how the Home Rule demand arose, and what meaning different parties attach to this term. In spite of what the political opponents of the Home Rule agitators may say or think, it remains a fact that the Home Rule cry was raised from patriotic motives. No one will deny that Ireland has for centuries remained in the most deplorable economic state. The extreme poverty of the bulk of the inhabitants is patent to all who visit the country, the mass of destitute labourers who swarm to England and America, and the large diminution of a population which never was sufficient for the country, testify to misgovernment of some sort.

Those who endeavour to explain the chronic poverty of the Irish by race theories stand confronted with the fact that Ireland has supplied to

z

England vast numbers of able men, that success has been achieved by a fair average of Irishmen in England, America, and the Colonies, in spite of the serious disadvantages they have laboured under, owing to prejudice against their nationality, their want of education, and training in special trades.

The Catholic Church has been sometimes pointed to as a cause of ruin to the Irish people, and the Protestant religion in the north of Ireland has been credited with the economic advantages that part of the country presents. To this we reply that nowhere can be found a more thrifty and more Catholic population than the peasantry of France, and as to the prosperity of the north of Ireland, it originates from potent economic causes to which we shall presently return.

There is no denying the fact that a great deal of thriftlessness exists in Ireland, Ulster excepted. This is, however, by no means an inherent defect of the race, but an outcome of national idiosyncrasies which under different circumstances might, and will one day, bring about opposite results. The Irish are an imaginative race, kind-hearted and open-handed, fond of display and keen to enjoy. When such people are born in poverty; when they inherit debts they cannot pay; when circumstances compel them to incur new debts; when the shopkeeper, the money-lender, and the landlord have constantly a right to seize upon any capital which the indebted man might have in his possession—all inducements to thrift are nipped in the bud, carelessness is fostered, all hope of economic independence is abandoned. To spend as soon as possible his earnings before the creditors can seize them appears the most philosophical course to adopt under the circumstances. To many an Irishman what is spent is saved—from his creditors.

Nothing is therefore more pardonable than that the Irish themselves should have come to the same conclusion as impartial outside observers, namely, that the government is responsible for the poverty of Ireland. This conviction is certainly entertained by the Liberal party, or its agitation would be criminal; and the sanction which the Conservative party has given to measures which involve interference with private contract and the remedial measures they attempt, reveal that they have been converted to the same opinion.

It is natural, therefore, that the discontent in Ireland should be directed against the British government. So long as Parliament obviously depressed the people of Ireland or neglected their interests, it was easy for the patriotic Irish leaders to maintain a large Irish opposition party. But there came a time when public opinion and Parliament were led by men who evinced the strongest desire to do justice to Ireland; and when the followers of Isaac Butt complained of the economic condition of Ireland, they were met with the assurance that the government was willing to do their best for that country if the Irish patriots would only tell them what to do—if they would only form a programme capable of bringing about the desired prosperity.

This the Irish could not do. What they might have suggested constituted such a glaring violation of the laws of Political Economy—which at the time were respected even by thinking Irishmen—that the votaries of Economy could easily demonstrate that the remedies were worse than the evils. For want of a proper programme the Irish leaders failed to unite the Irish members in one party, and the majority of these was assimilated by the two great parties.

But when State-socialistic tendencies superseded in England the faith in Political Economy, the Irish were induced to change their tactics. The growing protective spirit which has proved such a curse to continental states gradually invaded England, and the people began to look to government for remedies against all evils and for initiative in all progress. When government came to be regarded as the only source of good, its constitution assumed vital importance. In advocating the successive stages of the franchise, the Liberal politicians insisted upon the necessity of a broad basis of representation because such representation alone would compel the government to carry those State-socialistic measures which were supposed to be productive of happiness to the people. The indispensable condition for prosperity was, according to such views, a parental government in as close contact as possible with the people.

When, therefore, the Irish leaders, baffled by the repeated demand for a programme for their country, raised the cry for Home Rule, they placed themselves in entire sympathy with the socialistic spirit of the age, at the same time freeing themselves from embarrassing controversy with the economists. There can be no doubt that when the Irish leaders first raised the Home Rule cry they had so little hope and intention of carrying their proposed reform, that they never took the pains to place the outlines of a Home Rule scheme upon paper. They saw their country in a miserable state, they wanted to coerce the government to do something for Ireland, and the Home Rule cry gave them the means. It was a handy stick with which to belabour Parliament; it was a grievance of which they could not be deprived, and which promised to be perpetual.

Their expectations were soon realised. There came a time when Mr. Parnell held the balance of power in his hand, and, by simply shifting the dead-weight of the Irish vote from the Ministerialists to the Opposition he could render any government impossible. Through the first election, after the latest extension of the franchise—which had been sedulously manipulated by the Irish party—the number of the Liberals was exactly balanced by the Conservatives and the Home Rule members combined.

Here was a new and startling situation which was bound to produce far-reaching results. Whatever minister in power, Mr. Parnell would govern the country. Instead of England dominating Ireland, Ireland would dominate the Empire.

To old Parliamentary hands the situation was intolerable. It was all up with the old parliamentary chess-game of 'ins' and 'outs,' for an outsider could move the pieces at his will. Had Mr. Parnell and his followers possessed an economic programme for Ireland, had they known the secret of making their country prosperous and happy, now was their time. Mr. Parnell had more power than he would have possessed had he been the king of Ireland, for he wielded power over the mightiest and wealthiest Empire of the world; and any measures capable of conferring real prosperity on Ireland would have been sanctioned by both the parties and hailed with enthusiasm by the industrial and commercial classes of Great Britain.

But in the case of Mr. Parnell and his followers history repeated itself. For it is a fact over and over again confirmed by history, that when a people suddenly find themselves in the possession of unwonted liberty and power, the first use they make of them is to get rid of them. The first thing the Parnellites would have done, after their acquisition of supremacy in Parliament, would have been to vote themselves out of that powerful assembly, if the Conservatives had not prevented them.

Mr. Gladstone at once found that parliamentary life would be insufferable were Mr. Parnell permitted to pull all the strings. The remedy conceived was to expel the Irish from Parliament altogether. There were two ways by which this could be done —by violence or by diplomacy. Mr. Gladstone chose the latter.

By joining issue with the Home Rulers, he not only concentrated their attention on that measure of an abstract political nature, but induced them to swell his following and to part with their independent position, from which such immense power sprang. Home Rule being the measure so long demanded by Ireland and the boon which Mr. Gladstone promised them, it became necessary to give some definition to the term 'Home Rule,' which so far owed all its usefulness to its vagueness.

The first definition of Home Rule which saw the light was contained in Mr. Gladstone's two Bills.

The fundamental provision in these, and one emphatically dwelt upon by Mr. Gladstone at the time, was the exclusion of the Irish members from the British Parliament. It is only just to the

Parnellites to say that this proposition was somewhat coolly received by them, though it has now become historical that they were prepared to vote for it. This act of self-annihilation, this spontaneous rising to the tempting bait of Mr. Gladstone, has by cynics been attributed to the fact that many of the Parnellites, who for the first time sat in Westminster, were men with but small resources, that the subscriptions from the United States were dwindling, that there was no chance of the members being paid in Westminster, and that it was plainly understood that the members of the proposed Dublin Parliament would be paid.

It might suit their political opponents to thus represent the Home Rule members as selling their own and their country's birthright for a mess of porridge. But it would be invidious and hypercritical to look for any other cause of the action of the Home Rule members than in their firm belief that Home Rule was identical with prosperity—a belief which was fostered by sheer reiteration, and shared by many a man acknowledged as their superior in intellect and statesmanship.

Those who doubted as to the practicability of Home Rule received a striking confirmation of their opinion when Mr. Gladstone brought in his Bills. Home Rule, like Socialism, is most attractive while left hovering in the hazy atmosphere of sentimental dreams. Even as the practical socialistic programmes, at times issued by indiscreet Socialists, reveal to working men how Socialism cannot increase their wages by a single penny, so Mr. Gladstone's Bills proclaimed that Home Rule means not more but less liberty for Ireland.

The singular foresight which Mr. Gladstone has repeatedly shown, his immense diplomatic power, and his frequently avowed recourse to the expediency of withholding from his most devoted followers his real aims, might well cause close observers to suspect that he did not intend by his Bills to pass Home Rule but to render it impossible. Home Rule was popular because undefined. Mr. Parnell was far too shrewd to undertake its definition and thereby destroy so useful a weapon. Is it then unlikely that Mr. Gladstone took advantage of so good an opportunity to bring Home Rule into that fierce light of discussion which was certain to dispel the charm which environed it?

The only point which has been fully discussed

and the working of which Mr. Gladstone has been
called upon to explain, is the exclusion of the Irish
members from Parliament. It was very soon found
that this would be an injustice to Ireland of such
magnitude that all other acts of injustice would
pale before it. As both the Irish members and
Mr. Gladstone recognised this, there is no need to
dwell upon the sacrifice it involved for the Irish
people. It will not reappear in any future Home
Rule Bill. But does the abandonment of this clause
amount to the abandonment of the Home Rule
scheme altogether, or is there any other difference
between Home Rule and local government than the
presence or absence of Irishmen at Westminster?

If the other points in Mr. Gladstone's Bills
were thoroughly examined and placed before the
Irish people in a true light, they would have to be
abandoned in the same way because they could be
proved detrimental to the Empire and unjust to the
Irish.

Let us glance at some of the chief points. The
Queen was to have the veto of any Act passed
by the Irish Parliament. This seems at first sight
fair and constitutional. For has not the Queen the
veto of any Act passed by the British Parliament?

But what does it in reality mean? The Queen's veto in England has so far been nominal, and Her Majesty has been always wise enough (and will probably remain so) to be guided by her Ministers. The Cabinet is placed in office by the Westminster Parliament, and the Westminster Parliament is the essence of public opinion of Great Britain. The real meaning, therefore, of Mr. Gladstone's proposition as to the veto was to place the whole Irish nation under the absolute veto of public opinion of England, Scotland, and Wales. Considering that history is replete with warnings against such subjection of one nationality by another, it is impossible to suppose that Mr. Gladstone had any other object in proposing it than to show up the unreasonableness of the Home Rule agitation.

The scheme of prohibiting certain subjects from being discussed in the Irish Parliament has too much the air of burlesque to be taken seriously. Is there any civilised nation in the world that would send to a Parliament, supposed to inaugurate a new era of liberty, representatives who would consent to refrain from discussing points that might appear to them of vital importance to the country? If there be such a nation it would be a base calumny to say that that nation is Ireland. Anybody who knows the nobler side of the Irish character will feel sure that a Dublin Parliament would act exactly in the same way as the French Deputies did in the Tennis Hall when Louis XVI. forbade them to discuss the government of France. In face of the royal prohibition, before the muzzles of loaded cannons ready to blow them to pieces, they took a solemn oath not to separate until they had voted a free constitution for France; and this is what Irishmen would do under similar circumstances.

Though Mr. Gladstone's Bill does not mention the obnoxious word 'tribute,' the proposed contribution of Ireland to the Imperial expenses is nothing else, and would be regarded by the Irish as nothing else. Now we ask, what would the Irish people feel and do when they saw ten to fifteen million pounds sterling annually quit their poor country, passing over their own Parliament—the natural guardian and manager, according to European ideas of constitutional rights, of the nation's funds? Would not every candidate for the Dublin Parliament have to pledge himself to vote against the tribute? Of all the causes for the incitement to revolution and war, none is more potent than the attempt to make one nationality tributary to another.

Mr. Gladstone's Bill, instead of assuaging the grievances of Ireland, would create new ones of a formidable character—grievances which would secure for the Irish agitators the sympathies of every free nation. The connection with England would in the judgment of the Irish stand out more conspicuously than ever as the great barrier to prosperity, and the Irish agitators would possess not only greater cause but much more power to humiliate England.

For it should be above all borne in mind that Mr. Gladstone's Bills contain no measure for the economic amelioration of Ireland. He takes for granted that political reform suffices to cure economic evils, and shares the opinions of the Irish Home Rulers that Home Rule is the panacea for all Irish troubles.

If those who aspire to power in Ireland and are most likely to attain to it in the case of a Dublin Parliament, were sound economists, and if the connection with England really stood in the way of economic reforms, there would be some sense in the panacea theory of Home Rule. But, unfortunately for Ireland, the contrary is the case. While the Irish Home Rule members may be men actuated by patriotism and philanthropy, and while even their opponents cannot deny their eloquence and diplomatic powers, their best friends and greatest admirers will admit that all the Irish leaders are singularly lacking in insight into Political Economy. When asked by what means they propose to bring about the prosperity they so lavishly promise, they throw out dark hints about protection duties, State assistance to enterprise, interference with free contracts, and the raising of large State loans— measures which, by the most unimpeachable theories, confirmed by thousands of years of experience in all parts of the world, are mischievous enough to ruin countries far wealthier than Ireland.

Though, probably for diplomatic reasons, the Irish members are not prone to disclose how they intend to settle the Land Question, it is evident enough that the prosperity they hope for is expected to arise out of Land Reform; and this opinion is shared by most advocates of Home Rule.

The popular idea of the Irish Question is that prosperity can only come through Land Reform, and that Land Reform can only come through Home Rule. What shape this Land Reform is to take is very far from being settled, but, unfortunately, both political parties—Unionists and Home Rulers—seem to share one opinion alike, and this is that Land Reform in Ireland must be of a State-socialistic nature.

Now, we have shown in a previous chapter, how delusive State-socialistic measures prove themselves when applied in other directions, and how they must inevitably damage those whom they are intended to help, so long as we have not complete Socialism. We shall now show that the same result will follow if State Socialism be applied to Land.

Let us first remember that the fundamental principle of Political Economy—that which has proved itself to hold good in every branch of human activity—namely, freedom—has never yet been applied to trade in land. Many of our economic difficulties spring from the legal obstacles which stand in the way of transfer of land and special legislation relative to land. The inability of landowners to perceive what is their true interest, and perhaps the manœuvrings of the lawyers to maintain abnormally large fees, have unfortunately prevented the adoption of Free Trade in Land in Great Britain and Ireland. When the unnatural position in which the landlord stands produces an irresistible demand for Land Reform, the reform which is best for all, Free Trade in Land, looks far too tame, and thus a socialistic solution of the problem is the only one the public will listen to.

One of the meaningless cries which stir the Irish people to agitate is 'Down with the landlords.' The poor Irish tenant's idea of a landlord is naturally mediæval, because modern progress has not reached him; individual freedom, such as is the true aim of our civilisation, is to him an abstract idea he cannot grasp, for he has never experienced it. He frames his opinions on tradition, and this tells him that he would be happy had he a good landlord, and that he is miserable because he has a bad one.

In olden times, when contracts were made and carried out in primitive fashion, when the payment of coin was exceptional, when special bank legislation had not vitiated the relation between production and sale, and when the capitalist and money-lender did not hold the domineering position they now hold—in those olden times the solidarity which naturally existed between landlord and tenant had a better chance of prevailing ; a landlord had to be both careless and foolish not to understand that his interests and those of his tenants were parallel. The greater number of tenants, and the better those tenants were, the better for the landlord. His rent consisted of a share in a crop, and on this alone he lived comfortably. He had very small cash disbursements, and the coin requisite for these he obtained by the sale of surplus products.

The tenants were to him not only a source of supplies but one of social influence and political power. He had as strong inducements to see his tenants numerous, happy, loyal, as a modern sovereign has to please his people; the sweets of power and popularity were well worth the few paternal cares which produced them.

But when feudal institutions made room for the modern system of division of labour, when all contracts stipulated payments in coin, and when the foolish enactments of government respecting coin and banking made the capitalists and all dealers in coin the masters of the situation, the position was entirely changed. The coin disbursement of the landlord grew apace, and he was compelled to abandon the system of payments in kind and resort to rents in coin. The remaining expenditure of the farmers became payable in coin; all co-operation between the people was carried on with coin; the farmers were obliged to sell their products prior to payment of anybody; everybody wanting to sell for coin, the proffered products rapidly dropped in price; and the precious metal acquired a fictitious value which weighed down the farmers who were bound to pay so much of it in many directions. This change took place all over the civilised world, but it was most acutely felt in such countries as Ireland, where the people were chiefly agricultural, where the growth of trade and industry had not expanded the coin-holding power of the markets, where such prosperity and happiness as they enjoyed were the outcome of feudal institutions, and where such institutions were slow in dying out.

Under the altered circumstances it was no easy matter to be a good landlord. Only those could be good landlords who were good financiers, those who could keep free of debt, and hold capital enough in their own hands to allow such terms to their tenants as were calculated to assist them in the development of their farms. Those who desired to be good landlords could not always succeed, because greater exertion and greater sacrifice of capital were necessary than many could afford.

The landlord was not the only creditor who weighed down the tenant. The scarcity of mediums of exchange in face of an intense demand for them caused the whole distributive trade to function on a system of consumption credit. The tenants fell into a chronic state of indebtedness to the shop-keepers and other suppliers, and had to pay excessive prices for everything they purchased. At the same time they were compelled to sell all their products as soon as ready, and not infrequently before they were produced, to a middle-man, the first link in the chain of middle-men who constitute the mediums of exchange when truly economic ones are forbidden by law.

The exertions of the good landlords were thus counterbalanced to a very large extent by the artificially produced scarcity of capital and of mediums of exchange. The small results which the landlords obtained by their sacrifices, as well as their increased indebtedness, caused many to abandon all hope of improving their estates and renounce the part of Providence to their tenants which was the privilege of a landlord in olden times. Through the many points of contact which the landlords had with London and other progressing centres, they were as much affected by modern developments as business men in large cities: they had to discard every vestige of feudal life, and conduct all their transactions on strict commercial principles.

But with the tenants the case was very different. While, as we have already observed, the transition from a feudal to a commercial system affected them only by increasing the amount of coin they were called upon to pay; while the commercial system created free competition in their production—free competition in the supply of capital, credit, and mediums of exchange was forbidden. The change thus made them long more than ever for the paternal protection of the landlord, and when he responded by taking a strictly commercial view of his relations with his tenants, he came to be regarded as selfish, hard, and cruel.

The situation in Ireland might be thus briefly described: the tenants live and are compelled to live under the old feudal system, while the landlords live under a modern commercial system.

The consequence of this is that the interest of both, which naturally is parallel, appears to be antagonistic. The prevailing prejudice against Free Banking having prevented the extension of the advantages of the commercial system to the tenants, and having barred the way to every inquiry in the right direction, the tenants, as well as their spokesmen and sympathisers, have all come to the conclusion, firstly, that the landlord has not done his duty to the tenants; secondly, that he is too selfish to do it; and thirdly, that government must compel him to do it. The rent was the only point on which he could be attacked, and hence the anti-rent agitation and the successive Land Bills.

The Land Bills which have been so far passed have proved insufficient, and this must necessarily be the case with every Socialistic Land Bill in the future. If the circumstances of the Irish people could be improved in no other way than by the reduction of rents, the outlook would be dark indeed. It is a well-known fact that in many parts of Ireland, especially in Donegal, there are a great many cases where the total abolition of rent would not allow the tenants, under the present economic system, to get a decent living out of their holdings. Even in England there are farms now which would not be taken by a tenant rent-free. The reason for this state of affairs is that, when the exchanges are worked in a country on a system which involves a strong tendency to destroy profit on all production, as we have seen is the case in Great Britain, the chief industries of the country must suffer the most; and farming is after all the chief industry of this country, and almost the only industry in the poverty-stricken districts of Ireland.

We know that there are three factors in production—land, labour, and capital. None of these can be dispensed with, and if one of them is inadequate, hampered, or entirely withheld, the two others must suffer. If labour is withheld from capital and land, no production takes place, land remains waste, and capital perishes. If land is withheld from capital and labour, the disastrous effect on these two factors is evident. In Great Britain, and more particularly in Ireland, special legislation withholds capital from land and labour, and only a miracle could prevent land (that is the landlord) and labour (that is the agricultural population) from suffering.

No reduction in rent, no Land Bill, can remedy the evils of Ireland. If every tenant received his farm as a free gift, while the present economic system is upheld, the position of the tenants would in a few years be as bad as ever. The first thing the land-owning farmer would do, the first thing he would be compelled to do, would be to raise a loan on his new property. If the now existing loan institutions and money-lenders were not sufficient to hold the mortgage of every farm in Ireland, a land-owning peasantry would soon induce company-promoters to start Land Banks, that is, non-issuing banks granting loans in coin on mortgage. In a short time the interest which the farmers would have to pay to these banks and the usurers would probably exceed the present rent, and from these new landlords it would be vain to hope for any feudal paternity. The tenants would soon find how they had jumped out of the frying-pan into the fire.

This conclusion will be confirmed not only by all those acquainted with the financial condition of Ireland, but by all those who have studied agrarian questions in other countries. We shall here give some examples which, though drawn from countries where circumstances have differed and do differ considerably, all point to the fact that a defective economic system tends to destroy those who live on the land, be they farmers, landlords, or labourers.

In Russia at the time of the emancipation some 60,000,000 serfs were transformed into proprietors by having the land given to them, while no change was introduced in the wretched legislation which regulates, or rather vitiates, banking, credit, and coin in Russia. The result was that the new landowners rapidly fell into the clutches of the usurers. Each village had its mure-eater (or village-eater), and to these leeches the peasants lost not only the land, all their other possessions, but in many cases all their future work at a low nominal price. Large hordes of these now landless people keep drifting in search of work from one part of the country to another; and the poverty is appalling.

In Sweden and Norway the peasantry had been freeholders as far back as tradition goes. In olden times, before the commercial system was developed, these independent peasants held their ground against the nobility, and during periods when wars and revolts did not devastate their countries, the peasantry possessed large wealth and held positions which fully justified the name, frequently given them in the old chronicles, of peasant-kings. They withstood the sovereigns, the feudal lords, the crafty priests, the cruel devastating warfare of those days; but bank monopoly, land banks, and usurers were too much for them. Almost every peasant, every landowner of these countries is now indebted up to the utmost valuation of his estate. The profit on farming is extremely small and uncertain. The woods are ravaged to supply pit-props to England at a price that hardly pays for the labour and the carting to the ports. Though the population is scanty, emigration is excessive, and large numbers of landowning peasants quit their farms and emigrate to the Northern States of America, where a new Scandinavia is fast forming.

While similar difficulties afflict the farmers of Germany, Switzerland, and Italy, we find that in France—at least until recent times—the farmers have been able to remain in possession of their farms and keep free from debt. The cause of this is to be found in the economic system of the country. As we have explained in a previous chapter, the *banquier* system of that country supplies the producer with capital and mediums of exchange on a more rational system than in any other country, while it tends to lower the cost of production and raise the price of sale, thus rendering farming remunerative.

If, then, the free gift of land cannot benefit the agricultural classes in Ireland, it is vain to hope for a solution of the Irish question from compulsory reduction of rents; and the sooner this is understood the better for that reputation for love of fair-play on which Englishmen pride themselves. For it is an appalling injustice that the British Parliament should confiscate large portions of the fortunes of the Irish landlords in the hope of palliating the consequences of faulty legislation, from which the landlords have suffered in common with the tenants.

If there be any sincerity in the cry, 'Down with the landlords,' it cannot mean that the present landlords (many of whom have purchased their estates) should be replaced by new ones who would get them for nothing. Some plan of land-nationalisation must underlie this cry. Let us, therefore, see to what extent the appropriation of the land by the State would benefit the tenants and the nation at large.

The evil from which the tenants in Ireland must suffer, and which is at the bottom of the disproportion between the rent and the value of the crops, is the competition among the farmers to secure those farms which are in the market. This competition it is which has made rack-renting possible and placed the farmer under the heel of the agent. This fact has been used against the tenants; it has been said that they are themselves to blame if they sign contracts which they cannot fulfil. It is a pity that such things should be said at all, for many of these contracts have been signed under a system of compulsion which renders them invalid—if not from a legal, at least from a moral point of view. The extreme poverty of the tenants leaves them no other choice than to throw themselves on the mercy of the landowner. Many a tenant has had to choose between either leaving his cottage at once, or signing a contract for a high rent to be paid in the future. And who can wonder at the choice, when it is considered what it means for a man without resources, with a large family (including, perhaps, invalids), to be evicted during the autumn or winter months? Thus poverty compels the farmers to compete with each other and to bid up the rents of the farms, and if they were a little more independent they would probably not pursue so unwise a course. They have already proved that they can act in unison, and, if circumstances were not so terribly against them, they would take a leaf from the book of the English trades-unions as to the methods for the prevention of high rents. It would then of course be in their interest not to boycott, threaten, or shoot the farmer who pays his rent, but to visit their chastisement upon those who do not pay! Because it is evident that if a tenant knew that he would be shot at if he did not pay his rent, he would be careful not to sign a contract for higher rent than he was sure to pay. The reckless bidding for farms by men who never intend to pay their rent would cease, and all rents would be moderate. It is their utter destitution which causes the wrong men to be fired at; and this is not the only instance of poor people being compelled to make matters worse for themselves.

The advocates of land nationalisation seem to believe—and certainly wish others to believe—that their pet scheme would remove this evil of competition among the tenants for the holdings. But in this they are grievously mistaken. If the State is to be the national landlord, the question arises, How shall the land be meted out to the people? That great and influential section of the people which is not employed in agriculture, as well as the farm-labourers, would have a right to demand —and would demand—that the land should be given to the best farmers. It then has to be decided who the best farmers are. To leave this to bureaucrats would be to foster an intolerable system of favouritism and bribery which would be fatal to poor farmers. Competitive examination would be out of the question in this case, for it would leave the land in the hands of inexperienced theorists and deprive the State of a large portion of its revenue. Besides, it would again favour the wealthy classes. Only one practical way out of the difficulty is possible, and that one would surely be adopted—namely, to lease the land to the highest bidder. Land nationalisation would not, therefore, free the tenants from the evils of competition. The only difference would be that they would have no chance of a kind and charitable landlord, but would have to deal with the State—which, according to high ecclesiastical dignitaries, is not expected to act on the principles of the Sermon on the Mount. The loudly-complained-of wrong—absenteeism—would be magnified to its utmost extent, and the land-agents would be government officials who, if honest, could not deviate a hair-breadth from the fixed rules in favour of a tenant; if dishonest, would use their power for their own advancement, for the advantage of their kinsmen and friends, for political purposes, and for the extortion of bribes. Land nationalisation would therefore be an excellent thing for government officials, mostly recruited from the upper classes, but a very bad thing for the poor farmers.

Our land reformers persist in overlooking the fact that when government violently interferes with the liberty of proprietors in obtaining the market value as the price or rent of their property, neither the people in general nor the working classes are benefited. Only one individual or one private interest profits.

When government interfered violently with the free contracts between landlord and tenant in

Ireland it was often said that the legally fixed rents would in the long run benefit the landlord as well as the tenant, and the country at large. But some effects which have begun to show themselves already point in a contrary direction. Without desiring to dispute the fact that there are any number of farms let at too high rents to tenants who are dreadfully handicapped with respect to the supply of capital and the vitiated proportion between cost and sale, it is certain that in Ireland, perhaps more than anywhere else, there are farmers who are incapable of turning their farms to the best advantage. Such a state of things would, in a country enjoying a free economic system, rectify itself by a system of natural selection on the principle of the survival of the fittest. The incompetent farmers would have to make room for competent men rising out of the labouring class.

In a country like Ireland, where holdings are small, such an evolution would be natural and easy, and it will be more so when banking is made free. But by the interposition of government in fixing legal rents many a thriftless, drunken, and good-for-nothing tenant has been maintained in the possession of a farm which in his hands will always produce, even under the most favourable circumstances, miserable crops.

This of course reacts on all the inhabitants of the country; the whole of the working classes must in consequence suffer; and the injustice to the farm-labourers, owing to this violent interference with contract, is so glaring that Parliament could not deny them some kind of compensation were they to claim it. As a matter of fact, the farm-labourers in Ireland begin to understand, not that they are the natural victims of State interference with contract, but that the whole land agitation in Ireland is going on rather at their expense than in their favour.

The value of rents, like the value of everything else, is a question of supply and demand. If demand for farms has raised the rent to its highest pitch, the forcible fixing of a lower rent by the State constitutes a free gift to the occupant which is equal to the difference between the value of the lease before and after the reduction. The tenant can utilise this free gift in two ways. He can either retain the farm and add the reduction of rent to his profits, or he can sell out, pocket a premium and emigrate. When the rent is determined by free and natural competition, a compulsory reduction will *always* leave the tenant the option of sale : for it would not be a market value of the rent if it could not be at once realised. This is exactly what has happened in many cases in Ireland. The forcible reduction, instead of securing to the landlord a more prosperous tenant and greater regularity in the payment of his rent, places him in this respect, in the case of such sales, in a worse position than previously. The buyer of the lease generally obtains the purchase-money from a money-lender against exorbitant rates of interest, and, when the lowered rent is due, he is as incapable of paying it as the former tenant was of paying a higher rent ; and he is usually quite unable to farm in a rational way, the chief inducement to his purchase having been the hope of a further reduction.

In England, Scotland, and Wales, where rents are determined by free competition, a compulsory reduction would always mean a gift of so much cash to so many individuals, but would in no way improve the relations between tenant and landlord, and would considerably injure the labourers and the nation at large.

At the risk of appearing to digress, we must

here point out that what we have said about government interference with rent also holds good with regard to royalties on mines. The general impression is that the miners would benefit largely by the abolition of mining royalties. This is a gross mistake, for the holder of the mine is the only one who will profit. The price at which he sells his coal or ore is not determined by his own cost of production, but by the general demand and the general supply of coal all over the world. Were the English mining royalties abolished, the mine-holders' cost of production would be proportionately less. But they would not sell their products one penny cheaper, and, if nothing compelled them to do so, they would simply pocket the royalty, or, what is more likely, sell the mine to a new owner, or a company, at the higher value which the abolition of the royalty conferred upon it.

It is true that the competition between the holders of mines would produce a tendency towards a fall in the price of products, which again would produce an increased consumption. Now the popular theory is that this increase in consumption would cause an increased demand for miners, which again would allow these to demand and obtain higher wages.

But practice would not confirm this theory. In the first place the holders of those mines which government would have freed from the royalty would be very unwilling to reduce the price of their products at all. In the case of trade remaining brisk, reduction would be out of the question. As there are mines the products of which are not charged with royalty, or are too unremunerative to allow of a substantial lowering of the price of their products, the holders benefited by the abolition of royalty would be able to secure orders by means of a very slight reduction. Should they undersell their competitors to too great an extent they might compel the least profitable mines to close, and in that case the miners' position would be worse instead of better.

Besides, any abatement in price in England would be followed by an abatement in price abroad, and the extra demand which such universal reduction might cause would benefit all the mines of the world. A general reduction in price, however slight, would certainly be an advantage to the world at large, but it would be almost imperceptible, while the sacrifice which would be imposed on the owners of the soil by the abolition of royalties would fall very heavily upon them. The total result of the abolition of royalties might be summarised thus: the bulk of the confiscated royalties would go into the pockets of the mine-holders, and a small part of them would be distributed among all the people of the world.

It is a significant fact that when the advocates of confiscation of royalties and of land in general fail to show that any real economic advantages would accrue to the people from the reforms they advocate, they invariably fall back on the indisputable fact that such confiscations would allow a reduction in taxes. It is quite a usual thing to meet with speeches and articles on land confiscation beginning with the intention of pointing out an economic remedy against depression in trade and misery amongst the working classes, but in the end coming to the only conclusion that taxes might be reduced. Thus no economic advantage but simply a fiscal one is educed.

It is hardly worth while to write long articles to prove that if one class is plundered, and the plunder applied to the expenses of the State, taxation may be lowered. It is not from over-taxation that the country suffers. No one would mind the taxes much if trade were good. It is ridiculous to tell a man who is out of a situation that he will be benefited by a reform which will lessen his income-tax when he gets an income.

Fiscal measures can only produce fiscal results, and economic results can be produced alone through economic measures.

The would-be land reformers are generally tempted into adopting socialistic views because they can so easily find means of accomplishing the first part of their reform, the confiscation of the land by the State; but when they have to grapple with the second part, the application of the accumulated resources to the wants of the poorer classes, they find absolutely no other way to accomplish it than by complete socialistic measures, that is, pauperisation of the working classes and their subjection under bureaucratic masters.

That such land reforms as are advocated by the Home Rule leaders are not economic measures capable of economic results, but so many violent blows at the only base of genuine prosperity—freedom of contract—is not understood by the chiefs and still less by the rank and file of the Home Rule party. If it were, they would cease to agitate for measures which can only damage both Ireland and the Empire, and turn their attention to that other factor in the production of wealth—capital—the supply of which is curtailed, hampered, and vitiated by such a monstrous Act as that of the Bank Monopoly Act of 1844.

It will be easy to show that what in Ireland is regarded as a question of land is in reality a question of capital.

The possibility of a better, not to say a perfect system of supply of capital and mediums of exchange is so completely absent from the minds of the land agitators, that they look upon the miserable income which Irish tenants and Irish landlords derive from the soil as a stable factor in the land problem. They start from the evidently absurd supposition that the culture of the land is carried on in a perfect way, that the revenue cannot be raised, and proceed to level everything down to a miserable state which they take for granted to be normal. They suppose that the tenants can have no other supply of capital than from the gombeen man; that, for want of means, the farmers are compelled to produce the least paying products; that they must draw their supply at long credit prices from the last link in a chain of middle-men; that they are obliged to sell their products for cash to the first link of another chain of middle-men; that the supply of mediums of exchange of the country must remain of such a nature as to keep cost of production at a maximum and price of sale at a minimum; that they are compelled to live in a chronic state of indebtedness; all this is supposed to represent a normal state and the rent is to be adapted to it.

A little reflection, however, ought surely to make it clear that in a country where there is plenty of space and a considerable number of inhabitants making little use of their time, the establishment of an economic system which would be as favourable to production as the present antieconomic one is unfavourable to it would work an extraordinary change in the value of land.

Whether the vast tracts of uncultivated land which exist in certain parts of Ireland could be changed into wheat-bearing acres, and whether such a change would be a financial success, we shall leave an open question. That it would be ruinous under the present system is certain. But it should be remembered that under a system of Free Trade in Capital, cultivation in Ireland would mean the utilisation of land which has now hardly any value; of people who are unemployed; of resources which are wasted: and this without any of the financial drawbacks which under the present system upset all calculations by the necessity of attracting profit-destroying coin.

But it is not likely that the Irish farmers, under a sound economic system, would be tempted to enter into competition with America, Australia, and India in the production of wheat. They would have every facility and every inducement to embrace those branches of agriculture in which the great cereal products of those countries are used as raw materials.

Ireland is splendidly situated for the production of enormous quantities of other kinds of food than cereals which England consumes, and which would be cheapened by the supply of cheap corn. In England there is an immense and constantly growing consumption of foreign butter and cheese; foreign meat, fresh, cured, and preserved; foreign poultry, foreign eggs, foreign fruits and vegetables; and a whole mass of minor products, the production of which is becoming easier and more profitable through new scientific discoveries and new devices. The production of these articles of food in Ireland would form the basis of many new industries, and the prosperity which the export to England of so large a quantity of food-stuffs would call forth would cause an extraordinary rise in the price of land.

The reason why such large quantities of food are not produced in Ireland but imported into England from foreign countries is to be found entirely in the miserable financial system.

It is patent to everybody that the farmer who devotes himself to what the French call 'la petite culture'—the most paying of all farming—would be under the necessity of constant disbursement, for his production is quick, the turn-over of his capital frequent, and he must employ a great many hands. How is it possible for a farmer to enter upon such undertakings with no other mediums of exchange than the coin he can keep in stock, with no other source for the renewal of his capital than the money-lender? Were he to attempt it, his want of cash would drive him to desperation, and his first piece of bad luck would ruin him.

The success of 'la petite culture' in France is not due so much to climate and the subdivision of land under the cadastre as to the *banquier* system, and the ready supply of capital, low interest, and low cost of production which it involves. The extraordinary development in farming which in Scotland took place up till 1844 was due to the Free Banking which, as we have seen, benefits the country in virtue of the same economic laws as the *banquier* system does.

It is the prohibition of Free Trade in Capital alone which prevents Ireland from being the dairy, the kitchen garden, the orchard of England.

There are in Ireland the beginnings of many industries which only require those advantages which rational banking supplies in order to assume considerable dimensions. Many of these industries would go hand-in-hand with agriculture, and as Ireland would be essentially a food-producing country, cheap living—an important condition for the success of industry—would be assured. The ideal which some of our politicians strive for— namely, the working man in his own cottage, a garden, and a few acres of land—would be realised in Ireland as soon as banking were made free. The man, the cottage, the land are all there; but the capital and the mediums of exchange are wanting.

The introduction of Free Trade in Capital would in Ireland reverse the present relations between landlords and tenants. It is only the inability of the farmer to prosper which has changed his natural solidarity with the landlord into animosity. With Free Trade in Capital the natural relations—solidarity—would be re-established. With a plentiful supply of capital and normal cost and sale, the demand for farmers both in Ireland and the Colonies would certainly exceed the supply. In Ireland they could therefore dictate their own terms to the landlords. The rents would be probably in most cases three or four times higher than they are now, but the profits of the tenant would be higher in proportion, for the landlords would be compelled, in order to secure tenants, to leave them a large margin of profit.

With Free Trade in Capital none would more resent State interference with land than the Irish farmers, for such interference would prevent free competition for the best farms, would deprive the farmers of the power to sign such contracts as would be most favourable to themselves, would subject them to the tyranny of bureaucrats, would give rise to favouritism and establish a system of bribes. Government interference could not possibly be of any advantage to the farmers so long as in making contracts with the landlord the farmers have the pull.

When the full importance for Ireland of Free Trade in Capital is understood, the agitation for land reform will cease, because it will be evident that all the evils which now are supposed to spring from the land system are in reality produced by State interference with the supply of capital, and that the Land Question cannot be settled, nor even posed, until the Capital Question is settled.

And in all probability when the Capital Question is settled there will be no Land Question to settle.

Our contention is, then, that the demand for Home Rule is caused by the miserable state of the country and the discontent that poverty engenders; that the modern socialistic fallacies prevent the Irish leaders from conceiving any other remedies than socialistic ones; that poverty in Ireland is chiefly due to State interference with banking; that when banking is made free an unprecedented prosperity will follow, as it did in Scotland; that this prosperity would bring contentment and reveal to the Irish the enormous advantages they derive from the full citizenship of the British Empire which they now enjoy, and that they would jealously defend this privilege against all those who would deprive them of it.

If the Home Rule agitation were based on sentimental national aspirations and not on the desire for prosperity, the demand would be for national independence and not for Home Rule. The Irish agitators have found that to advocate entire independence does not bring them popularity, because most Irish people are aware what a loss it would be to them to be deprived of British citizenship and of their large stake in the Empire which they and their forefathers have helped to build up. The demand is therefore limited to that something which is not independence and not local government, and which is called Home Rule. The whole world is now waiting for a practical definition of this term, and it is no wonder that even Mr. Gladstone's genius is at a loss to supply it, for it involves a glaring contradiction. It means, in the opinion of the Home Rulers, more freedom than they have now, while to practical statesmen it means a curtailing of the liberties which the Irish now possess, jointly with the English, to govern the British Empire.

CHAPTER XXI

HOW THE ANCIENT PROSPERITY OF EGYPT COULD BE REVIVED

THE kaleidoscopic changes of modern events now and then thrust the Egyptian question in the background, but it is easy to foresee how it will soon be brought to the front again, and probably so forcibly that it will become impossible to refrain much longer from adopting a clearly defined Egyptian policy. The battle of Toski, far from bringing about that state of peace and security which is the avowed object of the English occupation and the indispensable condition for the withdrawal of the British garrison, has only demonstrated that invasion, devastation, and probably general anarchy, is prevented solely by English action.

Besides, immediately after the battle, a discovery was made which points to new and serious complications. It should warn us that a fresh departure in our Egyptian policy is necessary to prevent our interference from becoming a source of grave danger and endless trouble. We mean the discovery of a secret correspondence between the leaders of the dervishes and influential people in Egypt.

Our foreign detractors have not been slow to point out how the existence of such a correspondence shows that the English occupation, instead of pacifying the country, is in reality the cause of all the attempts at invasion. They argue that the Egyptian patriots, dissatisfied with the English occupation and fearing ultimate annexation, are willing to risk invasion from the Soudan in the hope that the fierce warriors from the south will assist them to drive the English from their shores.

So far, if we are well informed, only one culprit has been brought to book. But as he was found out by a mere chance the discovered correspondence between the Mahdists and the Egyptians is probably more extensive than appears. Concerted action between the dervishes and influential Egyptians explains so naturally the persistent attacks of the former, and is so much in keeping with what we have experienced from the latter, that it seems surprising that this simple explanation has not been mooted before. If, in case of more conspiracy, we have to proceed by arrests and executions in Upper Egypt, we should thereby inaugurate a far more dangerous campaign than that against the dervishes.

Both history and recent experience in Ireland teach us what such a campaign means. It would change utterly the part we have so far played in Egypt. Instead of the defenders we should appear as the oppressors of the Egyptians, as the destroyers of liberty and national aspirations. Though, to begin with, we should have to combat only certain classes, these would understand how to represent themselves as the true upholders of national and religious liberties. This would be easy for them, because we are foreigners who must compel obedience and make many enemies in order to accomplish the tasks imposed on us by circumstances. Besides, the miserable state of the country and the high taxes will surely create discontent, and it is a well-known fact, referred to before, that such discontent is sure to be directed against those in power, especially when they are of an alien race. It is only too evident that if we are to defend ourselves from treason we have to prepare for ourselves another Ireland in Egypt, more dangerous to keep and more dangerous to let go than the one we already have. If we let ourselves drift into the odious position of the oppressors of Egyptian nationality we create serious troubles in the future. There is only one way out of it, namely, by adopting a definite and intelligible policy in Egypt, one worthy of our nation, favourable to our interests, acceptable to the other great powers, and gratifying to the patriotic aspirations and the longing for prosperity among the inhabitants.

Such a policy might at first sight seem to belong to the region of unrealisable dreams, but if the Egyptian Question is studied in its most important aspect, viz. the economic aspect, it will cease to appear incapable of such a solution. Instead of having to deal with a number of conflicting interests, we shall find that all who are concerned in the Egyptian Question, except perhaps certain French chauvinists, aspire to the same thing, and that the differences arise simply out of the means by which the common object is to be realised. We come very near the truth when we describe this common object as the *prosperity of Egypt*.

There never was and nowadays there certainly exists nowhere any national aspirations which are not based on a desire and hope for increased prosperity. It is evident to all accurate observers of modern events, that the leaders of movements in favour of national autonomy derive their chief strength from the existing discontent, the prevailing economic misery, the inevitable consequences of maladministration.

A revival of prosperity in Egypt and the surrounding territories would satisfy every class and every race in those countries. All orientals are naturally keen business people, and even the fierce Arab warriors, were it open to them to acquire through legitimate trade and commerce the wealth which they now try to gain by force of arms and slave hunting, would prove, as they have done before, that under suitable government they can excel in the arts of peace.

Prosperity would make the payment of the Egyptian debts easy, and enable the country to balance its budget with light taxation only.

In presiding at the return of prosperous times

in Egypt, England could easily retain its protectorate without keeping a single soldier there and without any considerable expense. We should have all the advantages of annexation, without the dangers, expenses, animosities, jealousies, and responsibilities which it involves.

Prosperity in Egypt would benefit our industry, our trade, our shipping, and secure us the assistance of the natives in upholding national freedom and good government, which would constitute the best guarantee for the protection of the Canal.

Prosperity is impossible without Free Trade, and both combined would make Egypt and the surrounding parts of Africa a great market not only for English wares but for the products of other European nations; and if English influence in Egypt resulted in a large and free import of German, French, and Italian goods, popular opinion in those countries would support the English policy.

All this is undeniable, but the important question arises, Can such a state of prosperity be brought about, and can it be done so promptly as to produce the desired results early enough for practical political purposes?

That Egypt is capable of an almost incredibly

high state of prosperity is proved by undeniable historical evidence. Sceptics, who are always apt to disbelieve the records of the almost fabulous productive powers of ancient nations, must remain silent in the presence of such witnesses as the Pyramids and other gigantic monuments, the ruins of which now amaze us. These monuments were, so to say, the outcome of surplus productiveness, for most of them were constructed, not for useful productive purposes, but almost entirely in gratification of sentiment. Pyramids and temples were built, tombs excavated, obelisks and sphinxes were erected, only after the irrigation canals, roads, ports, bazaars, and dwellings were constructed.

The whole country was in a high state of cultivation, teeming millions were supplied and large quantities of corn were exported before the dead became the object of that vast expenditure of capital and labour of which the mummies and the tombs bear witness. No doubt the productive power of Egypt in olden times and during many centuries was then enormous, and the prosperity of the ancient Egyptians, regarded as a nation, far beyond that of any modern state.

In Egypt then our task should be easy and

our endeavours unfailing. We have simply to accomplish what has been accomplished before, and this without the enormous facilities which we now possess. The ancient Egyptians had not the perfect machines nor the scientific knowledge which render modern undertakings and modern production of wealth so easy and so sure.

So far the methods we have employed in Egypt are inadequate. For many years we have had our own way, and though some progress is perceptible, so small is it that if the ancient prosperity is to be emulated at our present rate of progress, our occupation will have to last thousands of years. Moreover, it is manifest that we are following in that country the same programme which has been followed in India, and that all European mistakes and fallacies are gradually taking root and producing the same bad result they have produced in Europe, in the United States, and many of our Colonies. If we do not change our programme in Egypt we shall, therefore, never arrive at that state of prosperity which is required to bring contentment to the masses, and which has here been pointed out as the true solution of the Egyptian problem. Instead of producing the prosperity of the ancient Egyptians, we are busy producing that of modern Ireland.

If we are to restore the grand past of Egypt we must first cease to ram our heads against the granite rock of Political Economy. We must, on the contrary, inquire in virtue of what economic laws the ancient prosperity developed, and then strive to give the same laws free play again.

Before we enter upon this inquiry let us first free our minds of the bias which has been produced by the explanation repeatedly given by historians of the decay of the ancient Empires in general and Egypt in particular. Their opinion is that the Empires, and their systems of civilisation, have crumbled because the people have degenerated. According to many historical authorities the race which worked such wonders in Egypt was vastly superior to the present Fellaheens.

This belief in the helpless inferiority of the bulk of the population of Egypt is one of the errors which the battle of Toski has scattered to the winds. The Fellaheens fought splendidly against men who always enjoyed a reputation for fierce courage, and whose very appearance was at one time a cause of terror along the Nile. What has then become of the theory of race inferiority? Has a few months' drill counteracted thousands of years of decay, corruption, and degradation? The theory of the degenerated state of the population must be dismissed, for we have now the most conclusive proof that it is the system which has been bad all these centuries, not the people.

When history comes to be rewritten in the light of modern Political Economy, it will be generally understood that it was not the degradation of the people, but on the contrary their moral and intellectual development, which caused the downfall of the ancient systems. This will be made clear by the following short reiteration of the economic explanation of the formation and downfall of ancient Empires.

All wealth is the product of labour. Division or organisation of labour determines its productiveness. Without division of labour, or organisation, human efforts produce but small results; but, under a well-developed system of division of labour, small efforts may produce enormous results. The great production of wealth which characterised ancient Egypt compels us to conclude that division of labour existed in that country in a very complete state, and the records prove such to have been the case. The country was like an enormous beehive, every individual having his appointed place and allotted share in the economic life of the people. Little time and little work were wasted, and the best methods available at the period were employed.

To bring about a state of prosperity equal to that of ancient Egypt we must, then, establish a division of labour as complete and as effective as that which functioned under the Pharaohs. We must have as powerful a motive for work, as large a supply of raw materials and instruments, as good a selection of leaders, as clever a distribution of special functions (according to abilities), as wise a selection of products to be produced, as careful an accumulation of capital, as stern a discipline in all ranks, and a life as frugal amongst the workers.

The idea of exactly copying the ancient mechanism is out of the question. It would not be possible; and if it were so, it would not be desirable, for the system would, in our modern times, when life is so intense and changes are so rapid, soon meet with the same fate it met with before, namely, collapse from inherent defects. The organisation of all the ancient Empires was based on and characterised throughout by compulsion. Political Economy, demonstrating the enormous advantages of co-operation through free exchanges, was unknown. The whole organisation was almost entirely on the principle of Domestic or Patriarchal Economy. The tribe was an overgrown family, the state an overgrown tribe. A central will presided over the whole.

Powerful monarchs, determined dynasties, superior castes, and strong-minded, cunning priests organised the labour in their own interest, and kept the people in bondage by military power or superstition. Fear of punishment was the great motive for work; the despots or slave-owners supplied the raw materials and the instruments; the accumulation of capital was in the hands of the State or the government classes; the discipline was that of slavery, and frugality was forcibly imposed on the workers but not practised by the governing classes.

Such an organisation was only possible when the bulk of the people were in a very low moral condition—when they had not enough moral courage to defy their oppressors, when they were too ignorant and helpless to combine; too weak-minded to throw off superstition. When, in ancient Empires, the accumulation of wealth in the hands of the upper classes and the craving for pleasure and enjoyment had fostered among the people skill, art, and knowledge; when favouritism and lavishness had formed the beginning of a middle class; when at last opposing political factions and court intriguers began to appeal to the progressing masses,—the old system began to totter.

The toilers began to chafe under oppression, and had to be reckoned with. The advantages they secured for themselves gave them more strength, and when they had risen enough to make slavery impossible, the whole system crumbled. If this is according to facts, the theory that the downfall of ancient Empires was caused by demoralisation must be rejected, for (as has already been said) the very contrary was the fact—the moral elevation of the people made a system based on slavery halting, unreliable, and often impossible.

While, then, we should aim at the most perfect division of labour, more thorough even (if possible) than that of ancient Egypt, we must accomplish it by other means than the ancient ones.

The only alternative for the economic system of the ancient Empire—that is to say, Domestic or Patriarchal Economy—is a system of Political Economy the characteristics of which are individual freedom and private property. The question consequently resolves itself into this: Can so complete a division of labour, as that of ancient Egypt, be attained under an individualistic system?

The individualistic system has proved itself capable of stimulating production, invention, and scientific researches, enterprise, daring, and personal abilities to an extent which may fairly be said to outshine the patriarchal one, or (to call it by its modern name) the socialistic system. Even when the two systems are compared in detail—as we have done in previous chapters—the palm must be given to the individualistic system, because it has been practically proved over and over again that free labour is more profitable to the employer than slave labour.

But at the same time the individualistic system, so far only fragmentarily tried by modern States, has been credited with social and economic evils of so exasperating a character that a very large proportion of the working classes, and sincere philanthropists throughout the civilised world, are ready to give it up and go back to the socialistic system, with all its compulsion, individual slavery under government, and a thousand other horrors.

We also know that for years (and especially lately, during the English occupation) the European individualistic system is supposed to have prevailed in Egypt, and that so far it has fallen fearfully behind the ancient socialistic system as far as productiveness is concerned. If, therefore, a somewhat complete division of labour has to be achieved in Egypt by the individualistic system, the system must be purged of those defects which produce the many evils so evident there and elsewhere.

We have already shown that the prohibition of Free Banking places enormous obstacles in the way of the extension of division of labour, and that nowhere in the world has it been permitted to fulfil the organising mission of which it is capable; we have seen how Free Trade in Capital rapidly increases wealth and causes the supply of credit and of mediums of exchange to regulate itself according to such demand as is favourable to prosperity and successful production, while it supplies the most effective checks on abuses of every description.

If we compare that free system of division of labour which is a natural outcome of Free Trade in Capital, we find not only that it supplies all the factors for the production of prosperity which the socialistic system supplied in ancient Egypt, but that each of the factors in the free system exceeds in potency the corresponding factor in the ancient system.

Instead of the fear of punishment as the motive for work we should have the desire for success, the hope of prosperity which has carried personal exertions to such a pitch in modern times; raw materials and instruments &c. would be supplied by competition between the whole world instead of being provided by government officials; the accumulation of capital would go on, not in the hands of a privileged squandering class, but in the hands of every individual, and would to a very great extent be applied to new production. The discipline would be that of our factories or farms instead of slavery; the selection of leaders would not depend on the caprice of a ruler, but would be the result of a natural selection of the fittest;

distribution of work and selection of products to be produced would depend not on the requirements of the governing classes but on the workers themselves, who best know their abilities and aptitudes; frugality would not be compulsory but voluntary, and actuated by highly stimulated thrift.

There can therefore be no doubt that the system of free division of labour would, wherever introduced, produce a prosperity far exceeding that of the ancient compulsory systems.

We have now to inquire whether Free Banking is possible in Egypt, and whether it would there supply such a division of labour as we have here described.

The moment it is clearly understood that banking, including note-issuing, is perfectly free in Egypt, there will be plenty of individuals and companies willing and eager to undertake the business. Mistakes might occur; but with the knowledge now available respecting the economic theories of note-issuing, it is almost certain that there would be far fewer mistakes in Egypt than there were in Scotland, where experience alone, unexplained by theories, presided over the development of the banking system. Whatever error however might be committed, the consequences would certainly fall on the banks and not on the public, for the system involves, as we have seen, a trusting of the public with the funds of the bank, and not, as our present system does, a trusting of the banks with the funds of the public.

It may therefore be taken for granted that there would be plenty of people willing to start banks, and that they would possess sufficient knowledge and capital to do so successfully. But most people would probably object that the Egyptians are not suitable customers for banks. This would be true if by the word banks we meant English banks of the ordinary type.

But needless to say we do not refer to such banks, but those similar to the small bank branches in Scotland. We know that the chief condition for the success of these, was that the district should be poor—too poor to allow the customers of the bank to become depositors using cheques as their chief medium of exchange, and poor enough to present a demand for cash-credits, and the corresponding mediums of exchange, bank-notes. This condition Egypt fulfils to perfection.

As to the ability of the Egyptians to make a

proper use of banks, notes, and credits, it will probably not be denied that they are as capable in this respect as the Scotch people were in the seventeenth century. We must remember that the fearful misgovernment of Egypt has for centuries deprived the people of all opportunities of displaying their business capabilities, and that when they are given a fair chance to do so, they might prove themselves as good cash-credit holders as they have proved themselves soldiers. We have already mentioned that orientals are naturally good business people. The Jews prove it every day; Arabs and Moors have at more than one period shown themselves to be keen financiers and intelligent traders. A very large trade is nowadays carried on in Africa, under the most difficult circumstances, by the same race. It is true that most of the enterprising African traders are not Egyptians, but the Egyptians have not had the same opportunity nor the same inducement as the Arabs. Good opportunities and powerful inducements will certainly influence the development of the people's character.

The first and most necessary qualification no one will deny them, namely, the love of gain. But the honesty? In Egypt, like everywhere in the

East, large transactions are entered upon on the system of long credit, which proves that commercial honesty exists. Anyhow it will be granted that when honesty becomes more profitable than dishonesty, as is the case under a free system of banking, most keen-witted people will turn honest. Besides, if, to begin with, Egypt should not possess sufficient able and honest people to assume the function of employers of labour, other nationalities would willingly supply this want.

Even if, for the sake of argument, we suppose that the Egyptians are incapable of developing into employers of labour, this would in no way prevent the Free Banking system from succeeding in Egypt. And the Egyptians, as mere labourers with high wages and low cost of living, would certainly be contented, because the want of ability to attain to a higher position in face of the greatest facilities, necessarily implies the absence of a desire for such positions.

It must therefore be conceded that when banking is free in Egypt, banks will be established wherever there are to be found people willing to work, willing to accumulate, willing to spend and to enjoy—that is to say everywhere. The country has already proved its capacity for production. There is a pretty general belief that railways, canals, and irrigation works are apt to produce prosperity, but it may be laid down as an absolute certainty that prosperity in Egypt would produce railways, canals, and irrigation works.

It is then no exaggeration to say that when we have introduced Free Banking into Egypt we shall have established a free system of division of labour which will present all the advantages of the ancient compulsory system plus all the advantages of our modern civilisation, without the disadvantages of either.

The results will be enormous progress, unprecedented prosperity, advancement of the sciences and arts, spread of education and refinement, elevation in religion, and a gigantic trade with England.

The Egyptians themselves would be anxious to maintain what England would have created, and as an immense prosperity would have resulted from English influence, this would remain paramount. The large market the French would find in Egypt and the absence of English military display in that country would satisfy France, even if England by treaties and guarantees maintained the protection of the Canal.

CHAPTER XXII

PRACTICAL IMPERIALISM

THE idea of an Empire like our own, on which the sun never sets, welded together into one vast body politic, is one of those dazzling visions over which the imaginative love to muse, but which the practical are slow to regard as destined to be realised. Our age has produced practical statesmen who, in order no doubt to be practical, have set aside all thought of consolidating the Empire, who have even striven to ignore and caused the English voter to ignore the very existence of a British Empire, and to concentrate all their attention on these islands.

It would not be fair to explain this exclusive home policy by a cynical allusion to the non-existence of voters outside Great Britain and Ireland.

To many popular favourites the consolidation of the Empire seemed synonymous with an interference with the liberties of our Colonies. In their belief, political reforms, the extension of the Parliamentary franchise to the lowest strata, were the means to prosperity. They were only consistent with their Home programme when they left the Colonies to their own devices, and even hinted that England could dispense with them. The extensions of the franchise however served to encourage this attitude among politicians in general, for as the balance of the voting power lapsed into the hands of those classes who knew little or nothing of our Colonial Empire, questions of wider Imperial interest were thrust further into the background.

Still, despite the indifference of the masses to broader Imperial questions, despite the necessity to heed public opinion, there were and there are in this country plenty of politicians well aware of the importance of maintaining, and if possible of consolidating, the Empire.

There are so many powerful reasons in favour of a closer union of the various parts of the Empire, that indifference on the part of any English statesmen would be difficult to realise were it not for their modern State-socialistic bias. We have planted English culture, English homes in the Colonies. The vast communities which now grow up there are English in their feelings, their views, their customs; and in maintaining a close relation with them we broaden our national life, we perpetuate English institutions, English ideas, and English love of liberty; we create a world-wide sympathy with English aspirations and a response to English impulse in every quarter of the globe.

So long as nothing severs England from the Colonies or the Colonies from each other, the English have for their literature, science, and art a wider field than any other nation. A political and military union between such large communities, in possession of resources so vast, would with but little military display and at an insignificant cost, command the respect of the world. The British Islands and British dependencies supplement each other in a most wonderful way, and, for the purposes of thorough co-operation, they could not possibly be better situated in relation to each other. Those of our dependencies which are populous countries are, with respect to climate and products, the opposites of our own country. While they easily produce necessaries and luxuries of which we stand in great need, we in our turn supply them with such goods as they cannot produce, or that it does not pay them to produce. On the other hand, those Colonies which present a similar climate and similar products to those of our own country are not populated, but offer, if necessary, homesteads for a hundred times the population of Great Britain and Ireland. It would therefore be difficult to over-estimate the economic, commercial, industrial, and maritime advantages which the Empire would present to each of its component parts, provided of course that government placed no barriers in the way of free co-operation.

It has been said that if our Colonies separate from the Empire and establish perfectly independent governments, the fact that they would be civilised States with English culture would be enough to secure for England both their sympathy and their co-operation. No doubt we should retain some of their sympathy, some of their co-operation, but what we should lose and what they would lose can best be seen by a glance at the United States.

Under the influence of the fallacious socialistic notions and the crass ignorance of the simplest truths of Political Economy now prevalent, a complete severance from England would, in many

Colonies, mean party strife, class tyranny, political upheavals, and a destruction of prosperity by excessive State interference. Complete severance might easily cause the first dispute to develop into threats of war and even war, create national jealousies, and change brotherly co-operation into competition to the knife. Absence of political influence would make us despair of our moral influence, and when a good reform was passed in England we should not have the power to accelerate its adoption in the disintegrated Colonies.

When, for example, Free Trade in Capital has been introduced into England, it will at once be adopted by all our Colonies, especially by the free-trading ones; but the capitalists who now ride rough-shod over the American people will certainly prevent its adoption there in the same way as they have blocked the way for Free Trade.

Moreover, the moral and intellectual sympathies which spring up between people who take counsel together on common interests exercise a far wider influence over material affairs than is imagined, and in ways that cannot easily be traced in detail.

The bonds which at present link the Colonies

and the mother country are bonds of sentiment alone. It is a theory with many statesmen that these are the only bonds possible. The loss of our American Colonies seems to have impressed the English people most deeply, and to have convinced them that any practical attempt to bring about greater harmony between the various parts of the Empire would be resented by our greatest Colonies as an encroachment on their liberties, and would lead to separation. It has been more than once contended that, by severing the administrative and legislative bonds, we knit the Empire closer together because we strengthen the bonds of sentiment. The political freedom enjoyed by the Colonies as constituent parts of the Empire has been represented as the greatest possible inducement we could hold out to colonists for remaining British citizens.

Owing to the prevalence of such views, the relations between England and the Colonies, as well as between the Colonies themselves, are regulated by a mass of vague enactments, haphazard clauses, and unrecorded understandings, based on no system, no general principle, except that of expediency.

'To leave well alone,' is a good proverb, but it is not applicable to our relations with the

Colonies. It is not well that some of our greatest Colonies should curtail their trade with us through Protection duties, that they should mismanage their Economy and their finances so as to hamper emigration from Great Britain and Ireland, leave undeveloped most of their immense natural resources, and plunge into useless indebtedness. The tyranny of the capitalist over the working classes which is growing apace in some of our Colonies, the socialistic tendencies which show themselves in others, bode no good for the Empire.

The economic advantages which the English, as a nation and a race, derive from their Colonies are a mere fraction of what they ought to be. England annexes extensive territories, where ownership of soil is unknown, where the population consists of a few savage tribes, but where there is fabulous wealth in the form of fertile soil, forests, and minerals; the English government administer and defend these territories at much expense and sometimes with loss of life, and the English nation is *de facto* owner of the new land.

But how much do these annexations benefit the English people? What becomes of the fabulous wealth they contain? Does it, or even a fraction of it, contribute to the payment of our military expenses? Or to pay off the National Debt? Or to lessen our taxation? Does the possession of these earthly paradises by the English allow them to secure healthy homes and flourishing homesteads for our underpaid farm-labourers, breathing-room for the pale and starving denizens of our overcrowded cities?

Nothing of the sort. The enormous wealth which the new country represents is lost to the English people. So soon as England has established security to life and property, the stream of emigrants sets in, not from our back slums and agricultural districts, but from every country in the world. Adventurers and desperadoes lead the way; prospectors and capitalists follow. The land is grabbed by company-promoters, trusts, financiers, and speculators of all descriptions by hundreds of millions of acres. The British government parts with its rights for a mere song, for barely enough wherewith to pay its local officials; and when the country begins to yield up its treasures in products, gold and other metals, the share of the profits which falls to the English people is small indeed.

When the population has somewhat increased,

the leading men of the colony form themselves into a State, and territories, too vast to be appropriated by private individuals, are secured as the property of the new government, to pass eventually into private hands. In this way wealth, to the extent of milliards of pounds sterling, has been flung away by the English Parliament.

In the new territories of the United States plots of land are reserved for school purposes, and though these plots are small compared with the land that is sold or given away, they generally more than suffice to cover all school expenses : because, as the population increases, the value of the school lands increases in proportion. Had the British Parliament proceeded on the same principle in our Colonies, and reserved for government purposes a small percentage of the new land in districts most likely to develop, the National Debt might have been paid long ago, and all our army and navy expenses could have been withdrawn from the budget for ever.

That our financiers should have overlooked such immense sources of revenue is amazing indeed. Such neglect of our colonial resources may, however, to a certain extent, be explained. English

Cabinet Ministers hold power by virtue of their popularity, and among those who for the most part sway public opinion, manufacturers, merchants, ship-owners, figure conspicuously. To them the indirect results of our colonial policy are of more importance than the direct ones. Reduction in taxation, and the National Debt &c., interest them but little. What they want is extended trade. To arrive at as large a business as possible they naturally wish the government to leave everything open in the Colonies, and would probably resent any reserve or any restriction on the exploitation of the natural resources of new possessions. A shopkeeper policy has thus got the better of statecraft.

Our financiers have no doubt also been influenced by a fear that by making any colonial interest, however small, subservient to purely English interests, they would fan the spirit of independence and precipitate separation. How far such fears are justified, and whether the apprehended danger can be averted by tact and good management, we shall not investigate here. But let it be remembered that all such apprehensions gather their strength from want of close cohesion in the Empire.

To strengthen this cohesion is Practical Imperialism.

The bonds of sentiment are indispensable to a closer union, and we are to be congratulated upon their existence. But to form one compact Empire these bonds must be strengthened by the bonds of interest. To render every part of the Empire more prosperous, more secure, happier, and more powerful, through a closer union, is the only practical way of solving the Imperial problem.

That the solution of the problem should be sought for in purely political and administrative reforms, is in keeping with the protective spirit which has invaded this country. To excogitate constitutions, to plan parliaments, councils, senates, —is not to establish the wished-for unity. These are but the outside trappings, and could be varied *ad infinitum*. When we have created a desire, based on reason, among the majority of English subjects here and in the Colonies, for a united Empire, then, and then only, have we solved the problem.

To strengthen the bonds of sentiment by the

bonds of reasoned self-interest is not so difficult as may at first appear.

We need not go back to the first principles of Political Economy in order to demonstrate the existence of a solidarity amongst the peoples of this Empire as well as among all the individuals of the world. Students of Economy recognise this truth; and others can infer, from the wonderful way in which (as we have pointed out) the mother country and the Colonies supplement each other, how the more closely they co-operate the better will it be for all. That the solidarity already exists is indisputable. But fallacious legislation has so far prevented its working out its splendid natural results. What we have to do, therefore, is simply to remove such impediments as have been placed in the way of that general co-operation which oneness of interests naturally suggests.

The incompleteness of Political Economy, resulting from the absence of the true economic theories of banking, has—in the Colonies as in Great Britain and Ireland—encouraged the protective spirit and promoted State-socialistic measures. It is State Socialism which destroys prosperity here as in the Colonies; and it is State

Socialism which prevents the splendid results that would flow from free and general co-operation.

The first thing, then, to be done in order to consolidate the Empire is to adopt in Great Britain and Ireland a sound, truly scientific system of Economy; then, without fear or hesitation, we can introduce the same system all over the Empire.

To do this, less heroism is required than might be supposed. As far as Great Britain is concerned we are already rid of the greatest obstacle of all—protection duties. Bank monopoly, though more terrible in its consequences than protection, is not so great an obstacle because it is a curse alike to all, and (when this is understood) its removal will hardly be opposed by anybody—not even by the holders of the monopoly themselves. Other monopolies and State-socialistic institutions we have, but their influence on the economy and the business of the country is small, and they would soon die a natural death. With Free Trade and Free Banking, the prosperity of England would be so conspicuous that all thinking colonists would be eager to follow our example.

Difficulties might be encountered in the abolition

of protection duties in some of our Colonies ; but it is absolutely necessary that they should be removed in the interests of the Colonies themselves and of the Empire. Parliament has the most legitimate ground for upholding complete Free Trade in every part of the Empire, as we shall see when we inquire into the workings of the protection system in the Colonies.

Let us take, for example, Canada, where the loss through protective duties is almost incalculable. That country opens up most magnificent prospects for farming and all the industries connected with it. Farming is, or should be, its leading industry, and on the prosperity of the agricultural classes depends the prosperity of the whole community, including the protected manufacturers. But farming and all the natural industries—that is, such industries as produce for export and consequently derive no advantage from protective duties—are attacked and undermined in every way by the protective system.

All the manufactured articles which the farmers consume are made dear by the extra price which the tariffs allow the manufacturers to extort : hence dear production.

Besides the tax extorted in favour of the manufacturers, the whole burden of taxation falls on the natural industries; because what the protected industries pay by way of taxation is only a small part of the tax they themselves impose on the natural industries. If a manufacturer, for instance, sells goods to the amount of 100,000*l*., and the protection duty, of which he takes advantage, is 40 per cent., the natural industries are taxed in his favour with 40,000*l*., whether he earns them or not. Whatever taxes such a manufacturer pays are consequently only a fraction of the taxes extorted in his favour.

But the protective tariffs subject the farmers and natural industries to a yet greater injustice. By prohibiting the large import trade from England which would result from Free Trade, a corresponding amount of export trade from Canada is prevented: for the export and import of every country stand in a fixed relation to each other. By not buying in England the Canadians deprive the English manufacturing centres of a certain amount of prosperity, and Canadian produce can only be sold there at a very low price.

The Canadian farmers are thus plundered in

their cost of production, plundered in their cost of living, plundered in their taxes, and plundered in their price of sale.

And to what end is this enormous sacrifice imposed on the farmers and the natural industries? The alleged purpose is the advancement of industry. Never was there a greater fallacy. The real purpose is to increase the profits of short-sighted and incapable manufacturers by screening them from competition, and this is not to advance industry but to murder it. A glance at the way in which protection duties affect industry will suffice to show this.

The products of one industry are raw materials of many others, and consequently the duty which is supposed to favour one industry by increasing the price of its products injures many others. Thus, the duty on cotton yarns in favour of the spinner damages the weaver, the printer, the dyer, the finisher, and every industry in which cotton-cloth is used. By way of compensation, heavy import duties are laid on foreign goods competing with all these industries, the result of which is that the protected industry of the country is no industry at all: for it is ridiculous to call by the name of industry work that is going on with a real economic loss which has to be made up by those who are engaged in the real and profitable industries of the country. The loss which Canadians suffer from this sham industry may be calculated by deducting the actual profits of the protected manufacturers from the total amount of the extra price Canadians have to pay for manufactured goods. Such a calculation will show that the manufacturers reap only a small part of the fearfully large direct loss which they impose on the natural industries. If to this direct loss we add the indirect ones resulting from stagnation, hampered export, and low selling prices, the manufacturers' profit will be found ludicrously small compared with the gigantic loss to the country.

The moral of all this is of course that the Canadians would gain enormously if they were to pension off their manufacturers at the rate of their present profits, and this would immensely benefit the industries of the country, which could then, like the English industries, co-operate with all the industries of the world and find markets for their specialities in every country of the globe. The now protected industries would find their home market considerably improved, and the rapidly increasing populations in the Western Territories would absorb large quantities of Canadian manufactured goods.

Advocates of protection always start from the supposition that England can turn out manufactured goods in unlimited quantities at a price based on starvation wages. They do not seem to realise how ready the English mill-hands are to take advantage of any improvement in trade to get their wages raised, and how, consequently, the adoption of Free Trade by one or two countries would raise the price of manufactured goods in England.

Protectionists hypocritically allege that the protective system is favourable to the working classes. Canadian manufacturers ought to know that the very contrary is the case. The effect of protection on the prosperity of the country is so baneful that the direct advantages to the manufacturers tend to disappear. But they have an indirect advantage through the low wages which protection involves. When the development of all the natural industries is effectively checked, and when the protected industries are limited to their narrow home market, the competition for workers is of course lessened, and the poor people have to be satisfied with less wages, while their cost of living is artificially raised.

The result of this plundering of the working classes is plainly visible in all the protected countries of Europe, where there is no other way of making good the enormous losses which an anti-economic system must produce than by an increase of the National Debts.

In America and Canada, and countries similarly situated, the evil effect of protection on the working classes is not so patent, because farming and other natural industries derive extraordinary advantages from the almost boundless wealth which is at their disposal, in the shape of vast tracts of fertile soil, forests, and minerals. The Canadian protected manufacturers are well aware that, if the natural industries were allowed to expand at the rate of which they are capable, the demand for workers would be so intense as to send up wages considerably. But what they do not understand is that the demand for their products would increase and their price advance in proportion; and, by taking a one-sided view, they wrong themselves, while at the same time they act as the enemies of their country and of their race.

The difficulties which block the way to the introduction of Free Trade in the Colonies may be gauged by the circumstances which have led to and maintained the establishment of the unpatriotic and ruinous protective system. Protection is possible in our Colonies only because those who enjoy, or rather fancy they enjoy, advantages from it—namely, the protected manufacturers—are men of education, fortune, and social standing, who generally live in populous centres, and who, wherever they live, can easily combine and intrigue together. They can influence elections, buy the press, and hire orators.

Their victims, on the other hand, live scattered all over the country, many of them in lonely places, and have no means of inter-communication or of concerted action; they are for the most part practical workers, of but little education and no knowledge whatever of Political Economy. They read few papers and books, seldom attend meetings, and readily yield to the influence of populous centres. The farming population and the workers in natural industries have a vague idea that they are being plundered by the protected manufacturers, but, as we have seen, their circumstances prevent them from protecting themselves and make it difficult for them to realise their situation.

In the protected Colonies the position is therefore this: the bulk of the people is overtaxed, deprived of prosperity and kept in economic subjection, by a small influential minority. What England has to do is to come to the rescue of the large majority, and confer upon them what ought to be the privilege of every British citizen, economic freedom. In those parts of the protected Colonies where the rich natural resources have already been squandered, protection begins to show itself, as it does in European countries, in its true character—that of slavery. To deprive a man of his best chances of employment, to compel him to work for low wages, and to raise the cost of his living, is slavery.

The boast of Englishmen, that they have abolished slavery throughout the Empire, is empty and vain so long as they permit the existence of a ruinous protective system in the Colonies. If Parliament had the courage to set its face against it, it would be backed by an enormous majority in the Colonies. The manufacturers and their satellites would probably do their utmost to rouse the people to resistance; but as Parliament has the means of making the issue clear to every colonial voter, and as the manufacturers, when called upon to supply rational arguments in favour of their absurd demands, would expose the utter fallacy of their theories, actual resistance would soon collapse.

Vested interests could be perfectly well protected in many ways. We will only suggest one. Such manufacturers who could prove to a Commission that they would not gain, but suffer loss, by the introduction of Free Trade could be liberally compensated either by a bonus on their products based on their present turn-out, or receive a pension based on an average of their last ten years' profits. The expense for the State would in the case of either of these schemes be a trifle compared with the enormous loss the Colonies now suffer.

The expended capital would be easily recovered if the government set aside for this purpose land where at present it is valueless. With Free Trade and a sound economic system such land would speedily yield sufficient income to indemnify the few manufacturers who would suffer actual loss. Thus the results of Free Trade could be made to compensate for the expenses of the abolition of protection.

But before Free Trade in the Colonies can be enforced we must extend Free Trade to Capital and credit in Great Britain and Ireland: for it would be illogical and dangerous to ask the Colonies to introduce partial Free Trade. To secure the sympathies of the colonists, now oppressed by capitalists, the programme we present to them must be complete.

Moreover, the adoption of Free Trade in Capital by England will enormously further not only Free Trade in the Colonies but all over the world. There are three great arguments on which the protectionists now base their reasoning—namely, that the protected countries have not enough work for the people, that they have not enough capital, and that England by adopting Free Trade has not saved its inhabitants from the curse of the sweating system and the destitution in which the farm-labourers and other workers live.

With the introduction of Free Trade in Capital the two first arguments disappear. It would demonstrate the economic axiom which says that every country has enough capital. It would show protection to be one of the most active agents for the destruction of opportunities of work. The prosperity which would extend to every class in England would practically illustrate the advantages of Free Trade.

Free Trade—including Free Trade in Capital—should not be adopted as separate, isolated measures, but as the natural outcome of the great principle on which the Imperial Constitution should be framed—which should be upheld by every free nation—that no individual or group of individuals should be permitted to interfere with the economic liberty of any subject. This means that one individual should not be allowed to keep the other in slavery, to tax him, or, for the sake of private gain, to raise obstacles to his work.

By enforcing this principle we should simply extend individual liberty in our Colonies; and, as such extension would mean (as we have tried to show) an immense increase in prosperity and happiness, our action would soon be appreciated by colonists, and go far towards demonstrating the advantages of closer union. As matters stand now, all such advantages are understood, with the exception of the commercial, economic, and financial ones. It is only by adopting economic fallacies that the Colonies have come to regard a complete union with disfavour. In all other Empires it has been found that the removal of custom-house barriers between their component parts has greatly enhanced the prosperity of all. Nothing can be more absurd than to suppose that the custom-house line, which is hurtful to adjoining provinces, is useful to the different parts of the British Empire because they are separated by seas.

If the new Imperial policy should at first meet with opposition and discontent, it would be unpardonable cowardice on our part to allow such a consideration to stand in the way of so glorious a mission. If the Colonies knew that England was determined, very little opposition would be offered, and the animosity which might arise would soon subside. The war between the Northern and the Southern States of America in which the North fought so gallantly for the preservation of the union, carried (for the time) party hatred to a point which it would be difficult to exceed. Yet every trace of animosity is fast disappearing, and the Southern States are becoming as loyal to the union as the Northern. This fact is all the more instructive as the Northern States (though abolition of slavery was on their banner) certainly did not fight for Free Trade and its blessings.

Another lesson to be learned from this great war is that if great economic mistakes, such as slavery or protection, are allowed to take root in a country, they may lead to internecine war and other national calamities. If we allow protection to work out its evil consequences in our Colonies, we may count on losing them.

The loss of the American States has, as we know, been held up as a warning to England not to interfere with the Colonies. What lost us the American Colonies was not the upholding of individual freedom, not the abolition of unfair taxation. On the contrary, the British Government wanted to deprive them of their individual freedom and to impose upon them galling taxes. If we allow the Canadians to be so shamelessly exploited by the protected manufacturers, we must not wonder if they break loose from an Empire which cannot even protect their individual and economic freedom.

The slow progress of Canada, despite its enormous resources, will exasperate the people, and gradually the small party, which now advocates union with the United States, will make headway. Without assistance from England absolute Free Trade would be out of the question in Canada, and what thinking man can doubt that the Canadians, under such circumstances, will long resist the temptation to acquire so much additional Free Trade as an union with the United States—now almost a world in itself—would afford them?

The statesmen, therefore, who maintain protection in Canada will be responsible for its loss.

There cannot be a doubt that, once Free Trade and Free Trade in Capital are introduced throughout the Empire, practical results will soon convince all our Colonies of the value of belonging to such an union. It would present an enormous market for every producer, free-trade ports for every ship-owner, the greatest facilities and lowest cost of production, the highest prices for products, supply of capital to every paying enterprise, general participation in the progress of new colonies, free emigration—not of State-aided paupers, but of men capable of raising a colony to prosperity—an extraordinary capacity for defence, with innumerable other advantages.

The conception of an Empire spread all over the world, containing incalculable latent wealth, with immense reserve territories, co-operating unimpeded by the errors and prejudices of the past, conferring on every British subject the highest liberty, the greatest scope for his work, and the best chances of happiness ever possessed by man—an Empire possessing free organisation of labour surpassing in completeness and productiveness the organisations of the ancient Empires, but offering to personal invention, exertion, and genius all the incentive of a purely individual system—the conception of such an Empire ought to induce every British subject to exert his uttermost powers for its realisation.

www.ingramcontent.com/pod-product-compliance
Lightning Source LLC
Chambersburg PA
CBHW032130010526
44111CB00034B/577